PSALMS 1–50

PSALMS 1–50

Sighs and Songs of Israel

ELLEN T. CHARRY

Foreword by William P. Brown

BrazosPress

a division of Baker Publishing Group
Grand Rapids, Michigan

© 2015 by Ellen T. Charry

Published by Brazos Press
a division of Baker Publishing Group
P.O. Box 6287, Grand Rapids, MI 49516-6287
www.brazospress.com

Printed in the United States of America

Library of Congress Cataloging-in-Publication Data

Charry, Ellen T.
    Psalms 1–50 / Ellen T. Charry.
        pages cm. — (Brazos theological commentary on the Bible)
    Includes bibliographical references and index.
    ISBN 978-1-58743-157-9 (cloth)
    1. Bible. Psalms, I–L—Commentaries. I. Title. II. Title: Psalms one–fifty.
    BS1430.53.C43 2015
    223′.207—dc23   2015012101

15 16 17 18 19 20 21   7 6 5 4 3 2 1

Dedicated to the Poets of Israel

CONTENTS

SERIES PREFACE

Near the beginning of his treatise against gnostic interpretations of the Bible, *Against the Heresies*, Irenaeus observes that Scripture is like a great mosaic depicting a handsome king. It is as if we were owners of a villa in Gaul who had ordered a mosaic from Rome. It arrives, and the beautifully colored tiles need to be taken out of their packaging and put into proper order according to the plan of the artist. The difficulty, of course, is that Scripture provides us with the individual pieces, but the order and sequence of various elements are not obvious. The Bible does not come with instructions that would allow interpreters to simply place verses, episodes, images, and parables in order as a worker might follow a schematic drawing in assembling the pieces to depict the handsome king. The mosaic must be puzzled out. This is precisely the work of scriptural interpretation.

Origen has his own image to express the difficulty of working out the proper approach to reading the Bible. When preparing to offer a commentary on the Psalms he tells of a tradition handed down to him by his Hebrew teacher:

> The Hebrew said that the whole divinely inspired Scripture may be likened, because of its obscurity, to many locked rooms in our house. By each room is placed a key, but not the one that corresponds to it, so that the keys are scattered about beside the rooms, none of them matching the room by which it is placed. It is a difficult task to find the keys and match them to the rooms that they can open. We therefore know the Scriptures that are obscure only by taking the points of departure for understanding them from another place because they have their interpretive principle scattered among them.[1]

1. Fragment from the preface to *Commentary on Psalms 1–25*, preserved in the *Philokalia* (trans. Joseph W. Trigg; London: Routledge, 1998), 70–71.

As is the case for Irenaeus, scriptural interpretation is not purely local. The key in Genesis may best fit the door of Isaiah, which in turn opens up the meaning of Matthew. The mosaic must be put together with an eye toward the overall plan.

Irenaeus, Origen, and the great cloud of premodern biblical interpreters assumed that puzzling out the mosaic of Scripture must be a communal project. The Bible is vast, heterogeneous, full of confusing passages and obscure words, and difficult to understand. Only a fool would imagine that he or she could work out solutions alone. The way forward must rely upon a tradition of reading that Irenaeus reports has been passed on as the rule or canon of truth that functions as a confession of faith. "Anyone," he says, "who keeps unchangeable in himself the rule of truth received through baptism will recognize the names and sayings and parables of the scriptures."[2] Modern scholars debate the content of the rule on which Irenaeus relies and commends, not the least because the terms and formulations Irenaeus himself uses shift and slide. Nonetheless, Irenaeus assumes that there is a body of apostolic doctrine sustained by a tradition of teaching in the church. This doctrine provides the clarifying principles that guide exegetical judgment toward a coherent overall reading of Scripture as a unified witness. Doctrine, then, is the schematic drawing that will allow the reader to organize the vast heterogeneity of the words, images, and stories of the Bible into a readable, coherent whole. It is the rule that guides us toward the proper matching of keys to doors.

If self-consciousness about the role of history in shaping human consciousness makes modern historical-critical study critical, then what makes modern study of the Bible modern is the consensus that classical Christian doctrine distorts interpretive understanding. Benjamin Jowett, the influential nineteenth-century English classical scholar, is representative. In his programmatic essay "On the Interpretation of Scripture," he exhorts the biblical reader to disengage from doctrine and break its hold over the interpretive imagination. "The simple words of that book," writes Jowett of the modern reader, "he tries to preserve absolutely pure from the refinements or distinctions of later times." The modern interpreter wishes to "clear away the remains of dogmas, systems, controversies, which are encrusted upon" the words of Scripture. The disciplines of close philological analysis "would enable us to separate the elements of doctrine and tradition with which the meaning of Scripture is encumbered in our own day."[3] The lens of understanding must be wiped clear of the hazy and distorting film of doctrine.

Postmodernity, in turn, has encouraged us to criticize the critics. Jowett imagined that when he wiped away doctrine he would encounter the biblical text in its purity and uncover what he called "the original spirit and intention of the authors."[4] We are not now so sanguine, and the postmodern mind thinks interpretive

2. *Against Heresies* 9.4.
3. Benjamin Jowett, "On the Interpretation of Scripture," in *Essays and Reviews* (London: Parker, 1860), 338–39.
4. Ibid., 340.

frameworks inevitable. Nonetheless, we tend to remain modern in at least one sense. We read Athanasius and think him stage-managing the diversity of Scripture to support his positions against the Arians. We read Bernard of Clairvaux and assume that his monastic ideals structure his reading of the Song of Songs. In the wake of the Reformation, we can see how the doctrinal divisions of the time shaped biblical interpretation. Luther famously described the Epistle of James as a "strawy letter," for, as he said, "it has nothing of the nature of the Gospel about it."[5] In these and many other instances, often written in the heat of ecclesiastical controversy or out of the passion of ascetic commitment, we tend to think Jowett correct: doctrine is a distorting film on the lens of understanding.

However, is what we commonly think actually the case? Are readers naturally perceptive? Do we have an unblemished, reliable aptitude for the divine? Have we no need for disciplines of vision? Do our attention and judgment need to be trained, especially as we seek to read Scripture as the living word of God? According to Augustine, we all struggle to journey toward God, who is our rest and peace. Yet our vision is darkened and the fetters of worldly habit corrupt our judgment. We need training and instruction in order to cleanse our minds so that we might find our way toward God.[6] To this end, "the whole temporal dispensation was made by divine Providence for our salvation."[7] The covenant with Israel, the coming of Christ, the gathering of the nations into the church—all these things are gathered up into the rule of faith, and they guide the vision and form of the soul toward the end of fellowship with God. In Augustine's view, the reading of Scripture both contributes to and benefits from this divine pedagogy. With countless variations in both exegetical conclusions and theological frameworks, the same pedagogy of a doctrinally ruled reading of Scripture characterizes the broad sweep of the Christian tradition from Gregory the Great through Bernard and Bonaventure, continuing across Reformation differences in both John Calvin and Cornelius Lapide, Patrick Henry and Bishop Bossuet, and on to more recent figures such as Karl Barth and Hans Urs von Balthasar.

Is doctrine, then, not a moldering scrim of antique prejudice obscuring the Bible, but instead a clarifying agent, an enduring tradition of theological judgments that amplifies the living voice of Scripture? And what of the scholarly dispassion advocated by Jowett? Is a noncommitted reading, an interpretation unprejudiced, the way toward objectivity, or does it simply invite the languid intellectual apathy that stands aside to make room for the false truism and easy answers of the age?

This series of biblical commentaries was born out of the conviction that dogma clarifies rather than obscures. The Brazos Theological Commentary on the Bible advances upon the assumption that the Nicene tradition, in all its diversity and controversy, provides the proper basis for the interpretation of the Bible as Christian

5. *Luther's Works*, vol. 35 (ed. E. Theodore Bachmann; Philadelphia: Fortress, 1959), 362.
6. *On Christian Doctrine* 1.10.
7. *On Christian Doctrine* 1.35.

Scripture. God the Father Almighty, who sends his only begotten Son to die for us and for our salvation and who raises the crucified Son in the power of the Holy Spirit so that the baptized may be joined in one body—faith in *this* God with *this* vocation of love for the world is the lens through which to view the heterogeneity and particularity of the biblical texts. Doctrine, then, is not a moldering scrim of antique prejudice obscuring the meaning of the Bible. It is a crucial aspect of the divine pedagogy, a clarifying agent for our minds fogged by self-deceptions, a challenge to our languid intellectual apathy that will too often rest in false truisms and the easy spiritual nostrums of the present age rather than search more deeply and widely for the dispersed keys to the many doors of Scripture.

For this reason, the commentators in this series have not been chosen because of their historical or philological expertise. In the main, they are not biblical scholars in the conventional, modern sense of the term. Instead, the commentators were chosen because of their knowledge of and expertise in using the Christian doctrinal tradition. They are qualified by virtue of the doctrinal formation of their mental habits, for it is the conceit of this series of biblical commentaries that theological training in the Nicene tradition prepares one for biblical interpretation, and thus it is to theologians and not biblical scholars whom we have turned. "War is too important," it has been said, "to leave to the generals."

We do hope, however, that readers do not draw the wrong impression. The Nicene tradition does not provide a set formula for the solution of exegetical problems. The great tradition of Christian doctrine was not transcribed, bound in folio, and issued in an official, critical edition. We have the Niceno-Constantinopolitan Creed, used for centuries in many traditions of Christian worship. We have ancient baptismal affirmations of faith. The Chalcedonian definition and the creeds and canons of other church councils have their places in official church documents. Yet the rule of faith cannot be limited to a specific set of words, sentences, and creeds. It is instead a pervasive habit of thought, the animating culture of the church in its intellectual aspect. As Augustine observed, commenting on Jer. 31:33, "The creed is learned by listening; it is written, not on stone tablets nor on any material, but on the heart."[8] This is why Irenaeus is able to appeal to the rule of faith more than a century before the first ecumenical council, and this is why we need not itemize the contents of the Nicene tradition in order to appeal to its potency and role in the work of interpretation.

Because doctrine is intrinsically fluid on the margins and most powerful as a habit of mind rather than a list of propositions, this commentary series cannot settle difficult questions of method and content at the outset. The editors of the series impose no particular method of doctrinal interpretation. We cannot say in advance how doctrine helps the Christian reader assemble the mosaic of Scripture. We have no clear answer to the question of whether exegesis guided by doctrine is antithetical to or compatible with the now-old modern methods of

8. *Sermon* 212.2.

historical-critical inquiry. Truth—historical, mathematical, or doctrinal—knows no contradiction. But method is a discipline of vision and judgment, and we cannot know in advance what aspects of historical-critical inquiry are functions of modernism that shape the soul to be at odds with Christian discipline. Still further, the editors do not hold the commentators to any particular hermeneutical theory that specifies how to define the plain sense of Scripture—or the role this plain sense should play in interpretation. Here the commentary series is tentative and exploratory.

Can we proceed in any other way? European and North American intellectual culture has been de-Christianized. The effect has not been a cessation of Christian activity. Theological work continues. Sermons are preached. Biblical scholars turn out monographs. Church leaders have meetings. But each dimension of a formerly unified Christian practice now tends to function independently. It is as if a weakened army had been fragmented, and various corps had retreated to isolated fortresses in order to survive. Theology has lost its competence in exegesis. Scripture scholars function with minimal theological training. Each decade finds new theories of preaching to cover the nakedness of seminary training that provides theology without exegesis and exegesis without theology.

Not the least of the causes of the fragmentation of Christian intellectual practice has been the divisions of the church. Since the Reformation, the role of the rule of faith in interpretation has been obscured by polemics and counterpolemics about *sola scriptura* and the necessity of a magisterial teaching authority. The Brazos Theological Commentary on the Bible series is deliberately ecumenical in scope, because the editors are convinced that early church fathers were correct: church doctrine does not compete with Scripture in a limited economy of epistemic authority. We wish to encourage unashamedly dogmatic interpretation of Scripture, confident that the concrete consequences of such a reading will cast far more light on the great divisive questions of the Reformation than either reengaging in old theological polemics or chasing the fantasy of a pure exegesis that will somehow adjudicate between competing theological positions. You shall know the truth of doctrine by its interpretive fruits, and therefore, in hopes of contributing to the unity of the church, we have deliberately chosen a wide range of theologians whose commitment to doctrine will allow readers to see real interpretive consequences rather than the shadow boxing of theological concepts.

Brazos Theological Commentary on the Bible has no dog in the current translation fights, and we endorse a textual ecumenism that parallels our diversity of ecclesial backgrounds. We do not impose the thankfully modest inclusive-language agenda of the New Revised Standard Version, nor do we insist upon the glories of the Authorized Version, nor do we require our commentators to create a new translation. In our communal worship, in our private devotions, in our theological scholarship, we use a range of scriptural translations. Precisely as Scripture—a living, functioning text in the present life of faith—the Bible is not semantically fixed. Only a modernist, literalist hermeneutic could imagine that this modest fluidity is a liability. Philological precision and stability is a consequence of, not a basis for, exegesis. Judgments about the meaning of a text fix its literal sense, not the other way around. As a result, readers should expect an eclectic use of biblical translations, both across the different volumes of the series and within individual commentaries.

We cannot speak for contemporary biblical scholars, but as theologians we know that we have long been trained to defend our fortresses of theological concepts and formulations. And we have forgotten the skills of interpretation. Like stroke victims, we must rehabilitate our exegetical imaginations, and there are likely to be different strategies of recovery. Readers should expect this reconstructive—not reactionary—series to provide them with experiments in postcritical doctrinal interpretation, not commentaries written according to the settled principles of a well-functioning tradition. Some commentators will follow classical typological and allegorical readings from the premodern tradition; others will draw on contemporary historical study. Some will comment verse by verse; others will highlight passages, even single words that trigger theological analysis of Scripture. No reading strategies are proscribed, no interpretive methods foresworn. The central premise in this commentary series is that doctrine provides structure and cogency to scriptural interpretation. We trust in this premise with the hope that the Nicene tradition can guide us, however imperfectly, diversely, and haltingly, toward a reading of Scripture in which the right keys open the right doors.

R. R. Reno

FOREWORD

Ellen Charry's commentary on Psalms is like no other. While form criticism has been, and continues to be, a staple of scholarly research, Charry's interest in the Psalter has more to do with what I would call "life criticism," but not in any piously anachronistic sense. Ancient Israel's travails and reforms are in full view throughout her discussion. Yet the *Sitze im Leben* of the psalms ultimately prove their value beyond their historical roots or formal settings. For Charry, the psalms are theologically and pastorally instructive for readers across generations, and she mines their edifying value for all they're worth. Her keen interest in ethics and historical theology, matched by her command of the Hebrew language and Jewish tradition, have equipped her well for engaging these highly charged texts of poetry. Drawing from a rich variety of patristic, rabbinic, and medieval interpretations, as well as from modern Psalms scholarship, Charry has produced a theologically robust, morally nuanced, honest-to-God kind of commentary. Whether the reader will agree with her at every interpretive move is beside the point.

The hermeneutical journey of commentary writing, particularly on Psalms, is invariably transformative. As she herself admits, Charry has discovered how central the issue of theodicy is in the Psalter, anticipated already in Ps. 1. Pain suffuses the book of Psalms, so much so that one could subtitle the Psalter "Pain Seeking Understanding." In Charry's words, "searing pain must be honored before it can be stilled." The psalmic attempt to "honor" the pain, to articulate it and understand it, even while raging against it, is consistently theological. While pain can rob us of speech, the psalmists of old were able to found a bulwark against silence-inducing pain, for they dared to give unfettered, honest voice to pain before God and community. Their doing so in the unsettling language of complaint, however, strikes many modern readers as audacious, even shameless. So be it. Charry has found a way to honor the psalmists' audacity, ambiguous as it may be, and turn it into hope.

As Charry observes regarding Ps. 16, the psalms teach us to "think and behave theologically when *in extremis.*" All the psalms, from laments to hymns of praise, are theologically edifying. They are meant for our good, Charry would say. Still underappreciated by many readers, the psalms were written and compiled *to be used.* They were written *for* others in various situations and contexts. They were designed to be "user friendly." Hence, the language employed in the psalms is open and instructive, as Charry demonstrates throughout her commentary. It seems only appropriate, then, that she concludes her discussion of each psalm with a reflection on its "theological pedagogy" (*not* "application"—a far too mechanical, superficial term). It is here that she deftly navigates between the ancient context of a given psalm and its instructive value for contemporary readers.

According to Charry, the psalms are fundamentally about faithfulness, about tenaciously holding on to faith in the one true God amid the temptations of despair and idolatry. As she aptly states, the poets of ancient Israel "know how difficult faithfulness can be," and their task was to make faithfulness "durable" for their audience and for future generations. It is in such faithfulness that Israel saw itself unwaveringly in relationship with God, even amid felt abandonment. The Psalms model demonstrates for readers, in whatever season of life, whether in crisis or in contentment, how to be faithful, empowered servants of the living God. That is Charry's fundamental conviction about the Psalter, a conviction that she elaborates with pedagogical vigor and a pastoral heart, a heart that has been broken and yet continues to find resolve in the struggle of living faithfully *coram Deo.* She is in good company with the psalmists.

William P. Brown

ACKNOWLEDGMENTS

No author produces a book without able assistance. In this case, I am deeply indebted to a series of devoted and able student researchers and copy editors who labored in this rewarding vineyard with me: Melanie Webb, Derek Taylor, and most especially Jillian Greene and Jeffrey Thompson who offered research help, Craig Rubano who did initial copyediting and proofreading and Kristin Wendland who transliterated the Hebrew according to SBL convention. Nancy Hazle read many of my comments as I went along. I am grateful to Rusty Reno (who assented to my request to comment on Psalms) and to the patience and support of the Brazos staff. Very special thanks go to Bill Brown for an eagle eye on a full draft as well as the gracious foreword. Above all, my gratitude is to the great poets of Israel who have blessed our lives with their profound theological honesty that clings to hope come what may. May their words resound in our ears forever.

INTRODUCTION

When I told an acquaintance that I was commenting on the psalms, he deftly probed, "What do you have to say about the psalms that has not already been said?" Truly, the Psalter may be the most commented upon text in human history precisely because these haunting poems provoke, shock, and soothe by turns, latching onto readers and resonating with the sufferings and strivings of each one afresh. Athanasius of Alexandria (ca. 296–373), the great formulator of Nicene theology, tersely annotated the psalms, claiming that each one holds up a mirror to the soul.[1] While in truth not all psalms offer comfort to relieve suffering, the fact that they contend with grief, humiliation, and God-abandonment is, in its own way, a refreshing type of companionship. They offer a ministry of understanding.

Wise authorities enshrined Israel's sighs and songs in Jewish and Christian worship, and later readers have countlessly copied and reprinted them in pocket versions for private meditation on the road and *in extremis*. The mishnaic tractate *Pirke Avot* (5:22A)[2] attributes the following to one of its sages: "Turn [scripture] over and over for everything is in it. Look into it, grow old and worn in it, and never move away from it, for you will find no better portion than it." Perhaps the observation applies, above all, to the Psalter.

When asked which book of the Bible I wanted to comment on, I immediately blurted out "Psalms." It has been the most liberating academic work I have ever undertaken, as I entered the tersely inflected elegance of the Hebrew poetry that often challenges translation. I rejoice in this opportunity to speak the theology and psychology of the poets into life once more. Even if my probing merely concatenates the insights of previous commentators, I fear no shame, for I dwell in the finest company.

1. Athanasius 1980, 101–47.
2. Neusner 1988, 689.

Despite the beauty of the language there are reasons to be shy of the psalms. Many countenance attitudes and policies of empire, conquest, revenge, and violence are deeply disturbing to modern sensibilities when read as scripture, even when one recalls that most of the poems are not proposed as from God but to or about God. These are not values that one necessarily wants to inculcate in one's children. While many commentators undermine the plain meaning of the texts by reading symbolically, I face the text as it is in order to live into the psychological honesty of the poets struggling with the challenge of religion and empire that is still alive in some parts of the world.

Perhaps one reason for the enduring power of the Psalter, despite its troubling aspects, is its blistering honesty; not only does the Psalter not shrink from owning negative emotions, but it also does not underplay the experience of abandonment by God voiced in the laments that dominate the first third of the Psalter. It is precisely this experience of abandonment, also placed in the mouth of Jesus as he died, that discomfits later theologians who have consistently sought to tidy up psalmic theology to protect a presupposed view of God as present, gracious, and powerful. Ironically, admitting that one does not always experience God this way vitalizes these poems. They showcase people struggling to make sense of God in the face of deep doubts and sometimes frankly failing in that endeavor. That the canonizers included this "counter testimony"[3] in the canon attests to their refusal to whitewash the problem of theodicy. The poets address people where they are, even when doing so flies in the face of authorized theological expectation.

Discovering the theodicy question at the heart of the Psalter was perhaps the greatest new learning for me in doing this work. In my reading here, theodicy accounts for Israel's great struggle against idolatry or "wickedness" within Israel as the poets urge loyalty to the ancestral faith even when cries for rescue from scoffers seem to be met with divine silence.

In keeping with the psalmists' refusal to avoid hard theological questions about the power and goodness of God—which they hold to overall—I do not shy away from the problem of theodicy as central to the first third of the Psalter. I honor the gift that the lament psalms in particular offer to those who suffer by honoring their worst fears. This desire to support the poets' honesty led me not only to face the theodicy issue but also to resist the temptation to anachronize the psalms by christologizing them in the manner of so much Christian interpretation. I do not interpret through a Nicene screen that relocates the Psalter in a Christian framework; these poems speak their own theological convictions and are honored for their integrity, contrary as that may sometimes be to later theological presuppositions.

How then, one may ask, can the psalms be read Christianly if one does not christologize them? We may read the poems in their own theological integrity and also engage with them through later Christian images, texts, and criteria, not in order to domesticate them but so that the soul-piercing questions that the poets

3. Brueggemann 1997.

raise in lament, supplication, and imprecation may expand Christian piety beyond conventional answers. Stilling the pain of abandonment and humiliation with a christological interpretation may comfort, but it can also belittle the pain that leaves people agape at the thought that there may be no justice in which to rest. The psalmists are convinced that such searing pain must be honored before it can be stilled.

While some theologians may disprefer theological ambiguity, people in anguish need the respectful space that Israel's poets permit readers in order to confront the deep fear that perhaps God is not "there" after all—or worse, that God is, finally, the enemy behind the enemy. The psalms entertain fear and doubt about God along with the incorrigible belief in the eventual triumph of good over evil. I rely on both Jewish and Christian commentators who, over many centuries, have worked to dispel the darkness of God that "shines" through these poems.

Tasks of Theological Commentary

Historically speaking, the primary task of commenting on sacred texts has been to render them spiritually and morally accessible to later audiences who are culturally and temporally removed from the original setting, circumstances, and perhaps values that gave rise to them. Prior to modernity, theological interpretation was indistinguishable from spiritual interpretation. In different climes, readers must be turned convincingly toward their sacred texts in order both to uphold the moral and theological continuity of the later community's values and norms and to nurture faith. Commentary sought to bridge gaps that time had bored into understanding in order to enable later readers to embrace the sacrality of their revered texts for their own well-being, especially when texts were asynchronous with later values. Classically speaking, theological interpretation is acutely warranted when the revered texts make claims about God and the things of God that, on the face of it, no longer readily compel assent. This is especially the case with the psalms, although no less true of other parts of scripture that lead to various forms of symbolic or figural reading.

Here are three examples:

1. The vast cultural chasm between the Song of Songs and the sexual anxieties of Origen's day led him (and others following him) to embrace allegorical interpretation so that the eroticism of the poems could be sublimated to the desire of devout souls for God.[4]
2. With less urgency, the Noah story, in which humanity is saved from drowning in a wooden vessel floating atop a flood, is interpreted by Justin the Martyr as a type of the true meaning of salvation—that is, through the wood of the cross of Christ and the water that flowed from his pierced side.[5]

4. Origen 1957.
5. Lampe 1969, 167.

3. Psalm 137:9 seeks revenge against the Babylonians for their treatment of Israel. Augustine cannot countenance revenge of one people against another as an appropriate Christian posture, and so "Happy shall they be who take your little ones and dash them against the rock!" (NRSV) becomes joy at having dashed one's bad habits against the rock of Christ: "When evil desire is born, before your bad habits reinforce it, while it is still in its infancy and has not yet fortified itself by alliance with depraved custom, dash it to pieces. It is only a baby still. But make sure it does not survive your violent treatment: dash it on the rock. *And the rock is Christ* [1 Cor. 10:4]."[6]

The desire to harmonize the text with later moral, spiritual, psychological, or theological sensibilities gave rise to figural readings that sought to close moral and cultural gaps between the text and later sensitivities. While all interpretation addresses its current readers, the downside of strategies that moot troubling texts is that the text loses its own voice on the assumption that this distance from later readers is unhelpful or even harmful. Yet recognizing our distance from the text may be edifying when it gives us a fresh perspective on our own time and place. In "cleaning up" the text it loses its repugnancy, but that makes later readers dependent on experts. In the case of allegory, this results in terms quite alien to the text itself. This presents a different sort of alienation from the text than the perceived offensiveness of the text itself, but no less an alienation.

Modern biblical studies, guided by Protestant desire to put the Bible in the hands of the people, undid the eisegetical strategies of figural reading, that the text might speak its own word. Yet those who pray may benefit from being both confronted by the text and lured by it so that it may penetrate the soul in more than one way. My comments seek to uncover the theology of the text on its own terms as well as in terms of my conviction about the theological foundation of the Psalter (explained below). I also try to tease out its psychological and spiritual helpfulness in our own time, often stopping in between to appreciate interpretive insights from other commentators both ancient and modern, including the texts used in the Younger Testament. Each comment is structured by its canonical context and themes, its structure and dynamics, and finally its theological pedagogy from which I try to wrest a gift from the psalmist to us.

Theological Foundation

The interpretation undertaken herein does not make a sustained argument about psalmic theology, but it does work from a conviction about the theological foundation of the first fifty psalms. The basic theological conviction that surfaces

---

6. Augustine 2004, 240.

throughout the poems, as well as in later Judaism and Christianity, is that the God of Israel is the only true God, the God of the world (Pss. 47, 67). This is the God whom Christians and Muslims worship. The "teeth" in that conviction is that one must make that claim central to one's identity and way of life. An urgency about the psalms arises from this duplex claim because it triangulates God, Israel, and the gentiles.

Psalms 1 and 2 sound this two-pronged theological conviction about the mission of Israel in the world. Psalm 1, although not specifying the Israelites, exhorts Israelite/Jewish readers to cling to the teachings of God and abjure the wickedness of those who scorn God's way. Psalm 2 goes in a quite different direction, identifying Israel's king as God's anointed regent who is divinely authorized to threaten and intimidate the foreign nations surrounding Israel into submission to Israel's God (to "kiss his feet" [Ps. 2:12 NRSV]). Israel's king is divinely appointed to impose God on the nations until they "take refuge in him," as Israel also must.

Both of these leading psalms bear progeny throughout the work. Psalm 1's division of people into the faithful and the wicked surfaces within the first third of the Psalter, in Pss. 3, 7, 11, 15, 17, 34, and 36. Psalm 2's insistence on the universal scope of God's intentions for humanity through Israel plays out in Pss. 18, 21, 29, 33, and 45–48. Yet these two themes are not as differently-pointed as they may at first appear. For if the God of Israel is indeed God of the world, a theologian-poet will understandably train one eye on the "home team" and the other on God's further target audience. If, as I propose, the ultimate theological goal of the Psalter is to advance the universal recognition of God, Israel's faithfulness is the key witness to God's presence, grace, and power abroad.

My read of the theology of the Psalter, and of the Tanakh more broadly, is that Israel is to model faithfulness to God not only for the sake of its own well-being but also to the end that God's universal reign may be acknowledged among the nations. The Psalter unpacks this duplex mission in the world one poem at a time. While the two themes interact in many of the poems, here I discuss them individually.

It is easy to read many if not most of the psalms as an elaboration of the basic commandment of Deut. 6:4, that Israel is to love the Lord with all its heart, soul, and strength. God has chosen Israel for himself, and the integrity of its life depends upon its loyalty to that election. This is the heart of the exhortation of Ps. 1 that clearly divides people into two stark categories. If Israel is unfaithful to its identity as God's own, it has no credibility offering God to the nations, and God is not pleased.

I read the individual laments that dominate the first third of the Psalter through the lens of Ps. 1. These anguished cries denounce "the wicked," depicted as disloyal to God's way. Although the suffering is personal and interpersonal, it is theologically freighted. The complainants often beg for release from suffering, for it would demonstrate to the scoffers within Israel as well as to the nations that God is present, gracious, and powerful. While there are compelling proposals about precisely who "the enemies" are in the lament psalms,[7] one possibility is that the speakers and their foes battle over whether God truly is present, gracious, and powerful. The poignancy of the debate lies in the fact that God's delay in rescuing the suppliant supports the opponents' case that perhaps God is not "there." The complainant struggles desperately to remain steadfast in the face of debilitating evidence of God's absence (e.g., Pss. 4, 6, 13, 35, 62, 74, 79, 80, 82, 89, 90, 119:81–88). An important psychological side effect of the theodicy struggle in the laments is the experience of being scorned for one's faithfulness against empirical evidence. The complainant is oppressed precisely because he trusts God, and others ridicule him for it. That is, the *Atheismusstreit* (the atheistic threat) here involves mocking and scorning the faithful who experience such contempt as shame. It is the shame of disgrace, not of guilt.

At the same time, Israel's own claim that there is no god but God, creator of heaven and earth, presses its theologian-poets to turn the community back to God in order to look outward to the international scope of God's reach. Although internally divided between religious and skeptical Israelites/Jews, the nation as a whole is to bring the nations to acknowledge God alongside Israel. Israel bears a burdensome election; it must itself remain faithful (always a challenge, as Ps. 78 lays bare) in order to bring God to outsiders—a delicate task to be sure, as Ruth and Jonah make plain. These theologian-poets work both sides of this twisted street.

The Tanakh does not address whether gentiles who acknowledge Israel's God— like Pharaoh, the widow of Zarephath, and the general Naaman, along with Ruth and the Ninevites—are expected to worship God as the one and only God. Rather, the burning question is the flip side of that coin: whether the Israelites are succumbing to idolatry. Idolatry is truly Israel's worst enemy. The Canaanites are infiltrating Israel's tribes—the opposite of what should be happening. Israel should be exporting God rather than being seduced by alien gods who pollute its accountability before God. The theological bottom line of the Psalter is that there is only one God, the God of Israel. The tension inherent in that basic assumption pops up throughout the Tanakh and pulses through the Psalter, which struggles with tribalism and imperialism in light of its conviction of divine universality.

Some psalms reduce Israel's situation vis-à-vis the nations to the speakers' enemies, and Pss. 2, 79, and 110 beseech God's wrath on them for the deliverance of Israel; several are clear that these nations are to know and glorify Israel's God and be judged by him (Pss. 2:10–11; 22:27–28; 57:9; 67:2–5; 80:8; 86:9; 96:3–10; 98:2, 9; 102:15; 108:3; 117:1; 126:2). Israel has a conflicted and ambivalent relationship with its neighbors in a political climate in which imperial power connotes dignity and honor. On one hand, Israel longs for its enemies to come to know the power of God through their military defeat by Israel's warriors. On the other hand, Israel is called to extend the reach of God's reign to

---

7. Fløysvik 1997; Miller 1983; Steussy 2008.

its enemies by demonstrating righteousness for them. Various psalms entertain alternate strategies for fulfilling this complex mandate.

In proposing that the Psalter promotes the notion that the God of Israel is the Lord of the universe, I link its urgent initial exhortation to piety within Israel to its mission to bring gentiles to God. While this linkage may seem odd at first because it forces Israel to face in two directions simultaneously, it is precisely this tension that makes the psalms so alluring. In truth, the employment of intimidation and military conquest, as well as the entreaty for God to destroy Israel's enemies (who appear in Ps. 2), might not advance Israel's call to bring gentiles to God. Elijah (1 Kgs. 17) and Elisha (2 Kgs. 5) employ a gentler approach. They heal gentiles rather than threaten them with harm. Offering help would commend a kind God to Israel's gentile neighbors rather than presenting God as one who brings destruction upon those he expects to honor him. The harsh approach taken by some psalms may not be appealing, but neither is it unusual. Christians have forced Christ on non-Christians, and Islam reached the pinnacle of its strength through military conquest in the name of God, although Muslims permitted conquered Jews and Christians to retain their ancestral faith notwithstanding civic disabilities.

The various expressions of these theological currents in the Psalter make Israel's triangulation between God and the nations particularly interesting. To get at some of these dynamics I have parsed the several conversations happening both within individual poems as well as those happening between the poet and the implied readers—sometimes this involves his immediate audience and sometimes the much later audience of today.

The poets operate on several levels at once. In a single psalm the speaker, the narrator, and God may all be conversing with one another, each offering his perspective to the others. Further, the poet's consciousness of the audience is evident as he overhears the conversation among the various characters in the poem. Changes of speaker, person, and addressee express not only the several conversations taking place in the poems but also the emotional tensions at work in them. My comments try to articulate the interest of each of these voices to discern the import of the conversation around the issue at stake. In doing so, the different perspectives of the various characters within the poems call all to be faithful to God in order to offer God to the world.

In this commentary, I try to discern the theology of the texts and ask how Israelite theology relates to or challenges later Christian theology and piety. To that end, I tend to the various voices in the psalms—the changes of speaker and of addressee in dialogues and monologues meant to be overheard by the worshiping community as well as foreign nations. My comments do not arise from following a particular scholarly school or discussion in an effort to contribute to it.

Still, a small conversation takes place concerning the theological implications of the changing voices and shifts of grammatical person (among first-, second-, and third-person speech) in relation to which I will briefly locate the approach taken here. In a two-part essay, Carl Bosma retraces the exegetical debate about whether the psalms should be understood as biographical self-revelation by the poet or as the cultic response of worshiping Israel to the mighty deeds of God.[8] The two positions in the debate recall Karl Barth's criticism of Friedrich Schleiermacher's theology, which influenced the nineteenth-century psychological or biographical approach to reading psalms, although that exegetical tradition reaches back to the fourth century.

While I do not intend to advance any particular scholarly conversation, it seems to me that choosing sides in this debate is unnecessary because polarizing these two approaches is fundamentally misleading. The public-worship-oriented approach assumes that the poems were written for that purpose while the older biographical-psychological approach assumes that the laments are outpourings of personal torment. It may be that, as Hermann Gunkel holds, cultic/liturgical psalms were adapted for personal use, although it could be that many of the poems began as personal expression and were later located in the public context for general instruction. Perhaps more likely is the possibility that both pathways lie behind different poems. Identifying psalms for one history or the other is not my concern here.

While locating many of the psalms in the setting of public worship is largely warranted by the texts themselves, the personal nature of many psalms, especially the plenteous laments found among the first fifty psalms, suggests that simply ignoring the psychology expressed in theological terms is an egregious misrepresentation of the poems and their function in public worship. Ignoring the pedagogy of the psychology in the texts risks neglecting the ability of the poems to comfort, confront, and even scandalize later readers seeking spiritual nurture and direction. My interest is not in discerning how the Psalter was shaped for Israel's worship but how the poems intend to spiritually and theologically shape later readers to be faithful Israel, for that seems to be the interest of the poets.

Here, I take the position that it is precisely the personal struggles so poignantly expressed by the poets and proclaimed in public that intend to draw Israelites into, or perhaps back into, faithful allegiance to God—not only in times of plenty but also in times of want. Whether these are the poet's own struggles or whether the speaker is a literary fiction is a moot point. Pedagogically speaking, the laments are warranted for public worship because everyone eventually experiences personal defeat of some kind and comes face-to-face with the searing question of theodicy. The theological pedagogy of these poems both prepares and shapes the community to confront the questions of theodicy and empire openly in order to sustain Israel's fundamental theological conviction that the God of Israel is the one and only God of the universe. That is, public worship is not an end in itself. Its design on the hearts and minds of the worshipers is to carry them faithfully through thick and thin. To read the psalms in either psychological or liturgical terms rather than both is to be driven by modern concerns that, in my judgment, miss the subtler point Israel's poets are making. Israel's faith and practice must

---

8. Bosma 2008, 2009.

be durable. The poets know how difficult faithfulness can be, and their poems meet people where they are.

Notes on Style

Readers will note that I use male pronouns to refer to the authors and the narrators of the psalms as well as God. This is in keeping with the general scholarly assumption that the authors who may or may not be speaking for themselves were men and that the author also assumed that the narrator or implied author (where there is one) was also male. I use male pronouns for God because the Hebrew, a strongly gendered language, uses the masculine forms consistently.

I also substitute the titles "Older Testament" and "Younger Testament" for the standard "Old Testament" and "New Testament." When the conventional terms were created to distinguish the predominantly Hebrew texts from the Greek texts of the Christian Bible, perhaps they were less value laden than they are today, given that in the ancient world novelty was not prized as it is now. However, it could be that even at their origin they had a supersessionist connotation.[9] In any case, Christian supersessionism is now increasingly recognized to be problematic, in light of its catastrophic consequences for Jews. The terms that I employ here are simply a nod in the direction of developing a new approach to the attitude of Christianity (and Christians) toward Judaism (and Jews).

I have uppercased Torah when it refers to the Pentateuch. It is lowercased when it refers to divine teaching more broadly.

Ancient Israel and the current nation-state are not to be confused. I have used the terms "Israel" and "Israelites" to refer to the ancient Hebrew-speaking people who wrote the psalms and for whom they were written. This designation overlaps with Jews and Judaism and the Jewish people, depending on one's dating of individual psalms. I rarely mention the current nation-state, but when I do, I refer to it as the State of Israel.

Translations from the Older Testament are my own unless otherwise noted. In some instances I use the New Revised Standard Version (NRSV). Versification follows the NRSV.

Italics in quotations from various commentators indicate scripture citations where these are so designated in the source.

Finally, the reader will be greatly assisted by reading this commentary with a Bible in hand.

---

9. This may be the case at 2 Cor. 5:17: "If anyone is in Christ, there is a new creation; everything old has passed away; see, everything has become new!" (NRSV).

PSALM 1

Canonical Context and Themes

The canonical authority of the opening poem of the Psalter is vast. Only the final poem has comparable rhetorical power. Here, warning prevails; there celebration triumphs. Psalm 1 is generally understood to have been intentionally placed—perhaps intentionally written—at the head of the Psalter to frame what follows theologically, and so I read it here. Psalm 1 depicts Israel as divided against itself. The spiritually strong who are able to resist bad advice to scorn God's teaching (torah) will thrive, like fruit-bearing trees, faithful to God's claim on their lives; those who scoff at torah and do not live by it are depicted as languishing sinners, perishing from their own cynicism.

In light of the psalms that follow, especially in Book 1 of the Psalter (Pss. 1–41), the issue driving the division is theodicy, the goodness and power of God in light of human suffering and Israel's public defeats. If God does not answer when we are in trouble, is he really "there"? Are we foolish to remain faithful? This penetrating question hangs over the Psalter, bubbling over in the laments and supplications. One of the psalmists' hopes in writing these poems is to strengthen faithful Israelites that they might cling to God's power and goodness, come what may.

The many complaints voiced by the confounded righteous, that they are not flourishing but languishing miserably and inexplicably in the dark despair of isolation, rivets the Psalter on theodicy. The faithful are neglected by friends, spurned by family, and even abandoned by God, while the faithless who have given up on God rudely scorn them, seemingly unchastened. Scoffers sneer and jeer at those who hold fast to the teaching of God. Cynical Israelites seem to have the upper hand, since the poem would console the faithful with the eschatological hope that they will ultimately be vindicated while the scoffers will perish. But at the moment, moral justice seems to be upside down! In light of subsequent poems, Ps. 1 daringly frames the persistent message of the Psalter: the faithful

1

who steadfastly cling to Israel's ancestral faith will eventually flourish; scoffers, who seem to have the upper hand now, will eventually falter. The message of this psalm anticipates the trenchant observation of Ps. 12:1 that faithfulness has vanished from Israel. The faithful feel isolated and ridiculed.

In the fifth century, Theodoret of Cyrus, perhaps sensitive to the dubiousness of the hope that the righteous will soon be vindicated while the wicked will languish, read Ps. 1 precisely this way.[1] The poet is not describing the experience of the faithful but the "dogmatic truth" of the text. This softens the implied anguish of the faithful by shifting their hope to the noetic realm where their vindication is not accomplished empirically but hoped for eschatologically. This takes the pressure off thinking that the vindication of the righteous will be realized any time soon.

The words "dogmatic truth" may not roll trippingly across many tongues today, especially when considering a poem that seems so upbeat on first reading, but Theodoret may have a point. That the wicked will not withstand judgment—presumably in the divine court—and that the righteous will be vindicated for their faithfulness is not a hope for empirical vindication but an exhortation to long-term hope that conceals a threat. If God will stand by this threat in some ultimate way (several of the verbs in the poem are in the future tense), one ignores this notice at one's peril. As a frame for the Psalter, Ps. 1 is exquisitely ambiguous, offering comfort and encouragement with one hand and challenge and threat with the other. Psalm 1 is a warning label.

Structure and Dynamics

Psalm 1's six terse verses depict the strength of the pious (1:1–3), mark the weakness of the impious and their ultimate fate (1:4–5), and commend the vindication of the righteous and the demise of the wicked (1:6).

Spiritual Strength (1:1–3)

The featured signature of the pious who prosper spiritually and morally, although they may languish socially or perhaps even physically, is their ability to resist the skepticism to which those who scoff at them succumb. By contrast, the wicked are those who scoff at faithfulness (*lēṣîm*), thus adumbrating the lament psalms that follow, in which the oppressed speakers chafe under the scorn of their opponents. That the opening verse of the Psalter abjures the ridicule of the faithful suggests that the lament psalms stand in the background and the theodicy question (which first appears at Ps. 3) in the fore. Strength here is the ability to resist the tempting advice of the wicked to abandon the way that God has set forth in torah (1:2). To be like a flourishing tree that bears fruit and whose leaves do not wither because it is planted near water (1:3) is not an absolute value or standard

---

1. Theodoret 2000, 50–51.

to which one adheres; it is an image of resilience, of one's ability to withstand drought—that is, resist the scornful ways of the wicked, who scoff at God's way because of God's silence before the suffering of his devotees.

The poet is exquisitely sensitive to the temptation to succumb to mocking godliness, and he exalts those who successfully resist. Those who thwart skepticism by remaining faithful are cognizant of how their behavior reflects God's teaching (1:2). They are Israel's true heroes.

Spiritual Weakness (1:4–5)

The weakness of the spiritually vapid who scorn God contrasts with the strength of the spiritually resilient who successfully resist the temptation to cynicism. The wicked are not evil in a criminal or psychological sense. Rather, they cannot withstand spiritual and theological challenge and succumb to skepticism; their weakness is elicited by God's hiddenness, evidenced by Israel's setbacks. Again, spiritually sturdy members of the community are not deterred by spiritually feebler members but see beyond spiritual weakness—succumbing to the temptation to religious assimilation—and tenaciously adhere to God's goodness and power on behalf of Israel, even when they are not evident.

Spiritual Vindication (1:6)

Not surprisingly, the final verse of the Psalter's opening poem reassures the psalmist's hearers that God will protect the righteous and abandon the wicked, even though the laments still cry plaintively for just such vindication. Thus the Psalter's brief opening poem anticipates the cry of later poems to resist skepticism. It proclaims God's ultimate alliance with those spiritually robust enough to hold fast to God's way, even when empirical evidence bespeaks a contrary reality.

Theological Pedagogy

Read in light of the laments that follow, in which the righteous are constantly assailed by scoffers and even tempted by the very doubts eloquently voiced by skeptics, Ps. 1 stands as a fiery gateway to the Psalter. Piety in Israel is not stress-free. God's power and presence are not evident in every circumstance; each Israelite must decide how to respond. If the laments, including their several imprecations, do stand behind the rallying cry of this song, Ps. 1 identifies the theological hope driving many of the poems in the collection. Even if the pious currently languish outwardly and the impious flourish outwardly, it behooves Israel to resist abandoning the ancestral faith. The theodicy question looms large over the Psalter, and Ps. 1 anticipates the concern even before it is voiced by Ps. 3. Israel simply cannot succumb to the temptation of abandoning God as some apparently have, worshiping other gods. Israel's very honor as the people of God is at stake; beyond it lurks the integrity of God's identity as the creator of heaven and earth, which the nations must eventually admit.

If the author of Ps. 1 does have the sufferers of the lament psalms in mind as he writes, he is preaching a searingly urgent message. "Happiness" lies not in the signs of outward success that others, including the wicked, may enjoy, but in the joy of a conscious faithfulness to the way God has called his people to go, regardless of the price. Even if God is silent and does not restore the godly to positions of honor and status in the short term, the faithful triumph spiritually because they are the strong trees that bear fruit and vibrant leaves; they know themselves to be so, and that is rewarding. The wicked may insult them, but their failure to defeat faithfulness in Israel renders their chatter like empty chaff that the wind disperses (1:4). No one of moral substance can be taken in by them; as for those lacking in moral substance, well, the godly need not be perturbed. They will compassionately seek to raise the faithless to a higher level, leading by example. Being a faithful Israelite, Jew, or Christian is not easy, but dignified and honorable, making it possible to rest in one's integrity as one of God's flourishing "trees."

PSALM 2

Canonical Context and Themes

Psalm 1 introduces God's demand for the faithfulness of people in general. But since the Psalter is directed primarily at Israel (with regular complaints about scoffing Israelites who ridicule faithful Israelites), it is reasonable to conclude that Ps. 1 has Israel primarily, though perhaps not exclusively, in mind. Psalm 2, on the contrary, extends the demand for faithfulness to Israel's God to "the nations," introducing a second great theme of the Psalter.

The two opening psalms are quite different in style and have been categorized as a wisdom psalm, reminiscent of Proverbs—and more specifically, as a torah psalm—and as a messianic[1] or royal psalm, respectively. Both articulate a common theme: God demands piety and obedience from all people, Jews and gentiles alike.[2] While Ps. 1 urges Jews to live by the received teachings of God, Ps. 2 lays a far more difficult calling upon the Jewish people. Not only are they to cling to the teachings that God mapped out for them in torah, but they are also to live into God's missionary call to bring the nations to him.[3] Here, that call is portrayed in terms of military conquest in much the same way that Islam would later adopt a missionary posture. Israel's imperial designs include both economic prosperity

---

1. Despite expectant Christian interpretation, it is unlikely that on its own terms this poem has messianic intentions. It is not clear that Israel harbored messianic hopes at that time, it being in a period of relative peace. Within Israel, messianism arises under repressive conditions. Here Israel is depicted as the power holder. Christian messianic hope is a longing for personal redemption from sin and guilt. In this psalm, those seeking "redemption" are seeking release from God's claim on them, not from their sin, as Christian theology later envisioned messianic hope.

2. Miller sees this as a "resonance" between the two poems (1986, 87).

3. Many commentators read Ps. 2 messianically through Younger Testament filters: recently (Gunn 2012), eschatologically (Høgenhaven 2001), and in a somewhat weaker vein, prophetically (Goldingay 2006, 94–95).

and religious hegemony. I read Ps. 2 neither messianically nor eschatologically but evangelistically. Israel's empire does not exist for its own aggrandizement or hegemony but as an instrument of God's universal claim on creation. Distinguishing one from the other can be challenging.

In Ps. 2, God puts a stressful second burden upon Israel. Israel's faithfulness, even amid untoward circumstances that may feel like abandonment, is essential for establishing God's reign over the nations of the earth, administered by his anointed king.

Structure and Dynamics

Psalm 2 is a dramatic confrontation among God, the nations, and watching Israel that is narrated by the poet, who tersely articulates the anxieties and delicate relationships among the principals. In addition to the narrator, who controls the flow of the poem, the speaking characters are the earthly kings and God. The poem easily breaks into four tercets.

The Nations Oppose God and His Anointed (2:1–3)

The opening tercet of this song portrays a dramatic battle of wills between God and the nations that adumbrates coming poems (e.g., Pss. 45–49). It opens with a general observation that sets forth the theme of the poem, so memorably vivified by composer Leonard Bernstein in his *Chichester Psalms*. Bernstein casts this psalm in dialogue with Ps. 23. Psalm 2 announces the second great theme of the Psalter. The poet envisions the nations surrounding Israel as vassals who should peacefully submit to the rule of God, administered through God's anointed king. Instead, they are aggrieved and restively seek their freedom from God's constraining tutelage. The language of conspiracy conjures up the image of a well-crafted plot by Israel's surrounding neighbors.

Moving clockwise from the northwest, the nations surrounding the united kingdom are Phoenicia (Sidon and Tyre in Lebanon), Aram (Syria), Ammon, Moab, Edom, and Philistia. The Older Testament is studded with stories depicting the course of international relations among these actors, with the Assyrian Empire (900–607 BCE) overarching the entire region.

While one might initially picture David as the anointed king in this psalm, lacking a superscription it seems decidedly undavidic, given that every other psalm in Book 1 that has a superscription is so identified. As John Goldingay points out, "While David and Solomon ruled an empire, we know of no time when Israel ruled the size of empire presupposed by th[is] psalm." Therefore, it is likely that Ps. 2 "deals with a hypothetical but destined sovereignty."[4] That is, God's sovereignty is identified with Israel's vaunted sovereignty.

4. Goldingay 2006, 95–96.

Depicting "the nations" as potential vassal kingdoms of Israel/Judah is designed to rouse support for Israel's imperial longings. The hostility between these nations and Israel/Judah is palpable. The gentile kings plotting against God's anointed have formed a conspiracy (at least in the imagination of the poet) and speak their objections and intentions forthrightly. They resist serving God and his anointed representative whose military strength already constrains them financially and perhaps religiously. They suffer indignity, and the narrator has them speak their complaint aloud before Israel/Judah, along with their plan to cast off the yoke of Israelite oppression (2:3) in order to free themselves from God and the power of Judah.

The vassal kings hide neither their irritation nor their plans. Israel/Judah is persuaded that the nations belong to God and have carried forward that sacred mission militarily. The kings now resist their conqueror, presumably on their own authority and with their gods in tow. Regardless of the precise historical situation behind the poem, Israel—or at least the psalmist—has embedded its territorial conquest in its theological mission and has been met with determined resistance. Assuming that the psalmist was aware of how deeply apostasy had taken hold of at least half of the tribes of Israel (Asher, Manasseh, Zebulun, Ephraim, Judah, and Benjamin are mentioned in 2 Chr. 30–31), Ps. 1 admonishes Israel to capitulate neither to idolatry nor to skepticism, and Ps. 2 intends to transform the sources of idolatrous influences (as far back as Solomon) that contaminate Israel into springs of living water from which the worship of God might again flow.

The Lord Addresses the Nations (2:4–6)

The narrator resumes addressing Israel in the second tercet, speaking for God on this matter to encourage Israel to persevere in its global mission in his name. Perhaps to reinforce Israel's mission among the nations, the narrator informs his audience in the name of God's authority that God is angry with those nations that rebel against Judah's might; God mocks and derides these rebels. In 2:4, the poet uses the same words (*yiśḥāq* and *yil'ag-lāmô*) and in the same order that the Chronicler uses them (2 Chr. 30:10). Perhaps the poet is indirectly likening the gentile kings who resist God's rule to wicked Israelites (mentioned in Ps. 1) who mock and deride faithful Israelites. The knife can plunge in two directions! God's derision at those who resist him applies equally to the nations who are to be brought to God and to Israel itself who must first be reclaimed for God in order to bring the nations along. The mission is both within and beyond Israel.

With faithless Israelites mocking and deriding faithful Israelites, severely distressing them as hinted at in Ps. 1, and with God mocking and deriding the kings who seek to escape God's authority, as conveyed by the poet in Ps. 2, a rather spectacular setting is portrayed at the opening of the Psalter. Taken together, the two opening poems stage high drama among both protagonists and antagonists who populate the work: God, the faithful among Israel, Jewish skeptics who mock faithful Jews, and the surrounding nations, some of whom will submit to God. The complex engagements are diagramed as follows:

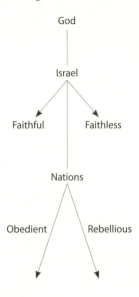

The Narrator Addresses Israel (2:7–9)

In the third tercet of this poem, the narrator turns from God's derisive address to the gentile kings and resumes speaking to Israel on God's behalf. The psalmist has God tell his expectant Israelite audience the same message he spoke to the foreign kings. God has formally declared himself to be the father of the anointed king, who will inherit the nations through violence mounted against them. God countenances Israel to use violence against the nations who resist his authority.

The Narrator Addresses the Nations (2:10–12)

In the final tercet, the narrator again turns from directly addressing Israel to addressing the foreign kings, this time on his own authority. He adjures them to serve Israel's God, implying that they must abandon their ancestral gods. Failure to worship Israel's God will result in disaster, for God will angrily destroy those who resist his authority. The poem ends on the threatening note of labile divine anger that may break free at any moment to consume its victims.[5] Yet the threat

5. The impenetrable phrase *naššĕqû-bar* is variously translated "kiss his feet" (NRSV), "kiss the Son" (NIV), "with purity be armed" (Alter), "submit sincerely" (Goldingay 2006), and "do homage in purity" (Jewish Publication Society). Whatever the precise intention of the author, the expected effect of the phrase is to intimidate the kings into submission under threat from divine anger.

morphs into a short but encouraging invitation. The nations are not doomed; they can enjoy equal privilege with Israel if they take refuge in God (as twenty-eight psalms frequently recommend).

Theological Pedagogy

This poem occupies an exalted place at the Psalter's opening, either as part of its introduction or perhaps as the first substantive psalm. Regardless of the editor's intent, the effect of placing this psalm at the head of the collection alerts the reader to the second great theme of the work. Israel may be tempted to read God's relationship to itself tribally, but prescient Israelites know that God's designs reach further. While Hezekiah may have had designs on all of Israel and Judah for God (2 Chr. 30), Jews in exile and afterward know that God claims every nation for himself.

Israel must nourish its ancestral faith amid temptations to apostasy, not only for the sake of its own well-being as pleasing to God but also toward a greater end—that God might be embraced by all the families of the earth (Gen. 12:3). The burden on Israel is pronounced, and its mission to pagans is stated here in harsh terms that are difficult for later moral sensibilities to appreciate. It seems that this psalm warrants war against those whom Israel is charged to bring to God, placing Israel in a most awkward position. Personal religious taste is seconded not for the well-being of the individual, as much later Christian theology would hope, but for the sake of God's universal reign, even if it needs to be imposed by intimidation. This poem pulls readers intent on their personal well-being to subordinate that selfish longing to the greater glory of God—for whom they play but a bit part. Psalm 2 presses thoughtful readers beyond self-assurance to genuine self-transcendence for the sake of others.

PSALM 3

Canonical Context and Themes

Psalm 3 inaugurates the sober tone so prevalent in the first half of the Psalter. Psalm 2 sets the frame for reading subsequent songs through a monarchical perspective, and Ps. 3 appropriately opens the collection of the "David psalms," which dominate Book 1, although with a more dour tone than Ps. 2 might lead one to expect.

A long descriptive superscription prefaces the text, setting it in one of several painful moments in the life of the king: his flight from Jerusalem after his son Absalom (whose name, ironically, means "father of peace") fomented a coup against him (2 Sam. 15). While the psalm surely predates the superscription, assigning this song to a poignant time in King David's life encourages later readers to contextualize it and interpret themselves through a salient moment in the biblical narrative. Poetry and narrative join forces to guide readers' emotions and behavior by offering both positive and negative incidents and role models. While this psalm can certainly be read in other ways, the superscription means to inform the reader's self-understanding; therefore, reading it intertextually is canonically warranted.[1]

The assigned superscription is obviously a "midrash" on Ps. 3. At the same time, it turns the poem into a gloss on a segment of the narrative of 2 Sam. 15.[2] Thus, quite apart from any original cultic or liturgical use, this poem becomes a spiritual guide, an imaginative reflection on a painful moment in Israel's history into which the reader is drawn. By means of the superscription, scripture is interpreting itself

---

1. Both Patrick D. Miller and James L. Mays encourage reading this psalm heuristically through its superscription for its theological, pastoral, and homiletical value (Miller 1986, 26–27; Mays 1994a, 127). Here I carry that recommendation forward.

2. Brevard Childs is one biblical exegete who welcomes the midrashic style invited by the addition of superscriptions (1971, 149–50).

so that the text may shape its readers for a noble or at least nobler life, inviting them to be transformed by identifying with Israel's greatest sinner-hero. Reviewing the story highlights both the poignancy and the theological pedagogy commended by the superscription.

Absalom's coup was one incident in the struggle for succession that anticipated David's death. Dynastic succession was not yet established in Israel, which had previously relied on charismatic leadership; David, having many sons, had not named an heir, perhaps fearing fratricidal intrigue among his male offspring whom he indulged to a fault. Absalom, David's third-born son, was ambitious. When David's first-born son, Amnon, raped his half sister Tamar, David failed to punish him. Absalom was outraged and, perhaps fearing that David would crown the rapist, stewed and plotted for two years, eventually arranging to have Amnon murdered in cold blood, at which time he fled to his mother's home country for three years, fearing his father's wrath.

Absalom managed to return to Jerusalem, and he formally reconciled with his father after two more years in seclusion (perhaps when David's wrath had abated), all the while campaigning among the populace for his own candidacy to succeed the king. The narrative indicates that people were suffering under a corrupt legal system, and Absalom promised them favorable treatment should he inherit the throne (2 Sam. 15:2–6). Gaining a following, Absalom made contacts throughout Israel, strengthened support for himself, and acquired a retinue. He waited yet another four years and, when ready to strike, returned to his birthplace, Hebron; under a pretext, he had himself declared king there and organized troops against his father.

Learning of his son's impending attack and his popularity among the people, David did not mobilize but, to protect Jerusalem from battle, went into mourning and fled the city, crossing the Kidron Valley toward the desert and taking people with him. "David ascended the Mount of Olives, climbing barefoot with his head covered and weeping" (2 Sam. 15:30).

Structure and Dynamics

Psalm 3 is often classified by modern commentators as a lament, but the opening two-verse lament is really only the gateway for a song of confident trust in God. Indeed, the complaint of 3:2 that the speaker's foes insult him saying, "there is no salvation for him in God," is rebutted by the last verse: "Salvation is of the LORD." The theme here is not human languishing but divine rescue and how people are to position themselves to expect and rejoice in it.[3]

The poem opens with the speaker explaining his circumstance to God using the form of direct address (3:1–2). However, the complainant immediately rebounds

---

3. The Hebrew stem is *yš'*, meaning "rescue, deliverance, or salvation." The word is ambiguous and can imply either material or spiritual release (or both) from an untoward situation, as in this psalm.

from self-pity, and the poem's remaining six verses sing of confident trust, proclaiming the speaker's deep sense of security in God's hands. Psalm 3:3–8 may be divided into four further subsections according to the function of the material.[4] Psalm 3:3–6 states the speaker's deep trust in God's unfailing care, and on that basis 3:7–8a issues a rousing call to God for rescue based on such faith. The last half of the final verse (3:8b) fans out beyond the complainant to conclude on a note of hope: a call for God to bless his people with deliverance.[5] This poem moves from anxious personal complaint to confident national optimism in fewer than sixty-five words.

The rapid changes of emotional tone and linguistic point of view in the poem cast it as a sort of shuttle diplomacy among parties who do not speak directly with one another. The speaker addresses God first and then his enemies, perhaps indirectly; the observer is always within earshot. The various linguistic points of view taken by the speaker not only engage various audiences, but they also aid the pedagogical intention of the superscription that constructs an intertextual reading of the poem. Interpreting it through 2 Samuel invites the reader to read his own circumstance—or perhaps better, his own life—through David taking refuge in God's power to deliver him from his enemies, even his own son.

Rashi sets the ominous tone for interpreting the psalm intertextually by pointing back to 2 Sam. 12:11, Nathan's portent to David's life when calling him to account for both adultery and murder: "I am about to bring upon you trouble from within your own family."[6] David brought his troubles on himself. The message seems to be that untrammeled lust reaps disastrous consequences.

The Complaint (3:1–2)

The opening verses set the speaker's plight before God to get his attention and arouse his compassion. It is not clear that these are personal enemies, however, for the complaint against them is that they mock the speaker's trust in God. The speaker's enemies, then, are also God's enemies, for by insulting the faithful complainant, they insult God's ability or willingness to rescue those who trust him. From the first, the speaker allies himself with God against their common foe: those who distrust God.

Quite apart from any physical or material harm the enemies might inflict, the hurt they hurl is against the speaker's faith. They tease him for trusting God, and their taunt that the suppliant foolishly relies on God seems more piercing than

---

4. Dharmakkan Dhanaraj structures this psalm in three segments depending on the point of view taken by the speaker. Psalm 3:1–3 and 3:7–8 are addressed directly to God, while Ps. 3:4–6 is in the first person singular. However, these divisions do not take account of how the various points of view function in the overall movement of the poem (1992, 90–91).

5. Alter finds the national perspective at the end to be so jarring that he considers it to be a "tag from somewhere else introduced in redaction" (2007, 9).

6. Rashi 2004, 183.

any impending injury. Psalm 1:1 has already warned the reader against associating with taunting scoffers, skeptics who deny that imploring God for help does any good. Those who trust in God when in distress reap the scorn of skeptics who torment with sarcasm.

Deep Trust (3:3–6)

The complainant defiantly resists the temptation to succumb to the cynicism to which his opponents have succumbed. Psalm 3:3 remains directly addressed to God, but its tone is now confident. The speaker's trust will not be shaken; although enemies surround him, God shields him from them and holds up his head. While in 3:2 the speaker allies himself with God, Ps. 3:3 allies God with himself. His point is not only that he is faithful to God, but also that God is faithful to him.

At Ps. 3:4 the discourse switches from direct address to first-person musing (3:4–6). This soliloquy may be offered as a sotto voce retort to the foes who seek to turn the speaker from trust in God (3:2), as a way to let observers of the scene in on the complainant's plan to seek redress from God and his state of mind, or perhaps as a little pep talk to himself to sustain his confidence in the face of the taunts. In effect, it accomplishes all three purposes. Psalm 3:4 is an antiphonal dialogue the speaker has with himself: "I will call aloud to the LORD and he will answer me from his holy mountain." Psalm 3:5 relays a calm inner state in which the speaker sleeps well and wakes up feeling that God has sustained him through the night, and Ps. 3:6 reports that he will not fear, though myriads array themselves against him.

From the soliloquy, the reader learns that the speaker draws his dignity and inner calm from trust in God. Enemies cannot damage his dignity because they have no access to it. The speaker—no longer a complainant but now a strong defender of God—believes that God sympathizes with him because he is faithful, and he shores himself up with that knowledge. Overhearing the soliloquy, the scoffers are chastised, seeing their insults come to naught.

If one proceeds to read intertextually, a riveting scene comes into view. David in mourning—weeping, head covered, and barefoot—is climbing the steep Mount of Olives, refusing to take up arms against his son and in visible retreat from his stronghold. Jerusalem watches and weeps, the people covering their heads, mourning with him as he goes. Is he mourning for the impending loss of his life, assuming his son will slay him? Is it for the loss of his kingdom? Or is he mourning in penitent shame for his treatment of his son, for the desolate Tamar, or perhaps for his manifold sins and offenses? The reader does not know. What the superscriptor would like the reader to learn from this towering figure bent over in public humiliation before his people, crying aloud in earshot of his tormentors, is that David's mourning itself is God's shield about him; in mourning he lifts his head honorably high amid the mortification (3:3). Ironically, his humiliation crowns him with honor; his mortification is his vindication. The intertextual reading puts words of trust in God in David's mouth: "I will cry aloud to the LORD, and he will answer me from his holy mountain" (3:4). David, for all his foolish antics throughout his career, emerges heroic as he models humility and dignity in and through his shame by casting himself on God's care. This is a great reversal of conventional wisdom, including David's own, about power and honor.

The reader is drawn to read Ps. 3:5–6 with David at the summit of the Mount of Olives looking down on his beloved city, sustained by his trust in God, sleeping securely, unafraid of his son's legions seeking his life. Indeed, 2 Sam. 16:11–12 gives credence to this midrash-like interpretation. It recounts that David deters his men from harming a Saulide named Shimei who, seeking revenge against David (who murdered Saul's son Ishbaal in order to destroy the house of Saul and solidify David's control of the monarchy [2 Sam. 4:1–8]), understandably curses David as a murderous scoundrel (2 Sam. 16:5–8). The scene unfolds just as Absalom enters Jerusalem. David, acknowledging his past sin and perhaps wanting to end a vicious cycle of revenge, says to his handlers: "My own son seeks my life; how much more now may this Benjaminite! Let him alone, and let him curse; for the LORD has bidden him. It may be that the LORD will look on my distress, and the LORD will repay me with good for this cursing of me today" (2 Sam. 16:11–12).

David accepts being publically cursed for his murderous actions as divine sanction—as a gift really—and so he sleeps and awakes peacefully, as the psalmist puts it (Ps. 3:5), for his public shaming is warranted. David the scoundrel suddenly soars to moral heights in the crucible of humiliation. Although the poem does not mention confession or repentance, its unstated message is that if David can so rise to the occasion, the listener can too. Perhaps with this powerful image in mind, the psalmist writes, "I will not fear myriads of people who have set themselves all around me" (3:6).

Rescue (3:7–8a)

Turning from his musing back to the crisis at hand, the speaker again addresses God directly and urges him to rise up and rescue his faithful one, reminding him of his previous routing of enemies. God has punched his enemies in the mouth and broken their teeth in the past (3:7). The first two words of Ps. 3:8a—"rescue is of the LORD"—may be considered with 3:7 as a conclusion to the call to action, especially since it repeats the word "rescue," which is the main theme of the psalm first used in 3:2.

Returning to the intertextual reading, a call for vengeance seems completely out of place for a figure brought low, or in this case, lifted up by repentance. If one imaginatively sustains the reading of Ps. 3 as a gloss on David's life and character, perhaps the enemies of 3:7 may be read not as the speaker's external enemies, but his internal ones. Israel's most troubled king does battle with his unconstrained personality that committed dastardly deeds, which have haunted him from the beginning of his reign to the present day. The smashed face and broken teeth become David's smashed cunning and broken ambition. The call for God to rise up and rescue him in Ps. 3:7 is a cry to rescue him from himself. David cannot deliver himself from his weaknesses; only God can do that, for "rescue is of the LORD" (3:8a).

National Hope (3:8b)

The final three Hebrew words of this poem turn in a completely new direction, of which the preceding gave no intimation: "May your blessing be on your people!" (NRSV). Indeed, if God has finally broken David's worst enemies—the unbridled passions of his lust and ambition—through the words and actions of God's instruments Absalom and Shimei (and going further back, Nathan), it is a boon for God's people who are David's people. God's "deliverance of David the king" is indeed a blessing on all Israel. A transformed king, raised up by God's grace in the sight of his people, is God's good news for the people.

Theological Pedagogy

Identifying David as the speaker in this psalm may seem like quite a stretch and the story of his flight from Absalom a surprising choice. Although some readers or singers of this song may well find themselves pursued by their children with an army in tow, it is likely that dysfunctional family dynamics will work themselves out in more subtle forms of estrangement. Yet the association of the speaker of Ps. 3 with David points toward the usefulness of the psalm for those in analogous situations—such as those with the challenge of being the ambitious son of a famous and equally ambitious father who can be impulsive, extravagant, and crafty by turns, yet is unfailingly brilliant at his appointed tasks.

A second surprise in setting the psalm in the context of David's troubled relationship with one of his sons is that it invites the reader to identify with this less-than-virtuous father. Modern psychology emphasizes the negative effects of erratic and outright bad parenting on children, which arouses sympathy for the child rather than the parent. Abraham Ibn Ezra boldly takes David's side, however, and defines God's people as "those who fought on behalf of David. They and not those who aid a son to rebel against his father are truly the people of God."[7] Ibn Ezra both encourages a plan of action (fighting on behalf of David) and discourages a line of action (rebelling against a father).

Of course the psalm takes David's side, but so does 2 Samuel in at least two instances. On one occasion Ahithophel, David's trusted aide, deserts him; calculating that Absalom will usurp the throne, he seeks to ingratiate himself with the son, advising him on how to bring down his father. When David learns of his friend's treachery, he does not act vengefully but prays to God to thwart Ahithophel's

7. Ibn Ezra 2006, 37.

"foolishness" (2 Sam. 15:31), and so it comes to be. Absalom abjures Ahithophel's advice, and when the traitor learns this, he returns to his hometown and hangs himself, realizing that he alienated both father and son with his intrigue (2 Sam. 17:1–23). Another instance of God's support for David is that Absalom's rebellion fails, and he is put to death against his father's orders (2 Sam. 18). David is distraught, in emotional disarray at the death of his rebellious son (2 Sam. 18:32–19:4).

Cast as a comment on David's inner life as a result of the twists and turns of this tumultuous relationship with his son, the psalm is an opportunity for other fathers to review their relationship to their own sons and reflect on the impact they have. Similarly, it invites sons to reflect on how much they have been formed in reaction to their father's behavior toward them. For his part, Absalom seems to be something of a "chip off the ol' block." He uses some of his father's own deceptive and nasty tactics to advance himself. For instance, when he humiliates his father to impress the people with his power, provocatively violating his father's concubines and usurping the realm by exploiting his father's property (2 Sam. 15:16; 16:20–22).

God's role in the interplay between the story and the psalm is noteworthy. The speaker's staunch trust in God against scoffers is reinforced by the 2 Samuel narrative in which God acts behind the scenes. God brings David to repentance, punishes Absalom, and finally vindicates the repentant king. Proposing David in all his moral ambiguity as God's defender strikingly portrays God's empathy and compassion for those trapped in a cycle of sin and repentance. The superscription takes Ps. 3 out of the realm of generality and pious entreaties and concretizes the struggle to hold to God amid political, sexual, military, and dynastic struggles. By drawing the reader into this unsavory moment in Israel's history, the superscriptor uses the psalm as a therapeutic tool for the formation of the men of Israel, calling them to account as fathers and as sons.

Psalm 3's message should not be lost on those who trace their lineage through that other descendant of David, Jesus of Nazareth. Mention has already been made of the great reversal of strength in weakness that David finds at the hands of Absalom particularly, but also of Ahithophel and Shimei. David breaks the cycle of revenge, eschewing violence and cunning for the dignity and honor found in God's ability to rescue him. Indeed, his salvation is the forsaking of these vicious manners. Jesus models himself on David by praying and leading his disciples to the Mount of Olives (Matt. 26:30). When sought by his enemies, he gives himself over to them without fuss or fight. His death is the crowning moment of his dignity and honor. It builds on David's climbing that same Mount of Olives centuries before—barefoot, head covered, and weeping—"that all this assembly may know that the LORD does not save by sword and spear" (1 Sam. 17:47).

PSALM 4

Canonical Context and Themes

Like Ps. 3, Ps. 4 begins as an individual lament and quickly blossoms into a song of confident hope. Indeed, the two psalms have much in common. They are about the same length, and both are inscribed to David, although Ps. 4 lacks a narrative superscription. Instead, its superscription gives instruction for liturgical performance: to be accompanied by stringed instruments. Like its predecessor, Ps. 4 opens in the first person but shifts even more quickly to other voices (4:2).

Psalm 4 is not a prayer for deliverance from personal enemies (or at least external foes), for they are not mentioned. Rather, a psychological anxiety torments the speaker. It seems that his relationship with God, not his relationships with other people, is out of joint. This poem pleads for a good night's sleep that comes from peace with God. Perhaps it is placed next to Ps. 3 because they both mention the importance of peaceful sleep secured by God's answer to prayer.

At the theological level, however, this poem resonates with a central theme: election. The speaker's sleeplessness, which he seeks to be soothed away, is born from the fear that he might not be among those faithful to God who are set apart by God, presumably for blessing (4:3). No indications of divine wrath or threats of punishment are heard here; instead, the poet instructs his readers on how to obtain the same quiet conscience that Luther's doctrine of justification sought.

Without a narrative superscription, an intertextual reading is not warranted. Rather, I will chart a path through the various linguistic points of view, speakers, emotions, and themes as they overlap, diverge, and converge to disclose the theological pedagogy of the poem.

Structure and Dynamics

Like its predecessor, this psalm moves rapidly among speakers and audiences. Psalm 4:1 is the plea of the primary speaker to be listened to by God. Psalm 4:2 presents either the speaker speaking against his detractors or God speaking directly to humanity at large, admonishing those who dishonor him. Psalm 4:3 returns to the narrator—presumably the original speaker—who speaks to the same general audience just addressed by God to reassure them that God's followers will be set apart by God and presumably escape any divine censure, although none is specified. Psalm 4:4–5 provides advice on how to avoid being among the censured and how to quell anxiety at the thought that one might be among them. Psalm 4:6–8 returns to the first person and is addressed to God. Thus a conversation emerges between the one pleading for divine attention and God, with both parties speaking to the larger congregation of those who might also suffer anxiety at not knowing whether they are among those who dishonor God or among those who are God's faithful followers, set apart to dwell in safety.

The Plea (4:1)

Here the plight of the speaker is far less clear than it was in the previous poem, since enemies are not mentioned and no cause for the distress is given. The pleader opens the poem by asking God to answer him and heed his call because he (God) is righteous; he has gotten the speaker out of a tough spot in the past, thereby positioning himself to act graciously to those who implore him to listen.

In the *Midrash on Psalms*,[1] R. Ze'era comments on this verse as follows: "Suppose a man has a friend who so importunes him with his needs and his wants that the man comes to dislike him and tries to avoid him. But with the Holy One, blessed be He, it is not so. The more a man importunes God with his needs and his wants, the more God loves him."[2] By inverting the results of requesting too much too frequently from one's friends, Ze'era cultivates confidence in approaching God with one's needs. John Chrysostom, bishop of Antioch, encourages prayer from a different angle:

> Let us too study, therefore, how to converse with God; let us learn how we must make this entreaty. There is no need to take ourselves to a library, nor outlay money, nor hire teachers or orators or debaters, nor devote a great deal of time to learning this oratorical skill. It is instead sufficient to want to do it, and the skills fall in place. In this tribunal you will be able to speak not only for yourself but also for many others.[3]

1. The *Midrash on Psalms* is a compilation of mini-homilies on words and verses in the Psalter and related biblical texts. Attributed to various rabbis, it was compiled between the fourth and the ninth centuries (Braude 1959a).
2. Braude 1959a, 65–66.
3. Chrysostom 1998, 49.

An Admonition (4:2)

Surprisingly, 4:2 is not an answer from God but an irritated admonition to all people. The words come in the form of a cry that is familiar to readers of psalms, though it is usually found on the lips of suppliants: "How long . . . will you dishonor me by loving vanity and seeking out lies?" The speaker is exasperated. This untoward behavior has apparently been going on for some time. But how is this related to the plea in 4:1, registered by one innocent, for there is no indication that the call is from a penitent heart? A possible answer comes from Ps. 4:3.

Assurance (4:3)

It is unclear who the speaker is but probably the suppliant, since the second half of 4:3 restates his confidence that "God will listen when I call upon him." The first half of 4:3 speaks to those addressed by God's irritated admonition, encouraging them to remain calm because "God sets the faithful apart." Evidently, the challenge here is that people are asking themselves (or at least should be asking themselves) whether they are among those who dishonor God with vain and lying lives or whether they believe themselves to be among the faithful whom God will separate from the dross. This interpretation explains the unease in Ps. 4:1. The pleader is worried that he might not be among the elected faithful, yet confident that he can approach God openly, trusting that God will respond compassionately and look favorably on him.

Counsel (4:4–5)

Here the narrator (the pleader) counsels his auditors on how to deal with the anxiety created by the ambiguity of their situation, which is apparently keeping some of them up at night.[4] When distressed by worrisome ruminations that chase sleep away, one should not sin, for that would make matters worse.[5] Although anxiety may chase sleep away, the poet counsels thinking about it so as not to

4. The syntax of this verse is "choppy," as Alter notes (2007, 11).

5. The Hebrew verb here indicating disturbance is *rigzû*. The Septuagint translates it as *orgizesthe*. The Hebrew has a broader lexical range than the Greek word. The Hebrew meaning spans "being excited, agitated, irritated, bothered, angry, anxious, sorrowful, fearful, and disquieted," while the Greek word is limited to "being angry or furious." Since the church fathers worked with the Greek translation, they all counseled being still when angry and refraining from sin. The Revised Standard Version sustains the classic translation but the New Revised Standard Version uses the more ambiguous "when you are disturbed" instead, noting "are angry" as an alternative translation. Alter notes that the word actually means "quake" (2007, 11), giving rise to the broader lexical range in Hebrew since "quaking" can be produced by many intense emotions, of which anger is only one. The problem of selecting the best translation is compounded by the fact that in the Hebrew text the word appears as a plural imperative. It is not describing an emotional state but a command to do something: quake, be anxious, be afraid as an alternative to sinning. Any of these fit better with the interpretation that the sleeper's restlessness is caused by anxiety at his standing in God's sight; the idea of being angry with someone as a result of some incident that has occurred does not arise organically from the context of the psalm. If anyone has a right to be angry in this psalm it is God, who is being insulted by people's behavior. Before that knowledge, many are sleepless.

act upon whatever is bothering the guilt-ridden pleader. Self-calming is easier said than done. Augustine adds a thought on this point: "Even if there wells up a strong emotional reaction, which we cannot altogether help, because of our sinful inheritance, at any rate do not let reason and the mind collude with it. The mind has been reborn within and conformed with God. The upshot of this is that with the mind we serve the law of God, even if still in the flesh we serve the law of sin."[6] The second piece of advice is to offer right worship (sacrifices) and to trust God (4:5). Taken together, perhaps knowing that one serves the law of God and worships rightly will chase the demonic fear away.

Concluding Plea and Contentment (4:6–8)

The last three verses of this poem return to addressing God directly (as in the opening verse) and end on the note of trusting God, which is signaled at the end of 4:5. The speaker is no longer speaking for himself, however, but for the people. He informs God that people are asking for a tangible sign of his favor toward them (4:6). He then reminds God of the joy he experienced when prosperity reigned and food and drink were plentiful. Content himself, and modeling contentment for his hearers, he concludes: "I will lie down and sleep completely at peace, for you alone, LORD, return me to safety" (4:8).

Calvin offers a nurturing comment here: "This verse contains very profitable instruction. . . . Never, therefore, shall we obtain undisturbed peace and solid joy until the favour of God shine upon us. And although the faithful also desire and seek after their worldly comforts, yet they do not pursue them with immoderate and irregular ardour."[7] In this way, Calvin echoes the Augustinian notion of rightly ordered loves and uses it to motivate his readers to consider how, even when they are not being afflicted by the wicked, they are to live in accord with the urging of the psalm.

Theological Pedagogy

Psalm 4 seeks to embolden people to address God with confidence in regard to their anxieties and to find comfort and contentment in faithful living based on God's promise to set them aside for himself, even when he is displeased with them. The author is well aware of the distressing effects of anxiety and offers his boldness in approaching God as a model for others to emulate; in this way, fretful worry can be controlled, assuring sound sleep. All the while, the author counsels "do not sin" to quiet the soul.

The writer is psychologically astute. God must both set standards and be accessible to those who find themselves in that middle place between insulting him

6. Augustine 2000a, 88.
7. Calvin 1998, 49.

and being his faithful follower. This psalm does not espouse an all-or-nothing piety. People are not neatly divided into camps of "the faithful" and "sinners." Rather, everyone is striving for faithfulness and needing reassurance that God is open to their entreaties. The Lord's compassion is not to be presupposed, nor is it funneled through a juridical procedure as if suppliants were accused of heinous crimes, their heads on the block.

The pedagogy of contentment offered in Ps. 4 assumes an intimacy between God and the suppliant on which the latter can rely. Despite being exasperated by vicious living, God can be swayed by sincere entreaty. Perhaps more to the point, the author believes not only that one can control unruly emotions by trusting in God's past blessings of prosperity but also that one can sleep peacefully despite nagging doubts about where precisely one has been placed by God on the spectrum of faithless to faithful.

PSALM 5

Canonical Context and Themes

Following the pattern of the two previous psalms, Ps. 5 is dedicated to David and opens with a complaint addressed directly to God. Initially, this psalm might make Christians uncomfortable; rather than throwing himself on God's mercy as a sinner in need of forgiveness, as Christian piety encourages, the suppliant presents himself as a righteous and God-fearing Israelite facing deceitful rebels who deserve divine retribution for their wickedness against God. It follows the lead of Ps. 1 in dividing the wicked from the righteous, whose strength before God is their piety, before it turns vindictive in a way not previously seen.

The rabbinic sages were also uncomfortable with the vengeful tone of Ps. 5:10, and the *Midrash on Psalms* provides numerous imaginative plays on the superscription "[to be played] on the *něḥîlôt*" (flutes?) to invert its message so that the theological pedagogy of the psalm would edify readers. The rabbis note that the word meaning "possessions" is similar to *hanněḥîlôt*.[1] A place-name with the same root, *naḥălî'ēl* (God is my possession), appears twice in Num. 21, although it is probably unrelated to a musical instrument: "from Mattanah to Nahaliel, from Nahaliel to Bamoth" (Num. 21:19). Reading the place-name with its linguistic similarity to both "possessions" and an unknown instrument or song title of the psalm superscription, the rabbis interpret the latter to teach that the Israelites had taken possession of a false god. In regard to the place-name, the repetition is interpreted to mean that "there the children of Israel took possession (*naḥălî'ēl*) of the Holy One, blessed be He, as their God, and God took possession of them as His people," bringing Israel back to God.[2]

---

1. John Chrysostom also associates *hanněḥîlôt* with "possessions," although he interprets the text christologically (Chrysostom 1998, 78–81).

2. Braude 1959a, 80.

Structure and Dynamics

Like Ps. 3, this psalm begins as a personal lament and plea for God to respond to the speaker's cry, and it ends with a ringing sound of triumphant rejoicing for all who take refuge in God, confident that they will be blessed with divine favor. Written almost exclusively in the first person and second person, the tone of intimacy between the speaker and God places the psalm's singer in that relationship, giving him a place among Israel's faithful quite apart from evildoers. Psalm 5:1–3 states the suppliant's desire to be heard by God. The next three verses (5:4–6) remind God (and especially the psalm's audience) of God's standards of conduct for people. In Ps. 5:7–9 the speaker separates himself from the wicked and requests divine guidance, knowing that no good will come from listening to the advice of those who rebel against God. Psalm 5:10 stands alone as a call for God to bring down the impious because they have abandoned him. The final two verses (5:11–12) take a completely different tack by proclaiming the blessedness of the righteous in which they rejoice. Here the speaker is no longer referring to himself but to all those who, following his example and urging, take refuge in God as he did in 5:7. The psalm moves from a personal cry to God to a reminder of God's hatred for evildoers, followed by a confession of trust in God and a warning to avoid unjust companions. After this, the speaker calls for God to topple the unrighteous, and the psalm ends with confident hope in divine blessing for those who love the Lord.

Opening Address (5:1–3)

The opening clause of the psalm, "Listen to my words, O LORD," is reminiscent of the opening clause of Deut. 32:1, "Listen, O heavens, and I shall speak."[3] The Song of Moses, delivered to the whole assembly of Israel before he died, proclaims the greatness and righteousness of God against the already evident or anticipated degeneracy of those Israelites who have alienated themselves from God, polluting the land by abandoning the high standards of behavior and worship that God has set for them. The theme of Ps. 5 is the same. The speaker is not Moses but another who, perhaps recalling that thundering speech, calls to God in the morning—the time when one begins acting rightly, according to Jerome[4]—to pray and plead his case on behalf of the righteous against iniquity in Israel.

The three verbs in 5:1–2 are in the imperative and dramatize the scene: "Listen to my words . . . attend to my sighing . . . heed the voice of my cry, my king and my God." Patterning the psalm on the Song of Moses sets a dramatic and urgent tone for what will follow. The speaker states his plan of action in 5:2b–3. He will pray to God in the morning, and he reassures himself that God will hear him.

3. While it is not known for certain whether this psalm predates Deut. 32, it cannot be ruled out that the author of this psalm knew that text.
4. Jerome 1964, 17.

He will lay his case before God expecting an answer, assuming that he attends to the cries of Israel.

God's Standards (5:4–6)

This segment of the psalm continues addressing God in the second person, but not in the imperative. It reminds God—or perhaps the psalm's listeners or later singers—of the standards of righteousness that God demands of Israel by specifying behavior that God will not abide: general wickedness, unruliness, all evildoing, lying, bloodthirstiness, and fraud. God will tolerate none of this; he hates it all. It is a ringing denunciation with no quarter given. Calvin characteristically reads 5:4 as bridling us (a favorite theme of his, taken from Ps. 32:9) in order "to restrain us from committing sin, in the vain hope of escaping with impunity."[5] God is demanding. Here is the admonition that the opening verses prepare the listener to hear. Indeed, God's moral standards for Israel are stringent.[6]

Holding to God's Righteousness (5:7–9)

The standpoint of the suppliant contrasts with that of the wicked in Ps. 5:7–9, in which the speaker separates himself from the misdeeds of evildoers by speaking again in the first person. He sees himself as a model for those who would heed the message of his song, saying that he will enter God's house—that is, his great loving-kindness—and bow reverently in his holy temple (5:7). There the singer will rest in God's righteousness despite his enemies. He asks God to chart the best way forward for him, God's own way (5:8). Again, a sharp separation can be seen between the ways of the godly and the ungodly. While one may be tempted to take the latter's advice, 5:9 tells us that nothing that comes from their mouths can be trusted, for they portend nothing but trouble. They have nothing helpful to say; their throats are like open graves; their tongues are slick. Beware of their lure, he seems to say.

Condemnation of the Traitors (5:10)

Here the speaker seeks to assure his auditors that the guilty will self-destruct through the poverty of their own bad advice. He is sure that the enormity of their misdeeds will catch up with them, and he asks God to cast them off, for they have acted cruelly toward God by abusing the faithful.

5. Calvin 1998, 57.
6. It is worth recalling that the Tanakh presents no doctrine of fallen human nature, which is a Christian reading of Genesis inspired by Paul. In the purview of the Psalter, even if all persons commit sins, sinning is a matter of committing untoward acts. Free will is assumed, and serious evil can be avoided.

Final Blessing (5:11–12)

Psalm 5, like Pss. 3 and 4 before it, makes an abrupt turn at the end, concluding on a triumphant and hopeful note. Having taken refuge in heartfelt worship of God (5:7–8) and having sought God's guidance against those with slippery tongues, the speaker urges those who have the strength to rejoice and sing forever as they choose the excellent life, sheltering themselves in God's protection (5:11a). These last verses return to address God directly in the second person, with Israel overhearing the conversation. The speaker is sure that those who love and exalt God are righteous and will be blessed and crowned with divine favor.

Theological Pedagogy

Psalm 5 is often classed as a lament in the face of personal enemies or as an imprecation because of 5:10, which asks God to cast out the speaker's enemies. However, its dynamic movement, from personal plea to triumphant hope in God's blessing for those who follow the speaker in hewing to the path of pious obedience to the moral standards that God sets for Israel, suggests that the lament setting may be a literary device. The psalm's further spiritual and pastoral aims are made transparent by the use of the first and second person. The question of whether a psalm like this originated from a personal situation, or whether it is the artful creation of a sagacious teacher in Israel, fades behind the author's technique of placing the singer or speaker of the psalm in the role of the faithful against the wicked. The recitation itself gives the psalm's user the godly identity that its author intends, so that the "stirrings of our souls might be grasped, and [the psalm] be said as concerning us, and the same issue from us as our own words," as Athanasius puts it.[7]

Psalm 5's theological pedagogy follows the broad framework set forth in Ps. 1, which divides those who scoff at God from faithful Israelites. Whether sung in worship or later meditated upon in solitude, this poem gives corporate Israel and individual Israelites a self-concept worthy of their calling as God's possessions, according to the *Midrash on Psalms*.

This psalm gives little indication that the speaker is afflicted because of something he has done or even a position he has taken that is being opposed or thwarted by opponents. Enemies are mentioned once, in 5:8, presented as those whom God hates because of their immoral behavior. Although the speaker is in difficult straits, the complaint suggests that these people are the speaker's enemies because they are evil, not because the speaker is personally caught up in their schemes. Rather, the speaker's piety itself, his adherence to the life God has laid before Israel, is the cause of his distress, which has been brought about by seeing others debase themselves and bring Israel, and thereby God, into ill-repute. The issue this psalm sets before Israel is faithfulness itself, gauged not by personal experiences, inner

7. Athanasius 1980, 111.

feelings, or untoward thoughts, but by the very calling of Israel to live up to being the people of God. Each singer of this song calls Israel to God. Those who lack that strength and wallow in rebellion against God are not only the enemies of God but also the enemies of Israel within.

No suggestion is made that all are condemned while God chooses whom he will for special favor hidden from public view, as the Augustinian doctrine of election would lead western Christians to think. Those who lie and deceive, seek blood, and counsel others to evil deeds are wrong; they will fall by virtue of their iniquity itself. While anguished by the sight of such evil, those who give themselves over to divine guidance—who truly love God and protect themselves with the way of life he commends—will be blessed and rejoice forever. God has chosen this people as his own to live by moral standards that proclaim God's righteousness as the one true God, as the allusion to Deut. 32 suggests. God's intention will not be thwarted.

The psalm is teaching its readers what it means to be Israel. God has indeed chosen Israel, but if that election is to function as it ought—to be a blessing for all—Israel will need to eschew the foolishness that God despises. Psalm 5 places people in their proper faithful identity so that Israel may indeed be a light among nations. The psalmist's anguish arises from seeing Israel stumble before its high calling. If one thinks of this psalm as a motivational talk to create a high-minded corporate ethos in Israel, perhaps the Christian anxiety noted at the outset of this comment may be at least somewhat muted. Rather than viewing Ps. 5 as a pre- or sub-Christian complaint in which the speaker boasts of his righteousness while he should throw himself on the forgiving mercies of God, perhaps it should be seen as a training exercise that teaches those who pray it the fabric and texture of pious living by enabling them to think of themselves as those who love the name of the Lord and exult in it.

PSALM 6

Canonical Context and Themes

Psalm 6 is another distressed cry to God dedicated to David, although no narrative assignation specifies the situation. Its language is ambiguous, giving rise to various speculations as to what provoked its composition. It has been thought to be a prayer for healing from physical illness, but it is not clear whether a medical condition has given rise to anguish or whether intense anxiety caused by other factors is behind psychosomatic distress and, as in Ps. 4, sleepless nights.[1] Calvin takes the latter view, paraphrasing David as saying that "so severe and violent is the inward anguish of my heart, that it affects and impairs the strength of every part of my body."[2] In Christian tradition, it is also often read as the first of the Psalter's seven penitential psalms, yet no confession of sin and no plea for forgiveness are offered.[3] Nothing indicates that the speaker understands his adversity to be punishment for sin, only that it has apparently been going on for some time. The speaker cries out for healing, not forgiveness. It is best, however, not to argue over whether the cry is aroused by external adversaries or a medical condition since both could be considered to be the work of God's anger. Whatever the form of suffering, Ps. 6 clearly belongs amid this little collection of laments, which includes Pss. 4–7.

The speaker's belief that God is in control of events suggests to him that God must be angry with him and is disciplining him with these troubles. However, he does not lament this, and he is not experiencing Luther's *Anfechtung* (dread). His complaint is based on the assumption that life is normally orderly and fair, and so the assaults of his enemies—whether in the form of other people, illness, or

---

1. James L. Mays takes this view, adding that it became a penitential prayer when it moved into a cultic setting (1994b, 59–60).
2. Calvin 1998, 69.
3. Cassiodorus identifies seven psalms as penitential: 6, 32, 38, 51, 102, 130, and 143 (1990, 90).

perhaps some unnamed overwhelming anxiety disorder—bewilders him. Given his doctrine of providence, suddenly God makes no sense. The world is awry. His situation is Kafkaesque, and God—the power behind events—is its chief agent. He does not know to what end he is being corrected.

The speaker's confused cry to God intensifies the standard theme of previous complaints, with the experience of terror mentioned thrice in these eleven verses (6:2, 3, 10), and contextualizes it in another way. The speaker's doctrine of divine providence presses beyond whatever the presenting problem is to see that God is truly the one who threatens his life, be it literally, psychologically, or both. An ominous theme enters the Psalter: God is the enemy behind the enemy. Like lovers who need each other and yet are the source of each other's pain, God is both the problem and the solution.[4] The speaker struggles to regain his characteristic trust in God's goodness and mercy, imploring God to turn the tables on his experience of divine chastisement and be angry with his enemies instead. They are the ones who will be terrified; their nefarious plans will be thwarted, turning them back from tormenting him.

These ten crisp verses drip drama. Unable to attribute his suffering to any reasonable cause and confronting the horrible thought that the source of his hope is the reason for his languishing, he desperately throws himself on God's grace—in which he cannot bring himself not to believe and on which the order of normal life depends—to extricate him from the terror in which his body and spirit flag. He dangles between terror at this enemy behind the enemy and his desire for a tranquil trusting heart.

Like the preceding complaints, Ps. 6 resolves the tension and resolutely turns at the end to assert confident hope and trust that God's intervention will turn back the enemies. The issue being battled out is how to make sense of God when empirical evidence speaks against what one believes about and expects from him. The psalmist unabashedly invites the reader into that profound question.

Structure and Dynamics

Like other complaint psalms, this one begins by addressing God directly (6:1–5). The next two verses are a soliloquy intended perhaps for both God and the community to overhear. The psalm then turns abruptly to address the speaker's adversaries directly in a petulant yet exultant tone (6:8) and concludes with a triumphant statement to that same community for those who sing or pray this psalm after him in their own context (6:9–10). By speaking to four audiences—God, himself, the enemies, and the watching congregation of Israelites—the author invites each to see the situation from other points of view, including the speaker's own.

The intense opening address to God seeks respite from divine wrath and healing from terror (6:1–5). Within it, 6:3b stands on its own, offering one of the

4. Fløysvik 1997, 38–46.

most challenging ejaculations echoing in the psalms, if not all of scripture. The attacked complainant attacks God in return: "And you, LORD, how long?" But the complainant's anger immediately abates, and he meekly continues elaborating his earlier petition (6:4) as if his anger at God has ebbed. Psalm 6:5 reasons with God to back off. The next two verses (6:6–7) call for empathy from God because of the victim's languishing. Psalm 6:8, like 6:3b, also stands alone. It resumes the feisty tone of the direct attack on God but now attacks the speaker's assailants in a confident tone; although the speaker brings no evidence to support the claim, he is persuaded that God has responded to him. The final two verses of the psalm (6:9–10) address hearers quite outside the scene, for the speaker is simultaneously speaking to God and to the listening community of Israel's worshipers who have been watching all along. Confident now that God has indeed terrorized and shamed his enemies, the speaker simultaneously encourages and warns the community overhearing this intimate interchange not to doubt God or overstep the line that he maintains against the enemies of the faithful.

Opening Supplication to God (6:1–5)

Both segments of the opening isocolon of this psalm state the suppliant's belief that God is angry with him (6:1), setting a tone of fear in response to chastisement.[5] He does not cower subserviently but begs for a merciful reprieve, not because of his innocence but because of his despair (6:2). Even if God's wrath is warranted, the suppliant still feels confident asking for mercy. He does not shrink before God but presents his terror as grounds for healing (6:3a). His trust in God is absolute. While the plea continues in 6:4, seemingly out of nowhere the speaker confronts God with anger of his own (6:3b). His trust in God is so sure that he can blurt out "And you, LORD, how long?" He is patently irritated by the length of time God's anger has been unfurled against him, for it is out of keeping with his expectation of divine kindness; he is not afraid to say so. If God's anger is unabated and he does not limit it through compassion for his servant, something is wrong. With the whole community watching, the speaker (as the dismayed object of divine anger) is in a tight spot, caught between his irritation at God's prolonged anger directed against him and his belief in God's mercy, which must prevail for God to be true to the fullness of his character and thus truly praiseworthy (6:5). Standing before the gathered community, he appeals again to God to save him for the sake of his kindness (6:4).

As if appeal to God's merciful character were not sufficiently persuasive, in 6:5 the pleader reminds God of his value. If the suppliant perishes, one fewer Israelite will be able to offer thanks to God for his mercy. Israelites who trust God are more

---

5. The isocolon is the basic structure of biblical Hebrew poetry. It is a literary form that involves a succession of two, three, or four sentences, phrases, or clauses. These have a parallel structure using words, clauses, or phrases of grammatically equal length, sound, meter, and rhythm. In biblical Hebrew the (usually) two clauses of the bicolon express the same idea through different words.

valuable to God alive than dead, for in death they cannot attract others to God by praising him. It is in God's long-term interest to attend to this plea for reprieve so that knowledge and praise of God's mercy can spread abroad. The faithful can make deals with God for the sake of his reputation.

Soliloquy (6:6–7)

Amos Ḥakham notes that the addressee of Ps. 6:6–7 is unclear.[6] The soliloquy is addressed to himself, but presumably God, the gathered congregation, and later readers are listening attentively. The speaker muses to himself that his plight always appears worse at night when he is swimming, or drowning, in his own tears and moans. Anyone who has cried sustainedly knows that one's eyes ache for hours afterward. The writer knows whereof he speaks. Real men cry![7]

Direct Address to Assailants (6:8)

Yet, amid his exhausted self-pity, the speaker rouses the same feisty voice with which he confronted God previously, now using it to address his tormentors—be they real people, the pain and debilitation of a medical condition, or the burden of accumulated sins. "Be gone from me you wrongdoers" (6:8), he cries out. Something has injected tremendous courage into the one who but a moment before was awash in tears! He interprets this sudden burst of energy to go on the offensive against his assailants as evidence that God has indeed heard his weeping, and it strengthens him to conclude this song with a triumphant vindication of God's true character, which abides in loving rescue, not enduring anger. It is God who has been on trial here, and God is vindicated by the suppliant's strength to stand up to his enemies.

Proclamation of Triumph (6:9–10)

In Ps. 6:9–10, the speaker repeats his confident belief that God has indeed tended to his complaint and addresses not his enemies but the congregation of Israelites, who hang on his every word. The good news is that God has taken—or perhaps a tad more tentatively, will take up—his case, as the future tense *yiqqāḥ* indicates.[8] The speaker assures the congregation that God has indeed broken through the speaker's struggle to hold on to God's mercy; they may rest easy and trust that God will respond positively to them when they seek deliverance from the terrors inflicted by divine wrath. In the final verse (6:10), the complainant assures the gathered crowd that because of God's merciful response the complainant's

---

6. Ḥakham 2003, 29–30.

7. John Goldingay suggests that women might have authored some of the psalms, but no evidence can be found for that claim (2006, 31–32). The most celebrated example is Ps. 131.

8. The first clause of Ps. 6:9 is in the simple past tense while the second is in the future tense, although psalmic use of tenses is not standardized.

enemies will be frightfully terrified, shamed, and instantly turned back from their assaults on him. Perhaps his hope is that they too will be converted from their evil intentions in shame when God foils their plans (6:10).[9]

Theological Pedagogy

Claus Westermann finds this psalm disorderly because the verses do not follow a set pattern.[10] Perhaps that disorder is intentional, for it expresses the emotional thrashing the speaker is experiencing and is preparing his hearers to expect at some time or other in their lives. He lurches from meek supplication before God (6:1–2) to an intrepid challenge of God (6:3b) and eventually to a feisty charge on the workers of iniquity to turn back in shame before God's advancing cause on the speaker's behalf (6:8a). The unruly form conveys the inner tumult of the poem and its protagonist. What is one to make of this intense colloquy constructed by the psalmist as he turns to and from God, himself, his enemies, and the watching Israelites?

The turmoil invites readers into the various struggles and conflicts, and the extreme emotions that accompany them. The suppliant struggles against his human, medical, or theological enemies who evoke fear and confrontational anger (6:3b, 8a). He is also internally conflicted, wanting to trust God yet being pulled down by the haunting thought that God's anger might be more enduring than his kindness (cf. Ps. 30:5). This fear expresses itself in the confession of exhausted grief in the soliloquy of Ps. 6:6–7. Furthermore, one hears the argument of the suppliant for God to rescue him after having disciplined him, with the suppliant begging and demanding by turns. The congregation hovers in the background (until Ps. 6:9–10). The speaker is certainly aware of and concerned with his responsibility for their spiritual formation.

What is Ps. 6 finally hoping to do with and for the singers who will assume the voice of the speaker and inch their way through these complex relationships and roles? A number of theological lessons may be drawn from the energy that pulses through this poem. The salient points include: (1) God accepts the full range of human emotions; (2) God both chastens and listens; (3) conflict and struggle are an expected part of life; (4) God expects us to act on our own behalf; and (5) our personal struggles can help others.

1. God Accepts the Full Range of Human Emotions

The speaker here is comfortable expressing both positive and negative emotions to God. He freely confides his terror of God to him and to us, confident

---

9. Augustine interprets this verse as a prayer for enemies: "*May all my enemies blush with shame and be confused,* a prayer that they should repent of their sins, something which is not possible without confusion and turmoil" (2000a, 112).

10. Westermann 1989, 75.

that God will respond positively to that disclosure. He does not praise God in his misery but challenges him and even expresses anger at God for acting in a way contrary to the loving-kindness that he has come to expect. He is comfortable being candid with God as well as with us, secure that God embraces him even when angry. Thus, while the speaker is terrified by his suffering and what may lie ahead, he is not afraid of God—not even of stoking God's anger with resistant emotions—but he trusts that he can lay his misery before God and be safe, even if that misery is caused by God himself! Given that God is his true enemy, such trust in God is astounding. What makes our speaker sick makes him well.

2. God Both Chastises and Listens

The speaker's understanding of God is perhaps the most intriguing aspect of this psalm. God's character is complex, for he disciplines with anger and saves with kindness. As I noted, a high doctrine of divine sovereignty seems to be operating in which God is an angry, invisible force behind events; the presenting enemies are not the real source of the complainant's concern. Whether they be microbes, or neighbors, the enemies are not acting on their own but intrude on the speaker's life as God's agents. Thus the assailed one has two enemies: the presenting problem and God behind that problem. Yet this daring Israelite is not daunted by two enemies or even by his own terror. Although he moans and groans, showing the reader his tear-stained face in the night, he also finds strength to move beyond making a career of his suffering. And *that* move from tears to strength depends upon God's merciful hearing of his plaint. He could not do it on his own.

The message to later readers is that they cannot expect God to make problems vanish, but they can rely upon God's strength to address those problems, not simply endure them passively in the hope that things will change by happenstance or divine intervention. Psalm 6:1–7 assumes the passive recumbent position of submission to divine power. But Ps. 6:8–10 shows the suppliant arising from his tear-stained couch, convinced that God has taken his case. That conviction gives him the strength to be rescued. Climbing out of a victim mentality, he turns the tables on his enemies and uses his strength to shame them into repenting of their animosity toward him. Finding strength to take an aggressive posture against his foes *is* God's rescue of him.

In short, God does not resolve issues as a deus ex machina. Indeed, if the complainant is suffering from the "wasting disease" (cancer), he will eventually die. The point is that even if the suppliant's problems ultimately stem from divine anger at some unnamed human failing, God can still be relied on to provide the strength for the complainant to work though the terrible fallout of divine correction. What is missing here (and would that it were present) is the story of how and what the complainant is to learn from the targeted divine anger that is at the core of this encounter between God and his faithful servant.

3. Conflict and Struggle Are an Expected Part of Life

Although the complainant's world is not working well, the investigation of inner struggle, conflict with God and with "enemies" (be they other people, illness, or some sin that lies behind them) teaches later singers that struggle and conflict—including conflict with God—are part of life. They are not to be denied or avoided but dealt with constructively. God accepts one's struggle against him and on his behalf when believers challenge evildoers who salivate as they wait for their prey to fall away from God so that they may triumph.

No indication is given that the sufferer should put on a happy face, grin and bear it, or keep a stiff upper lip. Suffering is real, and one should prepare for it. The challenge that the psalmist lays before his hearers is how to handle the situation that is causing the distress. It is appropriate to articulate one's distress verbally and with tears. Self-reflection is essential, as the soliloquy suggests; it is appropriate to ask for help. Misery is not to be bottled up, and confronting one's foes is acceptable in the context of trust that the one who rights wrongs is not the suppliant but God.

4. God Expects Us to Act on Our Own Behalf

This point follows from the preceding one. The two challenges spoken by the complainant—one to God and the other to his immediate enemies—suggest that although God is finally the one who will both vindicate and punish, we are to act on our own behalf, even if that amounts to no more than telling those who taunt us that they are taunting us, although that simple appraisal may be demeaning. Assuming that the taunters (whoever they may be) are acting from their integrity—as the speaker certainly assumes God is—gives the opponent an opportunity to rectify the situation. It calls upon him to respond at his best and invites him to care for the complainant by responding to his cry (in the case of God) and by leaving him alone (in the case of the evildoers of 6:8). Indeed, this is a bold suggestion. The psalmist is not encouraging the protester or his listeners to take every possible action to right their situation, nor is he counseling that those in misery take matters into their own hands, come what may. Rather, he is encouraging the suppliant to engage those who hurt him directly. What perilous business! Assuming that God is angry and the enemies (assuming they are human) believe that their opposition to the suppliant is justified, the suppliant puts himself at even greater risk of rejection. The intrepid psalmist now presses his protagonist—and the reader through his protagonist—to let his needs be known in a way that honors the finest in those he petitions, though he risks being lampooned or dismissed. He calls on both God and his enemies to act mercifully toward him. Although he seeks his own well-being, he calls on their moral maturity at the same time. The psalmist dissolves the old "us versus them" binary and instead calls his adversaries to their moral height that all might flourish.

5. Our Personal Struggles Can Help Others

This very personal and agonizing drama is played out before the worshiping community to whom the speaker turns in the last two verses, telling them that God has and will take his case and that his enemies will suddenly repent. While this psalm may seem disorderly in terms of its various audiences and voices, the author ultimately has the spiritual formation of Israel in view. God is trustworthy, he reassures them. We can rest assured that when our time comes we can rely on God to thwart our enemies by strengthening us to act appropriately on our own behalf. Thus the plaintive song of one harried Israelite serves to strengthen others, teaching them what to expect in life and how to act both decisively and faithfully.

Finally, the psalmist has in view how this story—for it has become a story—can support and guide future generations who will, in their turn, be caught among their own needs and feelings, the sovereignty of God, and the designs of others, be these persons or cancerous tissue devouring the body. This point carries a comforting message to the psalm's later singers and hearers. In its haunting ambiguity, this story can help others—whether as a warning, an admonition, or concrete guidance for approaching God and other adversaries. First and last, the psalmist says, trust God; in between, act cautiously to the end that both you and those who strive with and against you can perform at their best.

PSALM 7

Canonical Context and Themes

This is the last of the opening group of five lament psalms following the Psalter's introduction. Like the others, it exemplifies Ps. 1's stark division of people into two categories: the faithful who follow God's torah-given way of life and the wicked who do not and trouble and scoff at those who do. These psalms illustrate André Chouraqui's characterization of the Psalter as a great struggle between the innocent and the reprobate, the way of light over the way of darkness.[1] Psalm 7, like the preceding complaints, presents us with a protagonist crying to God for vindication against enemies in pursuit, but it moves on quickly to address and shape Israel's understanding of God and the standards of moral conduct that flow from that understanding.

Each of these laments possesses its own unique flavor. Psalm 7 introduces the image of God as the great judge. To impress upon his hearers the import of that image, the speaker offers himself to be judged, even as he calls on God to judge his foes by offering to suffer just punishment should he be found guilty of having provoked the animosity he now experiences (7:3–5).

Structure and Dynamics

Psalm 7 can be divided into two major sections, depending on whether the speech is in the first or third person. Each of these may in turn be subdivided into three segments, depending on the orientation of the content of the discourse. Psalm 7:1–9 is spoken in the first person and addresses God directly for the most part, while 7:10 and following is spoken in the third person and addresses the speaker's human audience with talk about God. As in Ps. 6, this psalm shows the praying

---

1. Chouraqui 1995.

community both watching the intimate relationship between God and the speaker and seeing into the speaker's inmost being. All the speakers in these complaint psalms stand psychologically naked before their public.

The punch of the poem comes in its second half. While the first half teaches Israel that God judges both individuals and nations fairly, the second half warns the auditors that God is readying deadly weapons aimed at those who make mischief in Israel. In typical fashion, Ps. 7 ends in thanksgiving for God's righteousness, praising his name.

Addressing God (7:1–9)

The first half of this psalm not only complains to God but confides in him as well. Psalm 7:1–2 seeks refuge out of fear of the speaker's enemies. Psalm 7:3–5 betrays the speaker's candid anxiety that perhaps he has done something to warrant the treatment he is receiving from those who would tear him apart, and if so, he should bear their remuneration. Having exposed himself to judgment, the writer uses the last four verses of the first half of the poem to call upon God to rise up and judge not only his enemies but also the nations, that evil may come to an end and the righteous be vindicated.

REFUGE FROM LIONS (7:1–2)

Taking refuge—literally taking shelter—in God is one of the most salient images of piety in the Psalter.[2] That he does so establishes the speaker's *bona fides* with his audience. Here we have the speaker sheltering himself in God while pursued by lionlike predators who will slash open his life. He cries to God for there is no one else to save him.

IF I AM GUILTY . . . (7:3–5)

Three staccato conditional clauses punctuate Ps.7:3–5a: "if I have . . . if I have . . . if I have . . ." done anything deserving of this treatment, he says, let me bear the consequences and let this pursuer vanquish me and my honor. Both Robert Alter and Amos Ḥakham point out that with this standard form of oath taking (if I . . . , then may . . .) the speaker is proclaiming his innocence.[3] Even if the victim sincerely believes that in this particular case he is innocent of either having unjustly wronged his pursuer or betrayed his ally, the bravado of such an oath sounds cavalier to Christian ears.[4] Certainly, relationships sometimes rupture and former friends or lovers not only distance themselves but even seek to thwart the other's

---

2. This image appears both in Pss. 2:12 and 5:11.

3. Alter 2007, 18; Ḥakham 2003, 33.

4. James Mays captures the Christian sensibility well: "A prayer made on the basis of one's own righteousness and integrity poses a serious question. How can anyone possibly ground prayer on such a basis with honesty?" (1994b, 63).

best endeavors without explaining why. Despite his candor, the psalmist opens his audience to the possibility that the speaker may warrant the opposition, even if he is unaware of his misstep. Such disclosure should provoke soul-searching on the part of his listeners.

John Chrysostom, bishop of Antioch, takes these verses as an opportunity to discourse on anger, with prayer as its medicine, to teach love of enemies.

> You see, just as fever would not develop unless the bile flowed over and surpassed its proper limits, in like manner anger would not become immoderate unless the heart were ruptured. So just as if you saw someone falling victim to fever, and if its effects were multiple and dire, you would not want to become infected by the disease, so too in the case of anger. Far from imitating or mimicking that evil, have pity on that person who lets the wild beast within off the leash, and more than anything else harms and destroys himself.[5]

This last phrase intimates the psalm's conclusion in which the enemies self-destruct, falling into the very pit they dug for the speaker.

You, O Lord, Are the Judge (7:6–9)

The final segment of the first half of Ps. 7 carries forward the oath of the previous verses by setting the situation between the speaker and his adversary in a court of law; God is the judge, and the nations surrounding him are spectators (7:7). Israel's internal strife is on public display! Again, this is high drama.[6] The psalmist pits the righteous anger of God against the salacious anger of the speaker's enemies (7:6), calling on God—pictured sitting above the fray—to judge between them (7:7). With all eyes looking to God, the psalmist warns the observers that they too shall be judged, but here God will favorably judge on behalf of the defendant's integrity, which is besmirched by his enemy's hope to dishonor him (7:5). Please allow the evil of the wicked to end, the suppliant begs, and establish the righteous—meaning him. By publically supplicating God to end his righteous suffering, the poet puts God on trial. The scene is reminiscent of Elijah's public test of God's power before the prophets of Baal and Asherah on Mount Carmel (1 Kgs. 18).

Addressing Israel (7:10–17)

The second half of this poem speaks about God to the worshiping community in light of what has just transpired. The change of audience suggests that the personal lament is designed as a teaching tool. This half of the poem can also be

---

5. Chrysostom 1998, 123.

6. Far in the background here might be 2 Sam. 15:2–6. Apparently David had neglected to appoint jurists to hear cases, and people were disgruntled with their inability to receive justice through legal means. This psalm is dedicated to David. Setting God as the fair and supreme judge in Israel, through whom justice triumphs, is a warning to any monarch that justice finally belongs to God.

divided into three segments. Psalm 7:10–13 sustains the depiction of God as judge but adds the image of God as warrior armed with deadly weapons against the unrepentant. The subject of 7:14–16 is the evil ones whose nefarious intentions boomerang and bring them, instead of their enemies, down. The final verse stands alone in thanksgiving to and praise of God.

God, in Righteous Anger, Is Ready to Punish (7:10–13)

The righteousness of God on behalf of the "straight-hearted" (*yišrê-lēb*) is mentioned a second time. God is the defendant's shield. There are two sides to this righteousness. While the protagonist is judged guiltless, he depicts God as a vigilant and angry warrior or hunter poised to attack the unrepentant with whetted sword and taut bow (7:12). The praying Israelites, aware of the nations watching the justice of God unfurl before them—which is depicted as deadly flaming arrows unleashed by God's wrath (7:13)—are sure to shrink back in awe and fear.

Perhaps contrary to common expectation, Augustine, who is famous for bringing humility to Christian attention through his argument with Pelagius about the human inability to be righteous, is not bothered by the protagonist's self-identification as righteous. Relying on medicinal imagery (like his contemporary, John Chrysostom), Augustine co-opts the psalm for his Christian vision of righteousness wrought by Christ. In his commentary on these verses, he opines that medicine has two functions; it is both therapeutic and prophylactic. God's help is needed both to become and to remain healthy. Psalm 7 qualifies as divine assistance for the healthy, that is, those who have been made well in Christ: "It is given to one who is already righteous . . . For if God dispenses the medicine by which, in our weakness, we are healed, how much more should he provide the means by which we are preserved once we are well?"[7]

Mischief Is Self-Defeating (7:14–16)

As if the imagery of weapons of divine punishment were not sufficiently vivid, Ps. 7:14–16 uses the imagery of conception, pregnancy, and birth to paint a word-picture of those who lie to attack the integrity of the innocent (7:15). Such lies intend to be a pit dug for the innocent, but God will throw the liars into it instead. The very violence (cf. Gen. 6:11) that they have mischievously conceived will fall on their own heads (7:16).

I Sing with Thanks and Praise (7:17)

As with many of the so-called lament psalms, this one ends with the speaker thanking God for his righteousness and singing praises before Israel and the watching nations.

7. Augustine 2000a, 122.

Theological Pedagogy

Although this psalm begins as a personal lament, like Ps. 5 it quickly morphs into other topics and concerns. Psalm 7 is about righteousness (the word occurs five times) and the shame and dishonor that accrue to those brazen enough to desist from it by opposing those who live by it and seeking to defame the innocent. Righteousness is the characteristic of God in the fore here (7:10, 12, 17), and it is the characteristic that God seeks in those who come before him—be it with a particular complaint, as in the case of the protagonist, or at some future time, as will undoubtedly happen to the watching nations and listening Israel. If any are tempted to engage in nefarious mischief against the righteous, they are hereby warned that they will be shamed by the very tactics with which they seek to shame others. The complainant is a fiery preacher who ensconces his hearers between God's wrath (7:12) and his flaming arrows (7:13).

In this psalm, God is demanding, and the standard of justice he sets extends far. Hearers of this song are, at best, only indirectly encouraged. God bores into the inmost parts of the self to ascertain where integrity resides and where mischief tries to hide. The righteous judge will have his way, and the innocent will have their day when liars fall into their own trap.

With no threat of hell or suffering in another life looming large here, Israel's poet depicts divine punishment as public humiliation. Divine judgment is not handed out for a generic condition of sinfulness on the assumption that people are unable to refrain from evil and must throw themselves on God's mercy in utter helplessness to avoid being who they are. The issue here is specific. Someone has slandered an innocent person with lies, and God will not tolerate the injustice. The guilty party will not suffer forever but will be hit with the stupidity of the affront. "It will catch up with him" is the message.

Another outstanding and perhaps discomfiting image in this psalm is anger. The offending attacker is clearly angry with his prey (7:2). God's anger is desired to counter the anger of the enemy (7:6), and it seems to be the backbone of God's weaponry against the offender, which takes the form of fiery shafts. Those vessels of death are sent to strike the unrepentant (7:12). In light of the acceptance of anger, it is interesting to note that the speaker is not depicted as angry like the complainant in Ps. 6. Nor is he depicted as sleeping calmly like the speakers in earlier psalms. Here the speaker's emotional temperature is not important. What matters is that God is awake and aware of the need to vindicate the integrity of one against the dishonesty of another. The purpose of Ps. 7 is to persuade its later singers and pray-ers that God is to be thanked and praised as a righteous judge who will vindicate the straight-hearted against those who give birth to lies. *Caveat emptor* is its final message.

PSALM 8

Canonical Context and Themes

With Ps. 8, the reader encounters a completely different facet of the Psalter and ostensibly discovers a previously undisclosed aspect of David's personality and temperament, which renders him a most complex and interesting character. The biblical narrative portrays him as a warrior, womanizer, schemer, murderer, devoted father, and musician. It is intriguing that David casts such a long shadow in the Younger Testament. The Synoptics all refer to Jesus with the royal title Son of David (sixteen times), despite David's tortured relationships with his sons. Both Matthew and Luke trace Jesus's Davidic lineage to substantiate his authority. This is worth noting because it illustrates that even the Younger Testament is not embarrassed by a man with such a checkered past. While perhaps few people reach the depth or the height of David's exploits, as a character he stands in sharp contrast to the Jesus of western Christian piety, a model of sinless perfection that only the brazen would dare hope to achieve. David is all man all the time—passionate when conniving, passionate when grieving, passionate when repenting, and passionate when singing to God for Israel's edification.

This song is known as a creation hymn of praise that takes its cue from Gen. 1:1–2:4. It exudes energy and enthusiasm for God and for humanity as God's excellent creation. While its center is anthropocentric, the repetition of its first verse as its last (8:1 and 8:9) frames it as a fundamentally theocentric song that extols divine sovereignty within which governing authority is delegated to God's most powerful creature.[1] Unlike its predecessors, Ps. 8 addresses only God, and

---

1. Brueggemann 1984, 37. John Goldingay cites James L. Mays to the same effect: "We can say 'human being' only after we have learned to say 'God'" (Goldingay 2006, 161). J. Clinton McCann finds this movement from God to humanity and back to God troubling: "How are the 'glory and honor' of humanity (8:5) to be understood in relation to the 'majesty' and 'glory' of God (8:1, 9)?" (McCann and Howell 2001, 58). This is a problem only if one assumes competition, even enmity, between God and humanity. Goldingay

while it notes that God has enemies whom he dispatches with apparent equanimity (8:2b), it does not dwell on problems, evil, affliction, or rebellious kings and other unruly servants of God. It is decisively upbeat.[2] The world is a wonderful place to be, and human beings are to flourish in, though, and with it.

Structure and Dynamics

After acclaiming the magnificence of God (8:1) and illustrating the strength and wisdom that warrant such effusive praise (8:2), the psalmist muses thoughtfully on the dignified stature of humanity within the compass of the creation and under the reign of divine sovereignty (8:3–5). Next follows a pericope on humanity's awesome responsibility for nonhuman creatures, which corresponds with Gen. 1:28. The psalm ends as exultantly as it begins, praising God's name.

The Majesty of God (8:1)

The opening verse sings in praise of God's name and splendor, which permeate the entire earth and the skies. Like other jubilant hymns of the Psalter (e.g., Pss. 19, 104, 148, and 150), the world itself proclaims the nobility of its maker. That the first verse is repeated as the last verse of this song confirms the psalmist's insistence that human dignity enjoys its full stature within the grandeur of divine majesty.

The Range of Divine Strength and Wisdom (8:2)

The two clauses of 8:2 sit uneasily together. The first is one of the most arresting phrases in scripture—"You established strength from the cries of babies[3] and nursing infants"—after which the poet rushes to a shockingly different context—"for the sake of your enemies to make an end of the enemy and avenger." How are they related? Early Christian and Jewish commentators labored over this verse, especially its insistence that God established his might ($\check{o}z$) through the weakest and most dependent of creatures, human infants, who yet mature to become its most powerful.

Midrash on Psalms interprets this verse quite concretely and draws a harsh conclusion: "The Holy One, blessed be He, asked the sucklings and the embryos:

---

also remarks on this tension: "It implies that Gen. 1 was not devastatingly undone by that human failure" (2006, 161). However, Ps. 7 does not assume adversariality between God and humanity. The Psalter, after all, knows of no fall that has decimated moral life and alienated God and humanity from one another.

2. William P. Brown notes that the string of ten complaint psalms (Pss. 3–13) is broken only by this one praise hymn (2012).

3. The word *ʿôlĕlîm* is universally translated as "babies," following *nēpiōn* in the Septuagint. However, it also means "gleaners" (Lev. 19:10; Deut. 24:21; Judg. 8:2) and "those who are mistreated or are suffering" (Lam. 1:5, 12, 22). That is, it refers to the defenseless of any age in need of help. For a discussion, see Goldingay 2006, 156.

'Will you be sureties for your fathers, so that if I give them the Torah they will live by it, but that if they do not, you will be forfeited because of them?' 'They replied: 'Yes,' . . . Accordingly, when fathers in Israel—God forfend!—reject the Torah, their children are forfeited on account of them."[4]

Augustine reads the reference to infants in terms of Paul's image of Christian neophytes being fed milk before taking solid food (1 Cor. 3:1–2) and draws a far gentler conclusion. He reads *ʿōz* as "praise" rather than "strength," following the Septuagint, and makes the typically Augustinian ecclesiological point that the church is a mixed body, comprised both of the faithful who take proper nourishment (the infants) and those who are "not yet able to understand things spiritual and eternal [but] are nurtured by faith in the history which unfolds through time [the enemies]."[5] Thus the babies of the first clause represent faithful Christians and the enemies of the second represent those who need to be brought to God gradually—so God makes an "end" of them gently. This undercuts any suggestion that the second half of 8:2 depicts a summarily vindictive deity for whom bringing an end to the enemy and avenger means destroying them. Rather, the innocent infant represents those nourished on divine wisdom instinctively; the enemy is the one who has yet to do so in the mystery of God. It is not the person but the person's antipathy to God that is brought to an end so that the avenger becomes a trusting suckling (i.e., a faithful Christian). Thus Augustine is hopeful, encouraging both those who already and those who do not yet "know the love of Christ that surpasses all knowledge."[6]

For his part, Calvin interprets the strength of God touted in 8:2 by noting that infants, even before they can speak, wonderfully display the wisdom of God, who transforms their mothers' blood into milk for them and who brings them into the world knowing instinctively how to suck to get that nourishment.[7] Calvin goes on beautifully to connect the divine wisdom that preserves infants to the vanquishing of God's enemies:

> To express the whole in a few words: so early as the generation or birth of man the splendor of Divine Providence is so apparent, that even infants, who hang upon their mothers' breasts, can bring down to the ground the fury of the enemies of God. Although his enemies may do their utmost, and may even burst with rage a hundred times, it is in vain for them to endeavor to overthrow the strength which manifests itself in the weakness of infancy.[8]

Here I follow the path begun by Augustine and Calvin to interpret this challenging verse. A reasonable translation would read these clauses in reverse order:

4. Braude 1959a, 125.
5. Augustine 2000a, 131.
6. Ibid. See Eph. 3:19.
7. Calvin 1998, 96.
8. Ibid., 98.

"For the sake of putting an end to enemy and avenger you established strength in the cries of the defenseless and suckling infants." Without the parallelism, this translation offers an arresting "take" on the consequences of observing one scene for a particular set of onlookers. The cries of the weak and helpless are so poignant and compelling that they pierce the heart of those who might summarily take advantage of them. Their very existence proclaims the majesty of God, and that is what inhibits those who would harm them. Enemies of the helpless are, after all, enemies of God. Not only the vastness of heaven and earth but also the weakness of God's children testify to the majestic power of the Creator, and that testimony, through their cries, converts God's enemies into precisely the Christians Augustine seeks. Calvin is correct; helpless infants can bring down the enemies of God, that is, transform them until they cease being vengeful against the weak. Psalm 8:2 is thus a piercing elaboration of 8:1, which claims that earth and sky tell the splendor of God.

Human Dignity (8:3–5)

The first tercet of this psalm illustrates how powerful the most defenseless can be in displaying the sovereign power of God; the next tercet pauses to reflect on the stature of the human adult in that great scheme of things: "When I look at the sky, the works of your fingers, the moon and stars that you attune . . ." (8:3). The psalmist is again awestruck. In comparison with the orbits of the celestial bodies human life seems paltry. Why should God make much of humanity? The speaker is but properly humbled by the smallness of the human frame set against the wisdom of the entirety of God's oeuvre. "Why do you (God) even bother with us, since your creation works so flawlessly without us?" the speaker seems to be wondering aloud. The musing is prelude to the astounding observation that God has set humans as regents over the whole shebang! We are adorned with honor and respect just below that of the *'ĕlōhîm*, "the gods," a term that the Septuagint translates as *angelous*, "angels," and so it remains in most English transliterations.

The import of these verses is to impress upon the psalm's singers that within the vast scope of divine wisdom, which created and controls the cosmos, God deigns to treat humanity with incredible dignity and respect. It is a position that calls forth humility, even hesitation before the honor. Indeed, these three verses are the prelude to the weighty responsibility that falls on human shoulders as the appointed regents of God in administering earthly affairs. The reader ought to pause before the task God has given.

Human Responsibility (8:6–8)

Properly awed by divinely bestowed dignity, the psalmist turns to the concrete responsibilities humanity bears. Just as the speaker is awed by the works of God's fingers in 8:3, in 8:6 the works of his hands are lovingly and deliberately placed under human protection and authority. The verb *tamšîlēhû*, "you made him govern," has the same root (*mšl*) that occurs in the curse of Eve (*yimšāl*) in Gen. 3:16. Here, however, it is used not in the context of a curse but of responsibility for maintenance. By giving Adam responsibility for naming the animals, Genesis 2:19–20 also reminds readers of their call to steward creation.

Divine Grandeur (8:9)

The inclusio brings the reader face-to-face with the sovereignty of God, within which the governing responsibility deputed is ensconced.[9] Like the inclusio of Ps. 118:1 and 118:29 (also at 106:1; 107:1; and 136:1), this one instructs the reader in piety. While the inclusio of Ps. 118 instructs in giving thanks to God, this one instructs in praising him in light of his excellence. Praise melts into thanksgiving, however, because the animal kingdom, over which humans have been given stewardship, is for their own benefit.

Lurking beneath this inclusio of praise is a warning. Humans may be the most powerful of God's living creatures, but they are also the most unstable. Indeed, it is the stability of the animal kingdom that enables humans both to rule it and to protect themselves from it. Animal behavior is more predictable than human behavior, and animals' needs are more easily supplied so that some can be domesticated. Human ingenuity, intelligence, and thereby power are tied to complex and frequently discordant emotions that are not as readily satisfied or easily directed. The concluding directive to be ever mindful that human regency exists in the context of divine sovereignty is thus a warning that reminds the reader of the human capacity for emotional vulnerability, which threatens to disorder the beauty of divine handiwork.

Theological Pedagogy

Read in the context of the psalms that precede it, Ps. 8 pushes forward out into the world, away from self-preoccupation and anxiety, in order to explore and adore creation in God's name. Read against the earlier David psalms, Ps. 8 is an energetic reminder that relief from problems sometimes comes by relocating to another venue.

As different as Ps. 8 is from its predecessors, it is just as edificatory. If the other psalms teach trust in God, this one teaches humility in light of the enormous responsibility God has placed on human shoulders. While the use of the verb *mšl* may raise the specter of an exploitative human posture toward the nonhuman world, the framing of human responsibility within the confines of divine sovereignty and majesty actually teaches an ethic of care. After all, God has been deliberate and deeply thoughtful in creating the world for humanity's well-being.

---

9. "Inclusio" is bracketing a text by ensconcing it with repeated text at both its beginning and end.

The attentive reader will learn prudent stewardship in the service of enjoyment of God and creation.

The stunning power of 8:3 discussed above shelters a special pedagogy of its own. Those with eyes to see God's beauty—not only in the grandeur of mountain vistas and the starry night sky but also in the beauty of the helpless who are just as much, perhaps even more, beloved of God—have been granted the grace of a profound vision of God in this life. If their lives are transformed by that vision and if they have been brought to the knowledge and love of the God who transformed the powerless into the powerful, they cannot but tell it out in the midst of the community. Although the word *'ôlēl* does not appear in chapter 2 of Ruth, the touching story of Boaz—who is drawn by Ruth's character to become her protector and eventually her husband—speaks from this psalm more broadly. Boaz sees the beauty and power of God at work in this foreigner's devotion to her mother-in-law, risking danger to herself, and he rises to her stature to exercise shining stewardship of his land, his employees, his family's honor, and perhaps above all, his honor. Psalm 8:3 calls people to the stature of Boaz when he was confronted with the majesty of God made known to him through Ruth. Perhaps this is the hope for the oppressed: that by the grace of God hearts will melt before the beauty and innocence of God's weakest that they may indeed be rescued from their travail.

PSALM 9–10

Canonical Context and Themes

Psalms 9 and 10 were originally one acrostic poem and appear so in the Septuagint. In their present form they are an imperfect acrostic resting on eighteen of the twenty-two letters of the (Hebrew) alphabet, suggesting the brokenness that is the theme of the poem. Yet dividing the original into the two psalms of the Masoretic text is not unwarranted. Materially speaking, Ps. 9 largely, but by no means completely, celebrates God's judgment of the nations for having taken advantage of the weak. By contrast, Ps. 10 (although it mentions the nations toward the end) is predominantly a heartrending plea for God to intervene on behalf of the poor and oppressed against the wicked, who emerge as a nebulous yet vicious "they," engaging in creative machinations against the helpless. Although both themes appear in Ps. 9, orientation of the two halves of the song is markedly different, warranting separate yet coordinated treatment here.

Psalm 9 follows Ps. 7:6–11's depiction of God seated in court, judging the nations. While the speaker addresses God directly in the second person, the interest is in God's rebuke. Psalm 9 is not so much a lament (with the exception of 9:13–14) as a song of praise for God's equitable judgment of the nations. Although it is a song of victory over the nations who have forgotten God (9:17) or perhaps never known him, it is also an evangelistic discourse of sorts. God's avenging of innocent blood shed by these nations (9:12) chastises them. Using the theistic sanction, the poem admonishes the nations to desist from their wickedness because the Lord, although he makes his home in Zion (9:11), is the judge of all people.

Psalm 10 is almost the inverse of Ps. 9. Primarily a discourse on the ways of the wicked, Ps. 10 takes special note of how the wicked rationalize their bad behavior to themselves. Acting wickedly is a renunciation of God, who demands righteousness. As Ps. 1 teaches, God's law is of a piece with righteous living. Sinful living sneers at God. As in many lament psalms, Ps. 10 questions why God is far off when he is needed (10:1). The same cry for God to arise and show his true colors as defender of the poor and meek (*qûmâ yhwh*) appears in both halves of the original version of the poem (9:20 and 10:12). It concludes with a confident assertion that God will respond to the speaker's call to action and destroy the enemy nations (10:16–18), restating the report of 9:3–13. Both 9:5 and 10:16 contain the phrase "forever and ever" (*lĕ'ôlām wā'ed*), which reinforces both the permanence of the destruction of the enemies and the permanence of divine kingship. God is surely to be relied upon, even if those languishing must wait a long time.

Structure and Dynamics

Quite apart from its poetic disjointedness, the thematic movement of Ps. 9 is choppy and seemingly confused. It does not flow evenly but jumps from one orientation toward God to another, then back to the first, and once more back to the second. Here I treat Ps. 9 in four major segments. It begins with a ringing song of confident praise in God's triumphant judgment of the nations (9:1–12) then suddenly, almost as if the sections are in reverse order, jumps to a short personal plea for deliverance so that the speaker may praise God, which the long first section has just done (9:13–14).[1] Psalm 9:15–16 returns to praising God for having punished the wicked nations, as if the intervening plea for help is not there or that the verses are out of order. The last section (9:17–20) is written in the future tense as another plea for God to punish the nations and liberate the weak from the nations' intimidating might. Intriguingly, a personal plea for deliverance is interpolated into a poem of global scope that depicts Israel's God as bringing "the nations" under judgment, echoing the message of Ps. 2 that God's reach extends far beyond Israel.

Psalm 9 lurches from confidence in God's track record at having rebuked the nations to a plea to him for rescue, then back to a proclamation of God's executed judgment, and finally to another plea that God will teach the nations a well-deserved lesson. If the flow of the verses was penned by one intentional hand, and is neither a collage of cuttings from other poems nor the result of scribal error, the psalm's vacillation betrays a conflicted writer proceeding jaggedly yet movingly from a confident conviction based on solid evidence of divine intervention to a plaintive and perhaps doubting cry to be heard, then back to confidence and back to doubt again. Perhaps the two opposing emotional moments can be

---

1. Calvin seems puzzled over the abrupt change in tone both here and in the reversion to complaint in Ps. 9:17–18. He tries to encourage the confused: "Here, then, is described to us the sudden and unexpected change, by which God, when he pleases, restores to order things which were in confusion. When, therefore, we see the wicked flying aloft devoid of all fear, let us, by the eyes of faith, behold the grave which is prepared for them; and rest assured that the hand of God, although it is unseen, is very near, which can turn them back in the midst of their course in which they aim at reaching heaven, and make them tumble into hell in a moment" (Calvin 1998, 129).

explained away with recourse to issues of textual transmission, as Robert Alter suggests.[2] The jaggedness might be an intentional literary device. Canonically speaking, the man caught between trust and anguish in this Ps. 9 resonates with Julian of Norwich's swings from consolation to desolation and back again, as well as Luther's fear of divine wrath from which he fled to the cross, hoping to stop the trust-despair seesaw.[3]

Psalm 10 is written in two voices. Psalm 10:1, 12–18 address God directly in the second person, framing 10:2–11, which is written in the third-person plural. The framing verses call God to emerge from hiding and take action, and the framed verses depict both the mind-set and the style of the wicked that give reasons why God should punish them. It is not the brute fact of harming the innocent that God should avenge but the wicked's contempt for God, which is the deeper problem.

Being written in the third rather than the second person, 10:2–11 is a public announcement of sorts to whoever will hear or sing; it addresses the psychology of evil from the perspective of one who stands firmly lodged in faith in God's way. That is, Ps. 10:2–11 explores the contempt for God and for righteousness that the faithful assume the wicked cultivate. The section is both a condemnation of those who do, and a warning to those who might, slip into such thinking. Again, the stark contrast of the righteous and the wicked surfaces, as it is set out in Ps. 1.

Song of Confident Trust (9:1–12)

Psalm 9 opens with two verses of exuberant thanks and praise for God's wondrous deeds—a theme that, as John Goldingay notes, usually appears at the end of lament psalms (e.g., Pss. 13:6; 35:27–28; 59:17).[4] Like most of its predecessors, this poem addresses God directly and then launches into a rehearsal of why such effusive praise is warranted. The psalmist reminds God of his glorious deeds, hoping that God will again act in concert with them. Perhaps more to the author's point, however, it reminds or informs the poem's auditors of what God has done—and thus of who he is—so that they may take courage for the future.[5]

God is portrayed as an equitable judge. The speaker's enemies (foreign nations) have perished as a result of God's righteous judgment against them (9:3–4). They apparently have been defeated in war, for their cities are in ruins and their memory is forever erased (9:5–6). Their defeat—by whom?—is evidence that God "sits enthroned forever" (9:7), judging the world righteously (9:7–8). Whatever the

2. Alter 2007, 25–28.

3. As John Goldingay astutely observes, "The psalm looks as if it is affirming that life has the order of the alphabet but also acknowledges that this is not always so" (2006, 168).

4. Goldingay 1993, 166.

5. John Chrysostom offers a similar interpretation: "This is a particular habit of a lover. . . . since it is not possible to see God, he composes songs to him, holding converse with him in song, stirring up desire, and gaining the impression of seeing him—or, rather, stirring up the desire of many people through the singing of hymns and songs" (1998, 182).

victorious army may be (there is no indication that it is Israel, leaving the text ach-ingly vague), the true triumph has been accomplished in a supernal courtroom. The mighty military power is not even mentioned, for the poet is promoting a grand triumph of justice with no interest in the human stratagems through which it was won. The victory is God's alone. God, whose judgments and role as righteous judge over the nations are established forever, erases the speaker's (presumably Israel's) enemies forever. Utter clarity is established. Good triumphs; evil perishes. The psalmist proclaims hope for the oppressed in troubled times. Based on the history alluded to, the oppressed can confidently trust God and sing to and of him, for he avenges those who cry to him in need.

While the address to God sounds as if it comes from an individual, it is evident that the battle is between Israel and enemy nations.[6] Although the singer speaks in the first-person singular of his enemies and his just case (beginning at 9:13), those rebuked are global forces ranged against defenseless righteous victims, *ănāwîm*. The voice of the individual suppliant is a shill for the nation of Israel that God will vindicate before the nations. The first foray of this poem is a song of comfort offered by Israel in a moment of triumph.

Plea for Help (9:13–14)

From this song of hopeful comfort, the psalmist plunges into a moment of despair, speaking again in the first-person singular. Suddenly, the suppliant is frantic, tormented by his foes and at the gates of death. If God will rescue him, he will move to the gates of the daughter of Zion where he will publically dis-close God's salvation using the effusive praise modeled by the preceding passage.[7] Psalm 9:13–14 conveys that God wants to be praised honestly, not insincerely. The suppliant can evangelize others when and only when God truly vindicates those who suffer unjustly. The speaker cannot proclaim God's goodness without concrete evidence to bring forward in public.

The Nations Are Truly Foiled (9:15–16)

The pendulum swings again, and the psalmist once more rejoices that the wicked are sunk in the pit they have dug, recalling Ps. 7. These verses continue elaborating the theme of the downfall of the wicked that reveals knowledge of God. Chrysostom makes an important theological point regarding the paradox that God is the eternal righteous judge, yet evil behavior is finally self-destructive:

6. *Midrash on Psalms* also recognizes that the oppressed refers to Israel. "God will not forget Israel's blood shed by the nations of the earth" (Braude 1959a, 145).

7. Augustine offers several interpretations of the movement from the gates of death to the gates of Zion, all in terms of being personally lifted from sin to sanctity. He especially excoriates craving pleasure, singling out greed as the root of all evils. To move to the gates of the daughter of Zion is to be delivered to the most honorable pursuits (2000a, 149).

"he reinforces his argument from both directions."[8] God judges justly, yet a natural "moral physics" operates in the world. The two are complementary, for God wants people to practice virtue voluntarily; they fall by their own hands in order to teach virtue.

Plea to Judge the Nations (9:17–20)

Psalm 9:17–20 reverts to the complaint of the needy who feel forgotten in their languishing. The first-person voice is gone, and the psalmist implores God to rise up on behalf of the weak so that brute strength will not be allowed to prevail (9:19). The speaker prays not for himself but on behalf of those trodden down by the anonymous arrogant "nations." Chrysostom is quick to note "the [compassionate] feelings of holy people" who are concerned not only for themselves but for "the mass of humankind."[9]

The hope of the singer is both for the oppressed and for their oppressors: that the nations, whose existence may be blotted out because of their evil, will come to fear the Lord and be brought down from the arrogant perch from which they think they can get away with untoward treatment of the poor and remain unpunished. The evangelistic thrust of the psalm is clearest here. Only God can bring the evil nations to heel so that they recognize their own mortality and admit that they cannot prevail against the right might of God.

The Wicked Heart and Mind (10:2–11)

The analysis of the psychology of wickedness is perhaps the most original contribution of Ps. 9–10. The particular vices of the wicked are arrogance (10:2, 4), greed (10:3), and stubbornness (10:6). Evildoers scheme against their victims (10:2) and lurk in hidden places, waiting to ambush them, crouching like lions waiting to assault their helpless prey (10:8–10). Most frustrating to their victims is that the assailants seem to prosper (10:5a). Yet the psalmist warns that their words are not to be trusted, for they belie the speaker's deceitful intentions (10:7).

That the wicked calculate their own advancement by seeking to get the best of others is not surprising, or perhaps even interesting. What is theologically interesting is that these destructive patterns and habits are the result of a bad attitude toward God. The root cause of social injustice is not that people do not respect one another or their property; it is that the wicked renounce (*nī'ēṣ*) God (10:3, 13). The full stature of their evil arises from denying God. As a result, they do not seek him and act as if "God does not matter," as the *Book of Common Prayer* translates the phrase *'ēn 'ĕlōhîm* (10:4).[10] The wicked have persuaded themselves that God's judgments do not pertain to them (10:5). This lulls them into a false and stubborn

8. Chrysostom 1998, 194.
9. Ibid., 195.
10. *Book of Common Prayer* 1979, 594.

security that their misdeeds will never catch up with them (10:6). Later in this segment, the psalmist identifies the point at which the wicked make a crucial error: they think that God is not paying attention. The great fear of the faithful—God's absence—is the very point at which the wicked make their dastardly move.

The wicked rationalize their behavior to themselves on the ground that God has forgotten or intentionally hidden himself, so he will never see the evil deeds being done. Thus the perpetrator deceives himself, believing that he will escape punishment (10:11). Paradoxically, God's absence is the anguished fear of the faithful: "Why LORD are you so far away, why do you turn away, precisely when you are needed?" (10:1). The wicked are wicked because they can get away with it, at least for some length of time.[11] Faith seeks evidence that it can call the wicked to account. Complaints about the inaction of God are not uncommon in the Psalter. "How long, O LORD" is a familiar anguished refrain, previously met in Ps. 6:3 (and also seen in 13:1–2; 35:17; 74:10; 79:5 et al.). In hushed tones, the fear is whispered: perhaps God is not "there" or, like the Olympian gods, not interested, in which case the wicked will have the last laugh after all. God needs to answer not only to rescue his devotees but also to break the stubbornness of scoffers, the insouciant, and all who resist Israel's God. He needs to salvage his own tarnished reputation.

Arousing God to Action (10:1, 12–18)

The psalmist pulls himself up to the full height of theological conviction and denounces God's aloofness from those who need him in time of trouble. John Chrysostom, ever the eloquent Christian Stoic, is quick to make a startling moral point. The aggressor ought to be pitied more than the oppressed, for their moral bankruptcy is on display for all to see. The wicked hurt only themselves, while the righteous, though wronged, remain unharmed. Indeed, the long-suffering orphans and the oppressed possess an advantage, for they "emerged better and more conspicuous from their tribulation."[12]

The psalmist calls God to rise up and not forgot the poor (10:12, cf. 9:20). Some English translations obscure the precise rebuttal 10:13 makes to the thinking of the wicked in 10:3–4. "Why do the wicked despise God and tell themselves not to seek him?" (10:13) repeats the scoffing attitude of the wicked in the earlier verses (*nī'ēṣ* and *bal-yidrōš*). The psalmist turns back to address God directly and dramatically, for his faithful life depends on it. "But you do see!" he insists. "You are not disinterested in us for you have aided the orphan" (10:14). He reverts to the opening confidence of Ps. 9 to recall to God his destruction of the wicked nations (10:16). The psalm concludes on the triumphant note with which it began

---

11. *Midrash on Psalms* adds: "The wicked do not sin until they have persuaded themselves their sins are permissible" (Braude 1959a, 153).

12. Chrysostom 1998, 204. See also his whole treatise on this counterintuitive point in Chrysostom 1889.

but now looks ahead to God's renewed commitment to justice when orphans and the oppressed will never again be intimidated by swaggering strongmen.

Theological Pedagogy

Psalms 9 and 10 present two theological pedagogies—one for the oppressed and another for the oppressor. Before exploring these, however, a word about the portrayal of God is in order. God is presented as permanently installed as the righteous judge of the world who both punishes the wicked and acts as a refuge for those in trouble (9:7–9). While Ps. 9:12 depicts God being of sound memory in regard to the afflicted, the crisis facing the psalmist as he teaches Israel about God through his poetry revolves around the fact that God seems to have forgotten the afflicted (10:11) or simply no longer cares about them (10:13). In light of this, what does the psalmist have to offer the downtrodden, and how does he address their pursuers?

The theological pedagogy offered to the oppressed is perhaps a bit disappointing from a Marxist-inspired perspective, which urges the afflicted to rise up on their own behalf against oppressive circumstances. While it is clear that God sides with the oppressed and hates evil and those who perpetrate it, it is also clear that everyone experiences God as distant and silent—indifferent. Even in this case, the poor are not encouraged to speak for themselves but asked to wait expectantly for God to rise up on their behalf. However, the passivity of the afflicted may be more a matter of their wherewithal than an approbation of modesty on the part of the poet. Nevertheless, that the psalmist moves from petitioning God on his own behalf (9:13–14) to petitioning God to take action on behalf of others (10:12–18) bespeaks an interest in modesty. Bystanders are urged to tend to the needs of others.

While it is possible to read this orientation to modesty as pacification rather than empowerment of the wronged, Chrysostom, Augustine, and Calvin would disagree. When faced with the psalmist's admission that God seems to come to the rescue of the oppressed too late, they counter that divine delay is part of the plan to empower the oppressed, though not in the way one might expect. Being deeply committed to the value of humility, the church fathers agree that in making us wait for relief, God is either cultivating the virtue of patience in the afflicted or exercising a more refined judgment of when to manifest his grace than we can discern.[13] These doctors of the church are encouraging the sinned-against in the way they should—and if they are truly righteous, the way they should want to—go: toward virtue. For if the hope of the Christian life is to grow in spiritual strength and the knowledge and love of God, the opportunity for the exercise of patience is surely a God-given opportunity to grow further into the person one wants to become. This is deemed to be more desirable—indeed more powerful—than being rid of untoward external circumstances.

13. Augustine 2000a, 151; Calvin (1854) 1998, 123–24.

Surely, however, the assumption that enduring untoward circumstances constitutes training in virtue is questionable. Such experience, especially for an extended period of time (as is assumed by this psalm) may have a corrosive effect on virtue and character. Rather than encouraging patience and teaching forbearance, prolonged injustice may cultivate anger, resentment, despair, and the desire—even the impatience—for revenge. Thus victims are doubly wronged, for they languish both materially and spiritually.

While the weak of heart may indeed be psychologically set back in such circumstances, the psalmist's aim is primarily to give hope to the weary, especially when they lack the social and political capital to extract themselves from harm. That is the reason for rehearsing God's past action against the wicked before the complaint. Knowing that God is an asylum for the oppressed in time of need (9:9) enables present sufferers to remain hopeful. Indeed, unless people remain hopeful they will be discouraged from thinking creatively and constructively about their situation and from taking appropriate steps; the hopeless are more inclined to take rash action that could land them in the company of their enemies. Perhaps, then, Ps. 9–10's failure to urge the oppressed to rise up against their foes should not be taken as a discouragement against discerning action for one's own well-being but rather as a warning against becoming what one hates as a result of negative emotions and designs.

What then of the other pedagogy embedded in this psalm? What are the perpetrators of evil—who are, after all, the main focus of this psalm—to learn from this portrayal of God and the depiction of the victimization of the weak? As John Goldingay insightfully points out, readers of this psalm should see themselves as the people who are being prayed against.[14] While every person has the potential to oppress others—both knowingly and inadvertently—the psalmists have no thought of sinfulness as essential to human nature, although they certainly recognize a heart bent on harm when they see one. Even when overwhelmed by human malevolence, the psalmists do not posit sinfulness as a fundamental spiritual illness that renders everyone morally hopeless and helpless before God.

Psalm 9–10's denunciation of evildoers serves to wake them up to their ugliness so that they cease and desist from it. The assumption is made that the wicked can be saved from their despicable condition by realizing either that they humiliate themselves, as Chrysostom suggests, or that God will at some point wake up, calling them to account in direct combat with the forces of God arrayed against them. Hope for the repentance and thereby the salvation of sinners is deep and strong. These poets believe that things can be made right. The later Christian notion of original sin as a permanently debilitating condition is nowhere in sight, not even in Ps. 51:5, for it would undermine the hope being held out for both sinners and those sinned against.

14. Goldingay 2006, 184.

PSALM 11

Canonical Context and Themes

Like many of its predecessors, Ps. 11 elaborates the stark message of Ps. 1. People can be categorized as either righteous or wicked. Their deeds are not secret, and God will be their judge. Although not a complaint psalm in the technical sense, it prepares for such a setting. The scene portrays a speaker being advised by supporters to flee to safety in the face of advancing adversaries. This encouraged Rashi and Calvin, both of whom knew the pain of exile, to interpret this psalm as a nation's (in Rashi's case) or an individual's (in Calvin's case) expulsion from their homeland.[1]

Structure and Dynamics

Unlike most of the earlier psalms, Ps. 11 does not address God. Rather, it is a soliloquy in which the speaker reflects aloud on advice he has been given regarding his delicate situation as he decides his course of action. It falls naturally into two parts, a point noted (perhaps first) by Calvin.[2] Psalm 11:1–3 explains the precarious position of the speaker, a righteous person considering flight from a bad state of affairs. The second half of the psalm offers his answer. He decides not to give ground but to stand firm in his trust in God. He depicts the judging and punishing side of God's righteousness, which devours the wicked and loves the righteous, from God's heavenly throne. This psalm, like Ps. 9–10, is a confident statement that the backs of the wicked will be broken and the righteous will be vindicated.

1. Gruber 2004, 215; Calvin 1998, 160.
2. Calvin 1998, 158.

To Flee or to Stand? (11:1–3)

Psalm 11 opens amid an ongoing conversation in which the speaker presents a rhetorical question to his friends who have been offering him advice. "Why do you tell me to fly like a bird to the mountains when [you know that] I take refuge in the LORD?" (11:1). The Hebrew is even stronger since the punch line, "I take refuge in the LORD" (*bayhwh ḥāsîtî*), is the psalm's opening statement, rebuking the speaker's advisers. Friends are not always the most helpful, as Job also learned.

The speaker's supporters mean well, but they see things from a limited perspective. Understandably, they are responding to the imminent danger in which the confident speaker finds himself. The wicked aim their taut bows at the straighthearted from an ominous dark place (11:2). In light of the Davidic dedication, the theme of flight from danger encouraged Jewish commentators as well as Theodoret of Cyrus to place this poem in the life of David as he is being urged to flee his pursuers. Focusing on the opening phrase, Theodoret nicely zooms back from the text to suggest that it is appropriate for every wronged person to place his or her trust in God.[3]

The speaker "agrees" with Theodoret, if the anachronism be permitted. Even in duress, he has a broader view than his friends do, for he is thinking not in the immediate-term but farther out, from God's perspective. At the same time, he does not break off the conversation with his friends but continues to edify them, coming back with another question spoken from his confidence in God. "What [else] should the righteous do when the foundations crumble?" (11:3).

Which foundations? Both Augustine and John Donne (who preached a whole sermon on 11:3) respond that the foundations are the foundations of the church's faith, which heretics undermine. Augustine is reading amid the Donatist controversy in which the doctrines of church, ministry, and sacraments were at stake, and Donne is reading amid Catholic–Protestant wars in which the Protestants believed that Rome was denying the foundation of the church: Christ.[4] The question posed in 11:3 is purely rhetorical, however. The answer has already been given: "I take refuge in the LORD" (11:1). I will not flee.

There are, of course, other ways to interpret "foundations." James Mays reads "foundations" as a "metaphor for the bases of common life and social order."[5] Fleeing for personal safety is an abandonment of civic responsibility and only contributes to the anarchic social conditions that the wicked archers are fomenting. Those who take refuge in God cannot abandon civil society. Seeking personal safety in a distant land is a cowardly retreat. True safety is to be found in standing firm in the way of righteousness—that is, the way of God—even though that may be how the trouble started in the first place. The remainder of the psalm reinforces this view.

3. Theodoret 2000, 99.
4. Donne 1995.
5. Mays 1994b, 75.

The Lord Is Righteous (11:4–7)

The second half of this poem explains why the speaker has chosen to stand firm in God. Perhaps he is still lecturing his friends, but he is also indirectly addressing the wicked who, if Ps. 10 is referenced here, think that God is not paying attention to what they are doing. The speaker explains God's location, values, and actions to friend and foe alike. God is in his holy temple (presumably in Jerusalem), although his throne is in heaven (11:4). The text is not fastidious about divine bilocation. God's physical location is irrelevant; it is his all-seeing moral watchfulness that matters: he loves righteousness and hates evil. Regardless of how one understands divine presence, God examines people, testing righteous and wicked alike as one's behavior reveals one's true colors (11:5). With the punishment of Sodom clearly informing the text, the psalmist threatens that God will not only rain fire and sulfur on the wicked but also a tempestuous wind (11:6).[6] The wicked will suffer for their mischief. Natural disasters upon the wicked are evidence that God loves righteousness and that the upright will behold his face and presumably be spared these torments (11:7).

Theological Pedagogy

On one level, this psalm is designed to strike fear in the hearts of its auditors, exhorting them to join the straight-hearted (11:2) and flee from the misdeeds that would bring divine punishment upon them. Here the theistic sanction is operating at its purest. Psalm 11:7 says that God is righteous and loves the upright, and hates the lover of violence (11:5). That contrast, however, should not be read through the filter of later western Christian sensibilities that connect God's hatred of sin and sinners to their eternal damnation. Original sin and the bondage of the will that see sin as inexorable is not in the psalmist's purview. On the contrary, he offers people a clear choice; they can live righteously or wickedly. Further, divine election is not connected to this choice and is not a seemingly arbitrary decision emanating from the secret places of God's heart. Israel is the elect of God—full stop. Wicked behavior may grieve God, here even to the point of hatred, but it does not alter Israel's and Israelites' status as God's beloved; at best it increases God's distress. For the Older Testament, God's punishing anger is administered in this life and understood to be time limited. That is why the psalmists can cry, "How long, O Lord?" There is no notion of eternal punishment or reward after this life.

At the same time, it may be worth noting that there is no hint of what in Augustine's day would become Pelagianism. With no notion of eternal judgment the idea of imploring a positive judgment through what Luther called "good works" loses its power to undermine divine sovereignty. Here, should God choose to punish it is a free decision. There is no biblical analogue to attempting to earn salvation.

---

6. Sirocco (*scirocco*), jugo, or ghibli is a hot dust-laden Mediterranean wind that comes from the Sahara and reaches hurricane speeds in North Africa and Southern Europe.

Some may draw back from this psalm's pedagogy because it so readily divides the virtuous from the vicious and because it seems to extend no grace or forgiveness to miscreants. The scope of divine vision is harshly apparent. But it must be kept in mind that for these writers and his readers change is always possible. Indeed, the poets' pleas to the wicked are for them to change.

Yet where is there a place for those who find themselves at one moment among the upright and at another among the wicked—that is to say, most all of us? The scenario is too simple. But then, again, Christian theology and spirituality did not, by and large, value that ambiguity either.

Perhaps the nuance many seek lies in reading the theological pedagogy of this psalm through the other conversation being played out here. As the psalmist sets it up, two such conversations can be identified. While one is between the upright and the vicious, the other is between the speaker and his friends—between those who would seek (and advise others to seek) their own safety in time of trouble and those who, taking refuge in God, stand firm for the common good when the foundations of civil society shake. At this level, taking refuge in God is not, as the words might suggest, to retreat from public life, but to remain in the fray. Indeed, the psalmist conveys this in his reproof to his friends, telling them just who God is and what he is going to do under pressure. The psalmist not only invites all to join the ranks of the upright but also to consider carefully what taking refuge in God requires.

PSALM 12

Canonical Context and Themes

Although Ps. 12 is dedicated to David, it could have just as well been dedicated to Noah, who was singled out as a righteous man when "the LORD saw that the wickedness of humankind was great in the earth, and that every inclination of the thoughts of their hearts was only evil continually" (Gen. 6:5). Lamenting the condition of a society in which the common good falters, Ps. 12 follows well its predecessor, whose protagonist stands bravely against the tide when fundamental social structures fail due to unchecked wickedness abroad in the land. Certainly all suffer in such times, yet the poet pointedly identifies the poor and needy who are usually the first to feel the sting and feel it more acutely than those with resources do. Interestingly, sins of the tongue rather than violent crimes are targeted as the cause of social deterioration as the speaker lifts his own voice, pleading with God to lift the vulnerable to safety.

Structure and Dynamics

Psalm 12 is difficult to segment because several verses seem to be continuations of thoughts that are either not in the text or hang loose, waiting for another clause or phrase to complete the thought. For example, 12:1 states the poem's theme—the faithful have disappeared—while 12:2 speaks of liars, with no transition from one topic to the other. Perhaps liars are those who abandon God. Similarly, while 12:7 is a fitting conclusion to a lament psalm with its confident proclamation that God will protect the people, another verse is seemingly tacked on about the wicked who prowl, leaving the reader with the taste of evil in her mouth.[1] To continue

---

1. Robert Alter also notes this (2007, 37).

my practice of structuring the psalms according to the audiences and addressees of the text, it will be necessary to treat most verses individually.

Cry for Help (12:1)

The opening cry for help is from someone overwhelmed by the godlessness of the age rather than someone who is personally afflicted, as in the previous lament psalms. It seems that all have deserted God, and the singer feels like he is living in a moral wasteland. "Save, O LORD," he cries, though he does not mention an object for his prayer. The attentive reader will recall the names of Joshua, Isaiah, and Hosea, and the Christian reader will add the name of Jesus to that list of prophets whose very names derive from the word "salvation," which opens the poem.

John Chrysostom astutely notes that the speaker does not ask to be saved because of his personal righteousness. Rather, he is isolated "*because there are no holy people left*, indicating that those who were so have been lost, since evil has prevailed and infection overcome."[2] Perhaps they have succumbed to the viciousness of the age one by one. From this situation, Chrysostom draws the lesson that "while being virtuous is hard, and more challenging on one's own, it is particularly so when the one practicing it experiences a dearth of good men [for moral reinforcement]. . . . fellowship and fraternal encouragement are no little thing."[3]

Denunciation of the Ill-Tongued (12:2–4)

Like Eph. 4–5, which singles out sins of the mouth as contributing to moral decay, Ps. 12:2–4 names lying, flattery, hypocrisy, telling tall tales, and trusting in one's own articulateness as bringing harm in their wake. Psalm 12:3–4 prays for God to strike those whose tongues drip with vain or vicious speech or who boast of being their own master, derisively dismissing God and social responsibility with "who is our master?" (*mî 'ādôn lānû*). Robert Alter notes the "violent concreteness" of the psalmist's call for God to "cut off all smooth-talking lips" that speak from a two-faced heart (12:3).[4] Smooth talkers trust themselves to spin smoke and mirrors around the truth. Psalm 10:3 and 7 have already warned against the wiles of vicious tongues.

Theodoret of Cyrus excoriates those who believe they can control their lives by their clever words. "They cannot bear, he is saying, to keep their words in conformity with their nature, nor are they prepared to have regard for the divine laws; instead, with mouths agape they heedlessly utter whatever occurs to them, scornful of divine long-suffering and giving no thought to their falling under the lordship of God."[5]

2. Chrysostom 1998, 217.
3. Ibid., 216.
4. Alter 2007, 35.
5. Theodoret 2000, 102.

God Speaks and Will Act (12:5)

In response to both complaint and prayer, the psalmist puts a promise into the mouth of God that he will arise and save the poor and needy in response to their sobbing. Against the later Protestant teaching that nothing one does can influence God—making praise the only truly appropriate form of worship—John Chrysostom sees power in suffering. Following his train of thought noted above, he opines that it is not one's virtue but one's dire straits that stir God to compassion.

> Mighty is the force of groaning, calling down grace from on high. Be in fear of it, you who wrong the needy. You have power and wealth and resources and favor of the courts; but they have weaponry more potent than all those, groans and laments, and the injustice itself, which wins help from the heavens. This weaponry digs up dwellings, uproots foundations, lays waste to cities, this weaponry casts entire races into the sea—the groaning of wronged people, I mean. God has regard for their right attitude when the abused utter no recrimination, but simply groan and lament their own misfortune.[6]

Reassuring the People (12:6)

After his auditors have heard directly from God, the poet turns to them to explain the preceding verse in which God promises to rescue society's most vulnerable members—promises as pure as finely refined silver. The purity of God's word contrasts starkly with the self-serving words of the lying flatterers of the age. Augustine remarks that God's pure words are "without any alloy of deceit,"[7] as are the words of those who boast of being beholden to no one.

Confident Address to God (12:7)

The speaker, who has been so careful to explain to his auditors what they can expect from God—to the extent that he even puts words in God's mouth—turns to God, blurting out a direct and plaintive plea for protection from the iniquitous generation that seems to be of overwhelming proportion: "You will guard them, LORD" [won't you?] (12:7). Reverting from the third- to the first-person plural—his own fear spilling out in spite of himself—he continues: "You will keep us from this generation forever" [won't you?]. It is as though he does not quite believe his own reassuring words about the purity of God's promises and is attempting to reassure himself yet again.

Read in a calmer frame of mind, however, 12:7 is the kind of typical concluding statement of confidence with which most lament psalms end. Doubts about God's care and power to protect the weak are to be banished by trust, even when one can barely hold on.

6. Chrysostom 1998, 219–20.
7. Augustine 2000a, 171.

Residual Complaint (12:8)

As previously noted, the last verse of this psalm dangles anticlimactically and a bit sadly, for it carries the reader back from the vote of confidence in God achieved by 12:6–7 to a cry for rescue. Psalm 12:8 reverts to the complaint of 12:2, as if attempting to smooth the abrupt transition from the plea of 12:1 by supplying a more precise subject for 12:2. Taken together, 12:8 and 12:2 might read, "The wicked prowl around; baseness piles up for everyone. People utter lies to one another; they speak with smooth lips from a duplicitous heart."

Theological Pedagogy

Although I treat Ps. 10 as the continuation of Ps. 9, there is a sense in which Pss. 10–12 form a group. They all lament the situation of society in general, and they lack the personal appeal on the speaker's own behalf that characterizes other lament psalms.[8] While Ps. 12 stays close to the plight of the poor and needy, it also looks across society to lament the loss of the common good. The complaint is that the pious have vanished (*gāmar ḥāsîd*) from sight, as noted in 12:1. The view is panoramic, revealing a large-scale social crisis that echoes the anxiety of Ps. 11:3. The social foundations have crumbled; what should be done?

The picture is of a contemptuous community in which each one takes him- or herself to be his or her own master or mistress, beholden to no one. Neighbors mislead one another. Acquaintances lie to one another. As one would expect, the psalmist exhorts his listeners to cling to the purity of God's promises. Only God can be trusted; only he can protect the faithful from "this generation forever" (12:7), that is, from their own people for whom there seems to be no hope.

No doubt those who seek to follow a leader whose kingdom is not of this world find themselves at times alienated from the predilections of the age—its entertainments, gadgets, and amusements, its usual ways of doing business, its standards of success and its strategies for achieving it. Perhaps these distractions warrant a time for skepticism and a withdrawal into God's promises of protection of a good life without those toys. The psalmist permits his readers to rest from the fray when flattering lips and duplicitous hearts abound and the wicked prowl around like a roaring lion looking for someone to devour (1 Pet. 5:8).

At the same time, perhaps the psalmist speaks as one who is alienated from others who are similarly alienated; perhaps he hopes to bring others into that company through his word-art. Is he not breaking out of his own isolation by writing, seeking to draw others into his circle of criticism as he laments his age? His song creates a kind of support group for himself. Writing itself, especially with the prospect of publishing, is a therapeutic act of hope in defiance of the cynicism that threatens to overwhelm him.

8. The translation "Help me" for the first word of Ps. 12 in the *Book of Common Prayer* (1979, 597) adds the first-person perspective, which is missing in the original.

PSALM 13

Canonical Context and Themes

Psalm 13 is the quintessential individual lament psalm in short compass. Walter Brueggemann calls it a psalm of disorientation.[1] A human enemy is present, but God's silence is the deeper threat. Humans are expected to be fickle, but not so God. The poem begins as a pure cry of despair then turns abruptly—without giving reason—into confident hope and praise apparently based only on the speaker's trust that God is compassionate. It prepares the way for the searing indictment of practical atheists that comes in the next psalm—"Fools tell themselves 'There is no God'" (Pss. 14:1 and 53:1).

One has the sense that God will not actually abandon those who trust in his loving-kindness (*bĕhasdĕkā*). In this, the psalm's cry of dereliction—followed by the stark inability to believe that God would do such a thing—follows Pss. 9:10, 13–14; and 22:4–5 (among others), which point to God's past rescue operations as evidence of his compassionate nature in order to give hope to those in distress.

Structure and Dynamics

The entire psalm is spoken directly to God by someone in intense pain because God, like his human enemy, has apparently turned against him. It can be considered in two segments: one that accuses God of betrayal (13:1–4), another that sings God's praises in advance (13:5–6).

1. Brueggemann 1984, 58–60.

How Long? (13:1–4)

The fourfold repetition of "How long?" is a scorching indictment of God that reinforces the haunting thought of Ps. 10:4, 11 that God is not "there" to answer. However, the psalmist does not suggest a limited God who can cry only with the sufferer or a God who permits freedom to creatures, thereby agreeing not to intervene (as the medievals thought).[2] No, the psalmist assumes that God is perfectly capable of action but willfully refuses to tend to his proper job of caring for his people. The theodicy problem rings out its pathos and confusion.

Nor does God's inaction spur the speaker to self-searching. The reason for God's silence is not the speaker's sin; no thought is given to blaming the victim. On the contrary, God's failure to act reflects badly on God, for it enables the enemy to gloat (13:4). In the threatening twofold repetition of "lest" (*pen*)—"lest I sleep [unto] death"; "lest my enemy say . . . [and] my foes rejoice" (*yāgîlû*)—the speaker goes toe-to-toe with God, desperate to protect God's honor. God's reputation is on the line, and the complainant holds him accountable for the sorry state in which he (the speaker) languishes. He goads God to act in the full stature of his best self.

The speaker's supplication is a reprise of Abraham arguing with God to save Sodom for even ten righteous citizens (Gen. 18:22–32) and Moses quarreling with God to turn from his anger and spare the people, rebellious though they be (Exod. 32:9–14). Both succeeded in calming divine wrath. Here the situation is quite different. The plea is for the speaker's own salvation; it is not to stay God's wrath but to rouse him to action in order to save the speaker from humiliation at the hand of those who dismiss God. Still, from the standpoint of Christian piety, which exalts humility, to see the oppressed dispute with God indicates that even in distress the faithful are powerful enough to demand that God be God. Despair is resisted by not dissolving into self-blame, and personal agency is sustained by calling God to account.

"I Will Sing" (13:5–6)

Suddenly and without warning or warrant (as is also the case in Pss. 3:8; 4:7–8; and 7:17), Ps. 13 erupts in exultation at having trusted in God through it all. The speaker will rejoice (*yāgēl*) in place of his enemies, who would rejoice at his downfall (13:4–5). With God's expected intervention, the power dynamic reverses, and the one who trusts in God's kindness is vindicated for his faithful hope; he breaks out in joyous song. The triumph is as much for God as it is for the suppliant. Indeed, the psalmist has been advocating for God all along, through the voice of the suppliant.

2. Duns Scotus (1265/6–1308) distinguishes God's absolute power to do anything that does not entail contradiction from God's ordained power to do things only according to previously established laws.

Theological Pedagogy

This poem recognizes the theodicy issue, for the justness, goodness, and power of God are imperceptible except to the eyes of those with the most stubborn faith. Hope emerges seemingly out of nowhere; the suppliant cannot help himself. Be that as it may, he has no choice but to trust God, for if God's silence is absolute, the foundation of the suppliant's life is truly imperiled. Not only that; he must also defend God's reliability, lest God be seen as the enemy behind the human enemy. God's integrity is on the line. The suppliant is highly energized to defend God, and that energy combats his languishing.

Even if it makes sense to be a practical atheist, as Ps. 10 suggests, distrust of divine oversight is not psychologically possible for those who cannot but believe in both the loving-kindness and the punishing judgment of God as the moral grounding of society. To believe otherwise is to succumb to a morally chaotic reality in which might makes right and personal agency is denied, further robbing the sufferer of power. The struggle is between those who defend the power and grace of God and those who scoff at the same. Moreover, it is a debate about the character of God or, as some might say today, the nature of ultimate reality.

While Ps. 13 is reminiscent of a boxing ring in which God's defendants and prosecutors duke it out, one might recognize, without impugning the spiritual combat, that the match is held within every trembling heart that shifts with life's changing seasons. What is striking, even daunting, is that the vise of prolonged abandonment does not prevent the trusting one from bursting out in song for having been requited (*gāmal ʿālāy*), although he brings no evidence to that effect; the moral order of the universe is at stake.

PSALM 14

Canonical Context and Themes

Psalm 14 is the last of this group of lament psalms that began with Ps. 3 (with the exception of Ps. 8).[1] Building on the cynicism of those who find God inattentive to the cries of those in need in Pss. 10, 12, and 13, Ps. 14 presents the telling thought that doubt about God's power or goodness or even existence is the underlying cause of the moral decline of society. Perhaps it bears repeating that the complaint—which has been building since Ps. 3—is finally not against the impious so much as it is against God. Reading canonically, we may assume that the speaker (or at least the psalmist) is familiar with previous psalms that struggle with this problem; perhaps he wrote some of them. He complains that the languishing of the suffering faithful encourages people to act with impunity and commit dastardly deeds because they think they will not be held accountable. Immoral behavior is atheistic behavior. God's silence is the cause of both moral decay and practical atheism.[2]

While the psalmist does not know of the intellectual objections of modern atheism—which originally arose from the incredibility of miracles, the philosophical failure of the classical proofs for the existence of God, the inability to locate the traditional three-tiered universe through a telescope, and the ability to probe the course of disease through the microscope—he does identify what I will call a biblical atheism, grounded not in philosophical but moral skepticism. The point is not that "God" is an empty term but that God is ineffectual and that people are taking advantage of that silence, making matters worse.[3] Though

1. This psalm appears with slight variation as Ps. 53.
2. The term "practical atheism" was coined by Gerhard von Rad and is explained by Walter Brueggemann in his discussion of Ps. 14. It refers to "one whose conduct is disordered and without focus, because it is not referred to God" (1984, 44).
3. Miller 1986, 95.

they witness the suffering of the poor, they are not aroused to pity or energized to fight for them. On the contrary, the state of the poor spurs them on to further exploitation. This discouraging picture shows the need for the theistic sanction on one hand and codes of civil and criminal law with domestic police forces to enforce them on the other hand.

Structure and Dynamics

The problem of theodicy was openly discussed in Israel, as seen in Ps. 10. Unlike philosophical discussions of the problem, as one sees in the writing of Boethius,[4] the absence of God is a problem of morale rather than reason. Psalm 14 begins with the poet complaining to his audience about those who "live and operate on the secret supposition that God is not," as Patrick Miller puts it.[5] The psalmist then presses his listeners to examine themselves on this account by having God himself lament the situation that everyone seems to have abandoned him (14:2–4). Psalm 14:5 returns to the voice of the original speaker (the psalmist) as he addresses his audience, and 14:6 chastises the audience as the culprits. Psalm 14:7 cries for Israel's deliverance, and it is tantalizingly unclear whether the salvation sought is from external adversaries or from the corruption that grips Israel itself.

Practical Atheism (14:1)

Like the other psalms in this string of laments, Ps. 14 honors David. Chiming in with the psalmist against practical atheists who act as if God does not exist, Theodoret of Cyrus uses both the historical context and a more philosophical reflection as arguments for faith and trust in God. Theodoret heeds the psalmist's appeal to the past actions of God on behalf of those in need in desperate circumstances by adding another historical narrative to the ones that the psalmists allude to. He places Ps. 14 in the setting of 2 Kgs. 18, long after the death of David. At that point in the narrative the Assyrians had captured Samaria and exiled the northern kingdom of Israel. Eight years later the succeeding Assyrian king, Sennacherib, captured Judah's fortified cities and prepared to take Jerusalem. He sent an emissary to the pious king of Judah, Hezekiah ("God is my strength"), inviting him to surrender in advance and arguing that Hezekiah's God will not save Jerusalem any more than the gods of other cities that fell in the face of Assyrian might saved them: "Where are the gods of Sepharvaim, Hena, and Ivvah? Have they delivered Samaria out of my hand? Who among all the gods of the countries have delivered their countries out of my hand, that the LORD should deliver Jerusalem out of my hand?" (2 Kgs. 18:34–35). Hezekiah, of course, trusts God; through

4. Boethius 1999.
5. Miller 1986, 96.

repentance and prayer he appeals to God to save Jerusalem, and he is vindicated! The Assyrians are defeated and Sennacherib goes home, only to be murdered by his own sons (2 Kgs. 19:35–37). Theodoret reflects calmly on Ps. 14's report of practical atheism: "Those who mocked the counsel of poor and lowly Hezekiah for trusting in God rather than arms will realize that the one who made himself dependent on God enjoyed a hope that was not disappointed."[6]

To lend intellectual support to the psalmist's desire to rebut practical atheism, Theodoret muses on the seriousness of the problem:

> Some people utterly deny the divine, and profess that God is not the origin of things but that the name is without force and devoid of any substance. Others, on the other hand, give the name gods to what are really not, while rejecting the only one that is. Still others concede in word that he exists, but do not actually come up with evidence of his care for things on earth or his scrutiny of human affairs. They have all thus been caught up in the one doctrine of atheism, presuming there is no God.... In their hearts, at any rate, they persuaded themselves that there is absolutely no God, being quite foolish and stupid as they were ... Before the coming of our Savior, therefore, the whole of life was in fact like this.[7]

Theodoret concludes that Christ, being God incarnate, brought hard evidence of the reality of God into the world and did away with the grounds for such practical atheism.

God's Lament (14:2–4)

While many think that God is uninterested, the poet portrays God as watching everything, searching for those who are wise enough to seek him. *Midrash on Psalms* includes the following parable:

> An architect who built a city making secret chambers and hiding-places in it, and then was made governor of the city. When he set out to catch the thieves in the city, they ran off and sought to hide themselves within the hiding places. Thereupon he said: "Fools, would you hide yourselves from me? I am he who built the city! I am also he who knows all the secret chambers and the way in and the way out of the hiding-places, better than any one of you." Likewise, the Holy One, blessed be He, says to the wicked: "Fools, would you hide wicked counsel in your heart from Me? I am He who made man, and so I know all the inner recesses and secret chambers within him."[8]

Psalm 14:3–4 might be God's own words of despair that people have abandoned him and devour one another like bread. Indeed, it is the height of foolishness to

6. Theodoret 2000, 107.
7. Ibid., 107–8.
8. Braude 1959a, 181–82.

act in ways that pollute society, weakening life for everyone and allowing oneself to be pulled down with the whole, especially when self-destructive behavior is involved. The foolishness of not seeking after God (14:2) and not calling upon God (14:4) is the result of thinking in the short term and failing to think and act in concert with the long-term interests of society.

Athanasius has moments like these in mind when, in the second part of his great treatise in defense of the moral triumph of the incarnation against sorcery and paganism, he writes: "So, as the rational creatures were wasting and such works in course of ruin, what was God in his goodness to do?... But once he had made them, and created them out of nothing, it were most monstrous for the work to be ruined, and that before the eyes of the maker. It was, then, out of the question to leave men to the current of corruption; because this would be unseemly, and unworthy of God's goodness."[9] Therefore, God became a person so that the world would be drawn into his embrace and would abandon the wickedness that characterizes such foolishness, as lamented in Ps. 14.

It is worth noting that Paul cites Ps. 14:2–3 at the head of a catena of passages in Rom. 3 to support his point that all have sinned and are accountable before God; the law that seeks to restrain sin is to no avail. Though the function of divine law is not under discussion in Ps. 14, Paul does well to cite 14:2–3 as a ringing indictment of the human failure to internalize the moral standards that are necessary for civilization to thrive. In our own day, the superficial force of the rule of law is often disclosed in moments of social crisis; looting and random violence occur when external constraints that maintain law and order are temporarily suspended. The poet's sad observation that no one does good, not even one, reverberates down the ages.

Threats and Encouragement (14:5–6)

These two verses reinforce the basic psalmic theology sounded in Ps. 1. Because God sides with the righteous against the wicked, the latter, if they are paying attention, will be rightly mortified, chagrined, not only that their crusade against the faithful has failed, but that they face ruin. Further, they are wrong about God; they are embarrassed.

Whence Salvation? (14:7)

The poem's concluding verse is intriguingly ambiguous. It is unclear whether the salvation sought for Israel in the first half of 14:7 is from external oppressors or from Israel's internal decay. Perhaps the obscurity is intentional. Yet even if unintentional, the ambiguity is to the reader's benefit because more can be deduced by playing with the text both ways. If the oppression is from an external

9. Athanasius 1954, 61.

source, perhaps it indicates an exilic origin for this psalm, which the second half of 14:7 might suggest. While Theodoret's interpretation of the conflict between Israel and its external enemies is instructive, reading 14:7 as an indictment of internal corruption invites considered reflection on faith. While faith in God should protect Israel from the moral debilitation brought on by practical atheism, perhaps Israel's failure—humiliating though it may be—functions as an accessible model to the world. Practical atheism might be even more tempting today than it was in the poet's day, and seeing it revealed so starkly is comforting in a cynical age such as ours. In any case, when God redeems Israel from exile—understood either literally or figuratively as the exile of faithlessness—rejoicing will abound throughout the land.

Theological Pedagogy

The pedagogical import of Ps. 14 is that faith in God is the moral basis of society. For everyone to move in the same direction, there must be a shared center toward which all gravitate. The moral health of a society is only as strong as the moral health of its members.

The psalmists generally assume the moral integrity of the poor and needy in these psalms; the damaged moral integrity of their powerful opponents speaks for itself. While being the underdog in a de jure godless society might be a source of moral capital, the victims of injustice are not beyond moral risk. When God restores his people, either to their homeland or to their faithfulness, those who were most vulnerable may very well be faced with new challenges in changed circumstances, finding themselves tempted to eschew accountability before God.

PSALM 15

Canonical Context and Themes

Having concluded a cycle of lament psalms (with the exception of Ps. 8), Ps. 15, following its predecessor, sustains the theme of Ps. 1 in order to keep the behavioral patterns of godliness (and ungodliness) in the forefront of Israel's attention. The first verb of the Psalter, *hālak*, is the first word of Ps. 15:2, *hôlēk* ("The one who *walks* [purely]"). The Psalter is commending a holy way of walking through life. Perhaps the psalmist realizes that the prolonged suffering of those who complained of God's silence will cause them to be persuaded by their enemies' argument that God's silence suggests his absence, enticing them to abandon the godly life and engage in the untoward behavior of which they are, or might become, victims. In painting more portraits of the righteous and unrighteous, Ps. 15 acts as a concluding exhortation to the laments, though it does not present a specific individual view. By making a general statement, the psalmist points Israel's attention to the common good and the behaviors that promote it. The psalmist is public-spirited and seeks to enlist his readers and hearers in the cause of the common good.

Structure and Dynamics

Psalm 15:1 sets up the theme with two questions that have already been answered by Ps. 1. The remaining verses answer the questions with two triads of examples—the first set positive (15:2), the second set negative (15:3). Psalm 15:4–5 adds a further list of characteristically salutary character traits, concluding with an affirmation that the virtuous steadfastly model this way of life.

Who Abides Safely? (15:1)

The opening bicolon asks the enduring rhetorical question of the Psalter: Who are the virtuous who dwell in God's house? The poet never tires of explaining what virtuous people do and avoid doing or of proposing how people should conduct themselves so that the whole community thrives. Theodoret points out that these lists of dos and don'ts are the substance of divine assistance.[1] Walter Brueggemann, on the contrary, finds 15:1 offensive to his Protestant sensibilities because it seems to suggest that only the righteous may enter God's presence.[2] That interpretation, however, conflates being in God's presence with dwelling in the house of God, which is presented as a long-term experience. Indeed, Christian eschatology has always reserved the vision of God, eternal life, and/or heaven for the saints. But the poet's theology is not eschatologically oriented. Dwelling in God's house, like taking refuge in God, is a way of living, not a reward for a moral life when it is done. The thought here is that moral living is safe living.

Those Who Walk, Talk, and Do the Truth (15:2–5)

The rest of the psalm identifies those of laudable character in both general and specific terms. Perhaps the specifics are of greater interest as they are easier to model. The poet admires those who speak truthfully and with integrity. Those who avoid slander and do not take bribes, who protect both friends and neighbors, who keep promises even when it is disadvantageous, who lend money without interest, who are repulsed by contemptible behavior, and who do not comport with wicked companions but respect honorable people who "fear the Lord" all receive special mention. Honesty, integrity, generosity, and graciousness are the most desirable character traits.

While the themes here are familiar, two phrases are worth noting. Psalm 15:2 concludes with the phrase *wĕdōbēr 'ĕmet bilbābô*. It translates literally as "speaking truth in his heart" but might be rendered more colloquially as "is utterly honest with himself." The psalmist realizes that a pure life must rule out the self-deception that can rationalize untoward behavior. Here is a point at which cognitive behavior therapy and insight-oriented psychotherapy might engage each other. The former argues that behavior shapes thinking, while the latter claims that behavior expresses attitudes and beliefs. That is, behaviorism thinks from the outside in, while psychodynamic models think from the inside out.

Christian theology generally takes the latter position, holding that correct beliefs about God, humanity, and the world will lead to a morally good life. By contrast, Pharisaic Judaism holds that behavior shapes attitudes. For example, the biblical prohibition against eating blood but allowing meat eating (Gen. 9:3–4) also cultivates respect for life.

1. Theodoret 2000, 111.
2. Brueggemann 1984, 42.

Thomas Aquinas popularized the importance of "habits," or dispositions cultivated by practices that form people in virtuous living, in his massive system of ethics, which dominates the *Summa Theologiae*. While the exhortation to self-honesty suggests that the moral life requires a well-ordered mind or inner life, the phrase that begins 15:3—*lō'-rāgal 'al-lĕšōnô*, "his tongue is not accustomed to"—takes the behaviorist perspective that careful speech is a habit that can be intentionally developed. Perhaps the poet is sagacious in recognizing that dispositions are shaped both by internal self-regulation and by habitual practices.

Theological Pedagogy

While the pedagogy of other psalms previously examined has been indirect—with the poet speaking to his audience through intermediary characters or by having his hearers address God through his words—the pedagogy in Ps. 15 is direct and pointed. There are things one is to do, and there are things one is to refrain from doing. The pure life is not obscure or ambiguous. This is not to suggest that the psalmist believes the pure life is easy to accomplish. The guiding principle is like the first rule of medicine: do no harm. Although he does not go into further detail concerning cultivation of the virtuous life, the psalmist holds up a model for emulation: unnamed heroes who resist the temptations that assail the tongue and the wallet and generally comport themselves beautifully with neighbors and kin.

Needless to say, all of this is framed theologically. The Psalter is not articulating a belief system, although it assumes the reality of the God of Israel whom it defends against reasonable doubts and questions that it is not afraid to entertain. Rather, the way of God is a way of walking that pivots on the virtue of justice. Dwelling in God's house is neither the beatific vision that Augustine craved nor the complete knowledge of God in heaven that Aquinas sought. It is walking a pure and honorable life, one step at a time.

PSALM 16

Canonical Context and Themes

Psalm 16 is an oath of loyalty to God that the speaker addresses directly to God in the presence of his gathered (or anticipated) listeners, who both witness to and observe the scene. In this psalm the speaker models the ideal Israelite who is deeply and self-consciously dedicated to God. The superscription describes the song as a *miktām*, and it is dedicated to David. The designation *miktām* occurs in five additional psalms which appear in canonical order, (Pss. 56–60) and are also dedicated to David. The superscriptions of Pss. 56–60 include instruction to the leader and indicate what is perhaps the name of the tune to which the songs are to be sung in worship; Pss. 57, 58, and 59 are to be sung to the same tune, "Do Not Destroy," which might suggest a plaintive tone. Furthermore, Pss. 56–57 and 59–60 append long superscriptions that locate each composition at a stressful time in David's life, although the event mentioned in Ps. 56:1, "when the Philistines seized [David] in Gath," is not recorded in scripture. The last of these, Ps. 60, indicates that the poem intends to teach (*lĕlammēd*) at a time when David was imperiled.

Miktām then does not designate how a psalm is to be performed but is likely a type of psalm. Of this group of six psalms, only 16 and 58 do not specify a circumstance in David's life. However, Ps. 16 does begin with a cry to God for protection, and Ps. 58 denounces the wicked, suggesting that a *miktām* might be, as Ps. 60 says, instruction in time of danger. That is, a *miktām* would teach one how to think and behave theologically when *in extremis*. This definition suits Ps. 16 well, since it teaches Israel how to approach God with the speaker as exemplar. It opens with a cry for protection by God, although it does not go on to explain the threat at hand.

Structure and Dynamics

Psalm 16 teaches by example rather than by exhortation. It begins with an invocation for divine protection (16:1) after which the speaker turns to his human audience and teaches them what to say to God when in need (16:2). Psalm 16:3–4 explains attitudes toward both holy and impious people, although 16:3 is obscure. Psalm 16:5–9 expands upon the speaker's loyalty toward God and the benefits he draws from it. The final two verses (16:10–11) return to address God directly in the second person as the human audience listens (a common psalmic style). Like many psalms, Ps. 16 begins by addressing God, turns to the human audience to explain what is going on, and then models how they should address God properly.

Invocation (16:1)

The psalm opens by invoking divine protection, although no evidence of suffering or oppression by enemies is apparent. The call is warranted because the speaker is a faithful Israelite who takes refuge in God. Calvin agrees: "God is ready to succor all of us, provided we rely upon him with a sure and steadfast faith; and that he takes under his protection none but those who commit themselves to him with their whole heart."[1] Divine aid is not unconditional; people are accountable.

Loyalty Oath (16:2)

In Ps. 16:2 the speaker instructs the people on the proper posture they should take before God. Both Theodoret and Augustine (as well as most Christian exegetes who follow Acts 2:25–28) understand the speaker to be Christ, speaking from his human aspect. He turns to his listeners, telling them that he says to God that he has no good apart from God, who is his master. According to the Christian exegetes just mentioned, Christ acts as a human teacher modeling piety.

Abraham Ibn Ezra, instructing his Jewish parishioners on proper piety, addresses a possible objection to Calvin's (much later) comment cited above. Ibn Ezra insists that God is not obligated to do good to those who turn to him. He cites "Rabbi Solomon the Spaniard [who] similarly writes in one of the prayers that he composed: *I stand before You for Your sake, not for my sake. I stand before You for the sake of Your glory. I do not stand before You to receive a reward for my deeds.*"[2]

Holy Attitudes (16:3–4)

The singer specifies what he preaches by depicting both holy people whose desires are noble and those he abjures. The latter choose another path, which the

1. Calvin 1998, 216.
2. Ibn Ezra 2006, 165.

poet frighteningly characterizes as blood libations; to these he adds a curse: "May their sorrows increase" (16:4). Taking Christ to be the speaker of the psalm, Augustine does not abide the obvious meaning of the text but inverts it, having those who are sick with sin long for a doctor and seek healing from Christ. Augustine's interpretation is most encouraging. When those who offer blood libations are transformed, they will forget their past and become children of God through Christ's peace.[3]

Blessings and Benefits of Loyalty (16:5-9)

The central segment of Ps. 16 is an encomium on the experience of shelter in God that elaborates 16:2. To enjoy no good apart from God is to have God as one's portion (16:5), one's inheritance (16:6). It is to be comfortably pleased with one's life in God, blessing the Lord for his guidance and, as a result, experiencing bodily rest at night because of that firm foundation, even when one's "innards" (literally "kidneys") might otherwise have reason to be agitated (16:7). With God as one's portion, life (especially life in the body, tucked away) is morally serene and secure, having been well advised by God and having complied with that advice. As a result, the psalmist rejoices, "my flesh will dwell forever" (16:9). Christians take this as an allusion to resurrection.

Concluding Address to God (16:10-11)

In Ps. 16:10–11, the singer turns back to God, apparently picking up the opening cry for protection, telling his hearers that he believes that God will not let him die because God shows him the way of life (*'ōraḥ ḥayyîm*), enabling the singer to enjoy God's presence forever. While interpreters of Christian eschatology see the promise of personal salvation in 16:11b, Rashi (in typically Jewish fashion) interprets joy in the divine presence as "[that which is found] among the group of people which is [spiritually and ethically] near You."[4]

Theological Pedagogy

Psalm 16 takes its place in Christian scripture and eventually in the creed through Peter's speech to the baffled Jews gathered in Jerusalem on the festival of Shavuot (Pentecost), which celebrates the giving of the law at Sinai. Acts reports that the Holy Spirit rushed upon the disciples, undoing the curse of Babel to enable them to become apostles and proclaim the news in all languages; Jesus of Nazareth had risen from death (Acts 2). Peter quotes Ps. 16:8–11 (Acts 2:25–28) to explain that David (in Ps. 16) spoke of Jesus's resurrection in the psalm's promise of escaping

3. Augustine 2000a, 182–83.
4. Rashi 2004, 228.

death and abiding forever (16:9–11). Furthermore, the author of Acts reads the resurrection through Ps. 16 to suggest that Jesus was exalted at the right hand of God (Acts 2:33 reflecting Ps. 16:10). Reading this interpretation of the psalm in Acts (reinforced by Ps. 110:1), the later theological tradition inscribed it in the second article of both the Apostles' and the Nicene creeds to teach the ascension and session of Christ at the right hand of the Father.

The Christian reception of Ps. 16 illustrates a reading strategy that quite transforms the original pedagogy. The general counsel for a morally flourishing and satisfying life with God morphs into a uniquely Christian vision of adhering to the risen Lord, with the commendation to repent and be baptized in the name of Jesus Christ for the forgiveness of sins and the reception of the Holy Spirit (Acts 2:38). Christianity is born by wrestling with ancient texts in light of startling events that require textual grounding in order to be theologically warranted. The Christian reading of David's psalm is a fresh instruction for people in a quite different context than the one the psalmist originally attributed to David. But the underlying hope is the same. The psalmist reads David's life, and the author of Acts reads Peter reading the psalmist's read of David's experience to the same end: as the "way of life" (Ps. 16:11) for those who "set the LORD always before them" (Ps. 16:8).

PSALM 17

Canonical Context and Themes

Psalm 17 returns the reader to the individual laments that dominate the Psalter's opening poems. This one presents a prayer of David addressed exclusively to God. In keeping with Ps. 1, the speaker easily distinguishes the righteous from the wicked and counts himself among the former as he seeks deliverance from arrogant opponents who purportedly speak ill of and plot against him. The themes and several of the images are by now familiar, perhaps written by the same hand as some of the other psalms.

Structure and Dynamics

Typically, there are no marks identifying the situation that provoked this complaint, leaving the impression that the speaker is ridiculed and held in contempt by those who scoff at his piety. He likens impious people to waiting lions, as in Pss. 7:2 and 10:9 (appearing again in Ps. 22:13). Whether someone is really out to get him or whether the cry reflects a deep insecurity in the soul of the complainant—who "smells" the derision for his godly orientation—will remain forever hidden.

This song is a sustained call for rescue punctuated by the reasons that God should do so. It begins with a cry to God to be heard (17:1a) and then gives God a reason to pay attention: the speaker's purity (17:1b). It develops the opening cry for protection (17:6–8) and then offers a second reason God should intervene; the speaker faces impending danger (17:9–12). It concludes with a call for God to intervene, but more significantly, with a glimpse of God himself (17:13–15).

Cry to Be Heard (17:1a)

Like Pss. 4, 5, 12, and 16 before it, Ps. 17 begins with a cry of distress. Of its first six words, three are verbs that implore God to hear, pay attention, and listen to the crier. The verbs appear in the imperative form, giving the psalm an urgent intensity, as if the speaker anticipates that getting God's attention will not be easy. Unlike Pss. 6 and 13 (and others that will be discussed later), there is no indication that God is not "there" to answer or that God is angry, as Ps. 6 and later psalms explicitly state, although the insistent tone here may belie such fear. God is not hostile, and the speaker, though beleaguered, is still hopeful and confident of arousing God to respond as he does in Pss. 11 and 16.

Claim of Purity (17:1b–5)

Even as he pleads for attention, the speaker eagerly proclaims his purity as a reason God should turn to him. He is confident of his righteousness. God has tested and purified him—even at night when evil deeds are more likely to occur either because they are covered in darkness or, as Calvin thinks, because "when a man is withdrawn from the presence of his fellow-creatures, he sees more clearly his sins, which otherwise would be hidden from his view."[1] The opening verbs of listening are matched by the speaker, who claims that his speech is without deceit (17:1b) and that God has found nothing untoward issuing from his mouth (17:3). He does not disturb God.

Midrash on Psalms finds this testimony of innocence from David too much to bear, given David's history, and is perhaps a bit embarrassed by David's flagrant self-promotion. It protests that David was unable to stand up to the test God gave him, referring to Ps. 26:2 where David invites God to examine him because he thinks he can stand up to it. The midrash constructs a conversation between God and David:

> In no time at all the Holy One, blessed be He, put David to the proof, and he was unable to stand up to it. About to slip into transgression, David cried out, saying: *Hold up my goings in Thy paths, that my footsteps slip not* (Ps. 17:5). Thereupon the Holy One, blessed be He, said: "Did I not tell thee that thou wouldst be unable to stand up to the proof?" And David said: *I have called upon Thee, for Thou didst caution me, O God* (Ps. 17:6). *Show thy marvelous loving-kindness, O Thou that savest by Thy right hand them which put their trust in Thee* (Ps. 17:7). David said to the Holy One, blessed be He: Master of the universe, give me of that marvelous balm which is Thine. And what is that? It is pardon and forgiveness.[2]

The midrash deftly turns David into a humble suppliant who confesses his sinful inclinations and need for reconciliation with God, rendering him a proper role model for Jews.

1. Calvin 1998, 238.
2. Braude 1959a, 212.

Continued Cry for Protection (17:6–8)

Having shown why God should tend to him, the suppliant returns to his plea for aid, confident that God will respond. In Ps. 16, the notion of the delight of the righteous at the right hand of God (16:11) is appropriated by the Christian creed as a reference to the resurrected Jesus. Here the image of being at God's right hand recurs, this time for those seeking shelter from threatening insurgents.

Psalm 17:8 is home to a celebrated phrase that has been immortalized in the service of compline, the bedtime prayer of the church that seeks divine protection through the night. Its striking phrase, "keep me as the apple of the eye," attracted the attention of several commentators. Theodoret explains the image as the pupil, the most interior and protected part of the eye,[3] while Calvin chooses the literal meaning—the "daughter of the eye," the "tenderest part of the body"[4]—to convey the goodness of God for hapless creatures. Both commentators appreciate the delicacy of the eye as a fitting image for the delicate soul who feels exposed before the wicked and entrusts itself to God's keeping.

Threatening Danger (17:9–12)

This pericope offers God a second reason to tend to the suppliant's call for help. Deadly threats encompass him, as others have complained. Even if the dangers are psychological rather than physical, being encircled by critics feels deadly because one's expected community of support has become a place of danger rather than security; criticism and contempt may break forth at any moment, even as the speaker struggles to keep his footing in purity, at which the wicked sneer. The Hebrew *šaddûnî* in 17:9 evokes a demonic image.

Psalm 17:10 depicts his enemies encased in fat and closed off, presumably from graciousness, so that unlike the speaker's guileless lips the enemy's speech is haughty, harking back to the opening verbs that appeal to God's acute sense of hearing. The repulsive image of the pursuers being enclosed in fat, usually translated as a heart encased in fat, is explicit in Ps. 119:70, which depicts the arrogant smearing the suppliant with lies (v. 69) so that he feels hemmed in and scrutinized by prying eyes that seem like hidden lions and their cubs waiting to pounce (17:12). But in 17:10 the wicked one is simply "befatted." No bodily organ is mentioned. One might envision him (or them) as encumbered by fatness, unable to move with agility, yet nimbly able to bad-mouth the defendant in his marginality.

Indeed, danger lurks here, although the prowling lions may be of a different sort than appear on the surface of the text. The deeper danger to readers and singers of poems such as this involves the repeated theme of being surrounded by those who scoff at unsophisticated and naïve piety. While seeking to support those in need, Ps. 17 might inadvertently encourage believers to see enemies

---

3. Theodoret 2000, 120.
4. Calvin 1998, 242, 245.

lurking inappropriately. Where disagreements about faith and piety arise, one voice will always be stronger than the others, and plaints of this type may provoke suspicion. The faithful may experience themselves as marginal, misunderstood, and maligned in the presence of skeptics who flaunt the tradition and the faith that sustains the pious.

Call for Divine Intervention (17:13–15)

In Ps. 17:13–15 the speaker calls God to arise and strike his enemies who are depicted as mortals; like us all, their lives are fleeting. While the speaker clearly seeks refuge under God's wings (17:8) and by God's sword (17:13), he recognizes that the days of his enemies are limited (17:14a); their power will pass. It is an insightful and comforting, albeit counterintuitive, observation from one who is on the receiving end of disrespect. The taunts of the scoffers will end with their speakers' waning lives, which the speaker can anticipate, perhaps with satisfaction.

The second clause of 17:14 turns in a quite different direction, away from the wicked and back to those protected as the apple of the eye, hidden from the lurking lions under the shelter of God's wings. The speaker locates himself in this protected company. He is no longer alone, if ever he was. He calls on God to feed those who seek refuge in him and to satisfy their children. The image evokes Ps. 37:25: "I have been young, and now am old; yet I have not seen the righteous forsaken or his children begging bread." Here is hope amid distress. Such hope is difficult to muster and lovely to behold.

The song's final verse (17:15) sustains this hopeful tone by returning to the speaker himself, who ends his poem more than content; not only has he experienced the security of vindication, but he is also satisfied by justly beholding the face of God. The second clause of 17:15 stresses that seeing the face of God satisfies the speaker's longing when he is wide awake, which contrasts with his testing in the dark of night in 17:3. With their receding lifeline, the wicked can never experience this satisfaction. The reward of the righteous lies in their closeness to God.

Delight in the vision of God as the essence of salvation plays a central role in Christian soteriology beginning with Augustine.[5] It is central to Aquinas's eschatology as well. According to them, the vision of God is reserved for the saints, the goal for which the faithful yearn. It ceased to take center stage with the Protestant Reformation when other soteriological considerations took precedence. But it is here, at the very end of this song, succoring the chaste one being chased.

Theological Pedagogy

Psalm 17's message is that God should take care of those who are faithful and just. If the division between the virtuous and the vicious is that the former hold fast to

5. Augustine 2003.

the tracks that God lays down for them to follow while the vicious do not—either because they scoff at the common good promoted by the path, thinking only of their own short-term interests, or because they are agnostics or theological skeptics—an example of division within Israel is presented that does not often surface in scripture, given its frequent preoccupation with external enemies. Internal division within Israel took on adversarial overtones, pitting the virtuous against the vicious when Jesus (the great lightning rod of Israel) divided Jews from one another. This is plain in both Luke's and John's Gospels. Luke 12:49–53 depicts Jesus as intentionally divisive:

> I came to bring fire to the earth, and how I wish it were already kindled! I have a baptism with which to be baptized, and what stress I am under until it is completed! Do you think that I have come to bring peace to the earth? No, I tell you, but rather division! From now on five in one household will be divided, three against two and two against three; they will be divided: father against son and son against father, mother against daughter and daughter against mother, mother-in-law against her daughter-in-law and daughter-in-law against mother-in-law. (NRSV)

Jesus did not come to bring peace but division within Israel!

While the comparison between the situation in the Psalter and that in the Gospels may seem a stretch to current sensibilities, this is precisely the form of intertextual reading that can draw the two Christian Testaments into constructive conversation. In both cases, the parties to the debate believe their cause to be just and right and the others' to be false and misguided. Indeed, each side may see the other as condemning and contemptuous of its own faithfulness to God and God's way—be it one that has been publically received by Israel, as in the case of the Psalter, or one that is only now being revealed, in the case of Jesus.

In effect, the psalms' depiction of people who fall away from approved religious belief and practice demonizes them: their hearts are covered with fat; they track down the faithful like devouring lions seeking their prey. Indeed, when Jesus is the cause of division, those who do not follow him are quite literally demonized (see John 8:39–47). Zealotry is the mother of contempt.

In the case of Ps. 17, the theological pedagogy does not come from the text. It can be gleaned only from reflecting on both experiences of division within Israel. Setting these texts side by side provides a vantage point that neither can achieve alone. As much as the psalmists and Christian theologians have fought for truth over falsehood, virtue over vice, and faithfulness over doubt, there lurks the danger of damaging and even destroying community in striving to prove one's point. Indeed, a moral price may be exacted for being right; righteous indignation can become a demon of its own.

Underlying the claim to rightness in both cases is the assumption that one does not know and can never know the truth of God *in se*. Sagacious minds from Gregory of Nyssa to Immanuel Kant (on entirely different grounds) warn that the human mind functions within real limits that cannot be transgressed without succumbing to sinful pride. We cannot know God *in se*—that is, as God truly is—certainly not in this life, as Thomas Aquinas also acknowledges. Such delight awaits the saints in the next life.

Whether one discern knowledge of God in scripture, creation, reason, or some combination thereof, those who are intellectually honest and modestly minded agree that our knowledge of God is, at best, penultimate. In more specific terms, it is limited by scripture that is wrought by human hands, creation that is discerned personally through direct observation, science that takes place through controlled examination, and reason that is worked out with its missteps, conflicted dispositions, and culturally shaped questions. The reality is that God transcends even what one takes to be God's definitive self-revelation. Those who truly accept the reality of divine freedom understand that knowledge of God.

Even in the face of intellectual modesty, however, the concluding verse of Ps. 17 is noteworthy. It may not be necessary to claim definitive knowledge of God, as western Christian theology has longed to do, in order for the faithful to breathe deeply and satisfyingly from the wisdom of God's well. This psalm ends not on a note of eschatological confidence but with triumphant achievement in the face of those who scoff. Just as the bellies of the children of those whom God protects are full to satisfaction (*yiśbĕʿû*), the singer is personally filled up (*ʾeśbĕʿâ*) with the vision, literally the picture, of God.

PSALM 18

Canonical Context and Themes

Psalm 18 is a royal thanksgiving song. Like most of its canonical predecessors, it is dedicated to David; moreover, it appears with minor modification as 2 Sam. 22 with nearly the same long superscription, lending some credence to its antiquity. The duplication of the text assures David's place as the poet laureate of ancient Israel. To the superscription of the 2 Samuel version, the psalmist adds that the song is to be sung to the tune of "Servant of the LORD" (the same as Ps. 36), suggesting that it became part of the liturgy after it was composed.

The text is set as David's response to his escape from King Saul. The story of Saul and David dominates 1 Samuel, but the tentacles of that thorny relationship reach into 2 Samuel through family ties. While initially appreciating David's military prowess and bravery (1 Sam. 17:1–18:5), Saul soon becomes jealous of David's rising popularity and tries to have him murdered in various ways (1 Sam. 18–19). David escapes each time and expends much time and energy evading Saul and his plots until Saul finally dies in battle at the end of 1 Samuel. At that point, David assumes the kingship of Judah (2 Sam. 2), a development the reader has already anticipated, since Samuel anointed David as a boy (1 Sam. 16:13). The first canonical insertion of the text at 2 Sam. 22, which is attributed to David's escape from Saul, appears a considerable time after Saul's death and David's elevation to the kingship, perhaps attributing David's supremacy to his cleverness in evading his pursuer, eventually triumphing over him and his house. Royal triumph is central to this song.

James Mays points out that this psalm is a sequel to Ps. 2.[1] There, the Lord ordains the unnamed king as his regent, promising him dominion over the nations. Here, God shows that he has kept his promise in time of military need. Psalm 18:16–19 and 34–48, which elaborate the king's triumph over the nations and

---

1. Mays 1994b, 90.

is not related to Saul at all, explains Ps. 2:8–11, which celebrates Israel's military triumph over enemy nations that rebel against the Lord's appointed king in Zion, understood to be the Davidic empire. An important thread connecting the various texts is Samuel's anointing of David to replace Saul (1 Sam. 16) and the anointed king's triumph over the kings who refuse Israel's authority (Ps. 2), followed by the elaboration of David's triumph over his enemies by the power of God in Ps. 18. There, God proves himself both the Lord of history and the master of nature who controls both geology and geography on behalf of his king (Ps. 18:7–15). A casual read of the theological message carried by this thread points to God's authority over nature and the nations through Israel's king. However, perhaps the implied message of Ps. 18 is adumbrated in Ps. 2:10–11: "Now, O kings, wise up, be apprised earthly judges; worship the LORD reverently, and celebrate [his rule] with trembling." God's authority over the nations and nature is through Israel's king. While this is a nationalistic poem that follows the lead of Ps. 2, it also rehearses the theme of Ps. 1, as do many of these poems, placing personal holiness in a global political context. The king presents himself as righteous, and this, allied to his military victory over enemies, pulls together other themes the psalmists have been developing: refuge in God, the righteousness of the suppliant, and the power of God to vindicate the righteous through triumph over military opponents. In Ps. 18 the two themes—personal righteousness set forth by Ps. 1 and public triumph in foreign, especially military, affairs set forth by Ps. 2—join forces to picture a righteous leader who is devoted to and dependent on God for victory, ultimately God's victory over all the families of the earth, as Gen. 12:3 puts it.

Structure and Dynamics

Once again I will segment the psalm by the audience to whom each segment speaks rather than thematically, since a discourse on a topic may abruptly change audience mid-thought. This psalm moves around with the poet speaking first in the second-person singular addressed directly to God, next in the third-person singular about God to the speaker's human hearers, and then in the first-person singular about the poet's experience with God—although this last section overlaps with speaking in the third person about God to the poet's local auditors. The psalmist continues to dart back and forth among all of these voices, speaking very personally in order to impart to others his intense experience with God. The shifts come fast and furious as the words tumble out, keeping the audience on its toes as the psalmist moves abruptly from one form of address to another.

Saved from All My Enemies (18:1)

The superscription identifies David as bedeviled by enemies (which he was), extending the scope of Ps. 18 from his troubled personal relationship with Saul to a broad political panorama. I have already noted David's struggle with Absalom, which was, like his enmity with Saul, a dynastic struggle for the throne; the former was to protect his throne, while the latter was to wrest the throne from Saul. The phrase "all his enemies" in both 2 Sam. 22 and Ps. 18's superscription confers divine approval on David's imperial aims. Theologically, the expansion from a specific to a general context teaches that the virtuous pattern of life of the righteous works at both the personal and the international level. God commends a single standard of living no matter the setting.

Declaration of Devotion (18:1)

The striking word of 18:1 makes its only biblical appearance here; ʾerḥāměkā is an Aramaic cognate of the Hebrew verb "to have mercy" in the first-person singular with a second-person singular suffix indicating the object. It is translatable as "I am devoted to you." The nouns reḥem (womb) and raḥămîm (mercy) are cognates, so the verb means "to love as a mother loves her child from conception." The seventeenth-century Dutch theologian John Cocce remarks that it means "to love with the deepest and strongest affection of the heart, with the moving of all the bowels." By using the translation "bowels," he extends the intense emotion to include men.[2]

What is perhaps most interesting about this diction is not its intensity but that David uses it to express his feeling for God, for the noun raḥămîm and adjectival form raḥûm are commonly used as attributes of God, not people (Gen. 43:14; Exod. 34:6; Deut. 4:31; 13:17; Jer. 42:12; Pss. 78:38 and 103:8). In similar fashion, the common Muslim formulaic address, "in the name of Allah, the most compassionate, the most merciful," uses the Arabic cognate of this word to express God's character. It is noteworthy then that Isa. 47:6 castigates the Babylonians for failing to show compassion toward their Israelite captives, applying the virtue horizontally as a standard for victors in war. It is not, however, a virtue that is displayed by the victor in this psalm.

Therefore, the psalmist's use of this attribute to describe David's compassionate love for God is quite striking. Ibn Ezra was so taken aback by it that he translated it "I will seek compassion from you," although he knew that previous Jewish commentators correctly read it as "I will love you."[3] Robert Alter's translation, "I am impassioned of You," captures the tone well.[4]

The Story of Distress and Deliverance (18:2–14)

After the brief exclamation of devotion to God, the source of his strength, David narrates the story of God's vindication of his reign in cosmic terms. The

2. Cocce is cited in Calvin 1998, 259n1.
3. Ibn Ezra 2006, 185.
4. Alter 2007, 52.

rescue operation is so spectacular that it is graphically portrayed using dramatic meteorological and geological imagery. God calls all creation to aid in rescuing his adoring servant-leader.

Psalm 18 highlights God's acute hearing and vision in attending to the cry of his faithful in distress. In contrast to those complainants who experience God as far off and seemingly deaf to his faithful ones, the king's triumph occurs because God has heard him. The poet encourages those who will follow with similar concerns by saying, "He heard my voice" (18:6). When the suppliant is caught, squirming in the underworld in what he experienced as the throes of death (18:5–6), God suddenly breaks into his suffering, enraged at his opponent. God figuratively breathes smoke from his nostrils and fire from his mouth so that the earth shudders and the mountains quake. God descends from on high and speaks simultaneously in icy hail and fiery coals, upsetting nature. God flies in riding on a cherub (18:10); no holds are barred for his wrath against those who challenge his rule by attacking the one appointed as his king on earth.

The destructive power of great storms—perhaps a hurricane, typhoon, or tsunami—enlists wind, darkness, intense rain, thunder, and lightning that join forces to rout the king's enemy. The narrative conveys that all hell has broken loose from the sky, which represents God's anger scattering those who rebel against him. It is significant that God uses the weather, not David's military or political acumen, to vindicate the king so that neither he nor his listeners can possibly attribute the victory to the king but only to God. It is the storm rather than military action that defeats the enemy. The message of dependence on God is not lost on the listener.

Your Rebuke (18:15)

Seething with God's anger, the story has so far been cast in the third person, but 18:15 slips into the second person, apparently unselfconsciously since it does not begin a new pericope in that form of address but moves immediately back into the third person. The direct address is simply "Your reprimand exposed riverbeds and the breath from your nostrils laid bare the earth's foundations, O LORD." The poet is overtaken with intense excitement as he stands back at a safe distance watching God acting on his behalf. The change of voice leaves the impression that God is immediately present with the king all the time, even when he is speaking to his human audience.

The LORD Delivered Me (18:16–20)

Directly after addressing God, the poet returns to the third person to tell his audience not only how but also why God rescued him. God pulled him out of the storm's path and away from the enemy's path, setting him in a safe open space (18:19). Psalm 18:17 suggests that one reason for the storm is God's realization that the king's enemies were stronger than the king, but the speaker goes on to add that at another and perhaps deeper level it was a deserved reward for clean hands (18:20).

I Was Blameless (18:21–24)

After speaking of himself as the object of God's delight (18:19), the poet addresses 18:21–24 to his audience using the first person, explaining his current safety to them as God's reward for his "clean hands." Perhaps this is to impress upon his hearers that the one who rescues him is God and not himself, for in 18:24 he adds that it is God who sees his clean hands, implying that neither he nor others may see him this way.

Between the verses attesting to God's judgment on his righteousness, the speaker indulges in an unabashed rehearsal of his righteous pattern of life. He lists six ways in which he exemplifies the righteousness of the happy one of Ps. 1, including things that he does and does not do (as Ps. 1 lists them). For the most part, this includes keeping God's ways (18:21), the laws and statutes of the commandments (18:22). Like Paul in Phil. 3:6b, the king is blameless and pure before God.

The psalmist, of course, is innocent of Paul's seeming rejection of this way of life commended by God, just as the speaker has no doubt of his ability to live as God would have him do, both as an individual and as a public official whose salutary leadership of the people depends on his purity and commitment to God's ways. Christian commentators, however, are caught between respecting the psalmist and being embarrassed by his theology, which has David—of all people—claim to be free from guilt (18:23). It is hardly a claim that would stand up in a legal proceeding or in the court of public opinion, especially since the song in 2 Samuel appears long after David's adultery with Batsheva and murder of her husband. The attempt at whitewashing is transparent.

Augustine does not shy away from the psalmist's claim about David's righteousness but attributes it to Christ's mercy, which enables David to act rightly. His well-doing is not seen by other people but by God.[5] Further, Augustine stresses the value of the divine wrath on display here as medicinal rather than retributive. Operating from an extreme Augustinianism, Calvin finds his own high doctrine of grace pressed here. While Calvin personally identifies with David,[6] David's boasting of his righteousness makes Calvin nervous; he neutralizes it by seeing it, as Augustine does, as evidence of God's mercy toward David. That mercy is usually interpreted in Calvinism as forgiveness of sins, although here it extends to David's physical rescue. Therefore, the reward of rescue from enemies that David reports in this poem is not really a rescue of David but the rescue of God's mercy toward David. God rescues the king not because he deserves it; the rescue is God's self-reward, so to speak—a display of God's attribute of mercy. In other words,

5. Augustine 2000a, 193.
6. See Selderhuis 2007, 30–34.

God invested in David and rescues him to sustain the value of that investment. It pays off for God to sustain David as a model for Israel because David is one toward whom God is merciful. The reward is a pedagogical tool to teach gratitude.

It is more than that, however. Sustaining his investment in David as the anointed leader of his people is God's way of reassuring the people of God's trustworthiness, especially after he withdraws his favor from Saul. Although David is a major sinner, God's mercy on him is not finally the deliverance of an individual from danger. It is the deliverance of the whole nation. In this way, the nation is not made to bear the punishment its leader deserves for his personal conduct. The point is that God chooses to look at David as if he were innocent for the sake of the nation that is saved from its enemies by David's military skill.

God's Loyalty and Perversity (18:25–29)

Having heard from the speaker about his own character, the poet returns to second-person discourse to illustrate both God's character and the very personal connection he feels to God. Psalm 18:25–26 taps out a lapidary rhythm in two bicola, each clause having two sets of three syllables—two phrases in each verse—with one extra syllable in 18:25. Each clause begins with "with," the repetition pounding the meter home for emphasis. Consummating the poetry in three of the four clauses, the adjective describing the person becomes the verb that characterizes God's action toward him: "With the gracious you are gracious; with the pure you are pure; with the innocent you will be innocent but with the perverse you are perverse" (18:25–26). The message is clearly the law of just deserts; we will reap what we have sown.

The last phrase, standing apart from the others as it does, struck Calvin. He offers an inverse theodicy of sorts to defend the "tough love" God uses in this psalm:

> When God thunders in good earnest upon [the perverse], they transform him, through the blind terrors which seize upon them, into a character different from his real one, inasmuch as they conceive of nothing as entering into it but barbarity, cruelty, and ferocity. We now see the reason why David does not simply attribute to God the name and office of judge, but introduces him as armed with impetuous violence, for resisting and overcoming the perverse, according as it is said in the common proverb, A tough knot requires a stout wedge.[7]

God fights perversity in kind—not the best model for those who believe that love is the best instrument of transformation but warranted by those who believe that a strong hand is the best way to cow the obstreperous. Indeed, 18:27 carries forward God's policy of just deserts by treating different kinds of people with different strategies. He will save the humble and humble the haughty. It is a view not lost upon Paul (1 Cor. 1:28) and Luke (1:52).

7. Calvin (1854) 1998, 287.

Whereas earlier the speaker stood aside while God worked on his behalf through nature, here God's invigorating power is direct. Speaking to God directly in the second person yet addressing his human speakers so that they learn what is in the depth of his heart, he declares that he relies completely on God who lights his candle, dispelling the dark and strengthening him so that he can crush a battalion or scale a wall (18:28–29). One can almost envision the king addressing God in front of his troops girding for attack, and through the king's confident address being themselves girded not only with arms but also with confidence in God.

The depiction of God's loyalty and mercy to Israel in 18:21–24 sits uncomfortably with the theology of just deserts when God defeats Israel's enemies. Psalm 18 might have inspired Bob Dylan's 1963 antiwar song "With God on Our Side," which galvanized the young in protest against the Vietnam War, shaking people's certainty in divine support for war. Taken together, these two passages sustain the ease with which Ps. 1 distinguishes the righteous from the wicked. Psalm 18:21–24 portrays the king as blameless and clean, deserving victory, and 18:25–29 presents the enemy as crooked and haughty, deserving to be crushed. Such clarity may be necessary for military and political campaign rhetoric to arouse patriotic courage and confidence in times of national crisis. Rarely, however, are conflicts adjudicated that simply. The psalmist's goal is to unite the people not only behind the national interest but also behind God, who properly defines that interest. Arousing enthusiasm for obedience to God's ways among the psalmist's goals, as best these can be discerned in the pressured circumstance.

Preparation with Confidence (18:30–34)

At this point, one can envision the king turning around to face his troops, reporting to them what has transpired between him and God and inviting them into the courage that he draws from that interaction. Perhaps God's meteorological performance was only a warm-up for the pitched battle that the king would engage in with his flesh-and-blood enemies. The king gives his warriors a pep talk of sorts. God has made him surefooted, swift as a deer, and steady at arms. Based on God's past rescue operations, perhaps he believes that his way ahead is safe. The king leads courageously, confident in his abilities and skill to lead well because, while these strengths are his, in another sense they are gifts from God. God has trained him well, so the troops and the people for whom they fight have nothing to fear. Here is a leader who inspires confidence and loyalty because his confidence in God carries over to others. God, not the king, is the ultimate leader.

Battle Report (18:35–45)

The next set of verses resumes the intimate conversation between the speaker and God, which the audience continues to overhear in a detailed thanksgiving for each step that God has accomplished for him. Psalm 18:35–45 furthers the list of accomplishments and powers of God, who enabled the military commander to crush his enemies as they cried out to no avail. God has no mercy on them, and they are laid low; utterly demolished, crushed like dust, ground into the mud, and made to serve Israel's king, they are, by extension, made to serve Israel's God, for to be defeated in war is to have one's gods suffer defeat as well.

Calvin is dismayed by the ferocity (almost the enjoyment) of the way in which David vanquishes his hopeless and hapless enemies. Calvin's Christian charity is offended that David seems to have abandoned mercy in his triumph, and he tries to justify David's actions as godly because he was simply being obedient:

> But as he attempted nothing without the command of God, and as his affections were governed and regulated by the Holy Spirit, we may be assured that these are not the words of a man who was cruel, and who took pleasure in shedding blood, but of a man who faithfully executed the judgment which God had committed to him. And, indeed, we know that he was so distinguished for gentleness of disposition as to abhor the shedding of even a single drop of blood, except in so far as duty and the necessity of his office required. We must, therefore, take into consideration David's vocation, and also his pure zeal, which was free from all perturbation of the flesh.[8]

Of course, the excuse that a military commander was simply following orders would not stand up in a modern military court-martial. But this is not the issue for either Calvin or Augustine before him, both of whom read the battle scene in spiritual rather than military terms. The warfare is over the soul, not the body or the booty of an enemy's property. The contest is for the spiritual allegiance of those who may be estranged from God. Calvin sees David fighting for the repentance of sinners that they may be brought to "a right state of mind" by Christ.[9]

Celebratory Shout (18:46–48a)

This brief interlude in the speaker's interlocution with God joyously shouts the victor's triumph to anyone listening, both then and long after. It includes his thanksgiving for vengeance wreaked upon his defeated and longstanding foe. Revenge as an acceptable emotion occurs both here and in other psalms (58:10; 94:1–2; 149:7). It is an unpleasant emotion and one that Christians shy away from because Jesus not only rejects it but also promotes a counterintuitive moral standard that many admire but perhaps find unrealistic: to love one's enemies and turn the other cheek.

Shunning vengeful feelings may be wise if it causes people to sublimate rash behavior and pursue more reflective courses of action, but the aggrieved need help to do so. Modern police forces and legal systems are central civilizing

8. Ibid., 294.
9. Ibid., 305.

instruments precisely because third parties act in the stead of the aggrieved, enabling them to control and deflect destructive feelings into more constructive pursuits. Most significantly, third-party intervention enables the aggrieved to rely on others to turn the incident from a personal vendetta into the public achievement of justice. Cultures and countries that still rely on codes of honor and revenge and tribal warfare to settle disputes remind those who operate at a higher remove from such raw emotions that they are truly fortunate. Public justice advances more than retribution. It is a pedagogical tool that shapes citizens to look beyond personal experience to the common welfare. The psalmist's society lacked that advantage.

Exalting God (18:48b–49)

The colloquy with God resumes mid-verse with the speaker turning jubilantly to God: "You exalted me . . . you delivered me . . . For this I will exalt you, O LORD . . . and sing praises to your name."

The King Triumphs (18:50)

David speaks the final word to his human audience about himself in Ps. 18:50. God's victory is not finally for the king but for his people, and it is forever. Thus the specific events and intense emotions expressed in this poem involve more than historical interest. The victory there and then tells of the future of the Jewish people, David's descendants, for whom the victory is wrought for all the families of the earth.

Theological Pedagogy

Psalm 18's central message is that Israel is called to remember all that God has done for it and therefore to trust God and live righteously because God protects and vindicates Israel against its enemies. The evidence presented here is graphic and violent. Perhaps more moderate language would fail to attract attention sufficient to the day.

Remembering God's graciousness to David warrants Israel's trust in and compliance with the way of life that God commends, which Ps. 1 makes clear. Free, loving response to that graciousness is the *cantus firmus* of the Psalter and perhaps of the entire Tanakh. Recalling to memory past evidence of divine care for Israel is a central strategy of Israel's poets, who sing out to captivate Israel's heart and soul. Psalm 78 is perhaps the supreme example of this strategy, but it is used continuously in scripture and later in Jewish liturgy, which relies heavily on the memory of the exodus from Egypt as the expression par excellence of divine mercy (Deut. 7:7–9; 8:11–20; 26:5–9). Faithful obedience is warranted because God has proven himself to Israel. Israel is not to obey the commandments in order for

God to be gracious. Rather, Israel's own history invites Jews and Christians, who rivalrously see themselves as latter-day Israel, to entrust their lives to God based on the memory of divine goodness, which precedes God's expectation of righteous conduct from the people of God. Righteousness is the appropriate response to divine mercy and goodness.

PSALM 19

Canonical Context and Themes

"This is a very important psalm," Abraham Ibn Ezra writes, because its appeal extends beyond Jews.[1] By singing of the "heavenly apparatus," the psalmist proclaims that the sun and moon teach of God to anyone able to discern the truth of God. Likewise, the psalmist's transition to the witness of God's teaching on life through law, testimonies, precepts, and ordinances proclaims that God directs us on the straight path.[2] As with previous psalms, Ps. 19 reaches beyond its original Jewish audience, for the rightness of the precepts is recognizable by anyone and can take root in any human heart.

Readers accustomed to discussing God the creator apart from God the redeemer—as Calvin notes, both in his commentary on this psalm and in his *Institutes of the Christian Religion*—may think of the creator in terms of the Older Testament and the redeemer in terms of the Younger Testament. As a result, the two parts of the psalm may appear as conflicting theologies at work: a God of nature and a God of commandment or covenant, stuck together without so much as a transitional phrase.[3] Such a view of the text is anachronistic and artificial[4] both historically, because it knows no other scripture, and theologically, because its theological point is that such a division misunderstands who God is. It is not "a Torah-wisdom composition prefaced with a creation hymn," as Leslie Allen

1. Ibn Ezra 2006, 210.
2. Ibid., 221.
3. Knierim 1991.
4. Recent scholarship argues for the coherence of this psalm's theology, as opposed to an older view dating back to H. Gunkel that it was composed of excerpts of two separate texts.

notes,[5] but a guide for understanding the comprehensive reach of God's grandeur and power across nations as well as nature and history.

Psalm 19 rings like a sermon to Israel's cultured despisers, tempted by pagan gods crafted to lure them back to covenantal fidelity. It teaches that 'ēl of 19:1 (or 'ēl 'elyôn of Gen. 14:22) is the God of Israel (yhwh) mentioned in 19:7–9, 14. Like Ps. 1, Ps. 19 is a great torah psalm that directs the hearer to divine teaching as a sweet way of life. Yet it is also a wisdom psalm because a God-guided life is a wise one, and the song ends with a plea to be able to live by that salutary path. It is a hymn praising God for the natural order, a meditation on the commandments, an admonition to scoffers, and an ingenuous request for acceptance.

Patrick Miller notes that Ps. 19 is the most direct reflection of Ps. 1 because it spells out the "benefits for those who study and keep" the torah.[6] He recalls the suggestion that Ps. 19 may be at the center of a ring of psalms (Pss. 15–24) arranged in concentric circles with Pss. 15 and 24 as the outer ring, 16 and 23 as songs of trust, 17 and 22 as balancing laments, and 18 and 20–21 as balancing royal psalms.[7]

The canonical placement of Ps. 19 after Ps. 18 also testifies to the unitary theology of this psalm. In discussing Ps. 18, I noted that the first major strophe depicts God working through the weather and then through the military prowess of the king. Here God is evinced first through the movements of the heavenly bodies, which attest to another form of God's control of the natural order. Only subsequently is God evinced through the commandments.

Later Christian theology distinguishes the order in both psalms—first nature, then history—as two forms of revelation or sources of knowledge of God, known in Christian theology as general and special revelation respectively.[8] The former is, as Ibn Ezra notes, available to any intelligent person. Christian theology assumes that the latter is evident only to those who have faith, that is, Jews and Christians who identify God through history as recorded in scripture. Yet recognizing a divine hand in the movements of nature is not as self-evident as adherents of the teleological argument or the argument from intelligent design often suppose. Even the possibility of a "watchmaker" behind the orderliness of the cosmos (like Adam Smith's "invisible hand" behind the economy) assumes an intelligent, organized, and probably benevolent center of power that is personalized and conceptualized through written accounts.[9]

5. Allen 1986, 545.

6. Miller 2000, 272.

7. Ibid., 272n8.

8. Discussion of revelation as a theological doctrine developed only when knowledge of God from any source was questioned in the modern period, as noted by John Goldingay (2006, 298). Claus Westermann is adamant that this psalm is not about revelation, if by revelation one means divine self-disclosure. Rather, it is a hymn of praise (1989, 254).

9. Leslie Allen offers other interesting parallels between Pss. 18 and 19, concluding that "the purpose of juxtaposing the two poems was evidently to relate David's experience to the individual believer who sought guidelines for personal living" (1986, 546).

Structure and Dynamics

While traditionally considered in two parts, this psalm is better assessed in three strophes.[10] The first (19:1–6) points to divine control of nature for a person's physical well-being. The second (19:7–11) points to moral and spiritual well-being, which is wrought by adhering to covenantal precepts. The final segment (19:12–14) reinforces the need for the moral and spiritual guidance of divine precepts in a rather anxious confession of unwitting sins and concludes with a prayer for acceptance.

Orderly Circuits (19:1–6)

The first strophe is an artful polemic against worship of the sun god Shamash in order to proclaim that Israel's God is the power behind the sun.[11] The poet subordinates the created order to its creator and manager, who sets the sun and moon in the heavens and directs their courses in the sky, just as God's teachings direct the course of Israel in its life on earth. The pagan deity is sublated into the God of the covenant to show that God is ruler of heaven and earth.

Psalm 19:1–6 builds its case in two steps (19:1–4a and 4b–6), beginning with the first verse that states the thesis of the psalm: God has crafted the heavens that proclaim his glory. Heaven speaks. The daily cycle of day and night attests to heaven's maker. The stable natural order on which life depends volubly teaches everyone about God (19:2–4). Anticipating what is to come, no one and no place can ignore the fact that the life-giving cycle of work and rest—cool and warm—displays the wisdom of God, whose handiwork enables balanced life on earth (19:6).

Psalm 19:3 and 4a are often treated as antipodes—the first to the effect that the heavenly bodies are silent, the second to the effect that they speak. Robert Alter translates them literally: "There is no utterance and there are no words, their voice is never heard. Through all the earth their voice goes out, to the world's edge, their words."[12] The two verses are in flat-out contradiction. To capture the poetic intent of the strophe, the New Revised Standard Version adds "yet" to the beginning of 19:4a to make the verses contrastive. The idea is not that the heavenly bodies are silent but that their wordless speech resounds throughout creation. No one can experience the transition from day to night and back again without "hearing" day and night speak to each other (19:2) of their maker. Creation "speaks" of God just as the ordinances and commandments do, though it uses a different form of language. Both manners of expression reach to the human spirit, giving the wisdom of God in multiple formats.[13]

10. See Nel 2004.

11. Brown 2002, 81–103; Harrelson 1999, 144–45; Sarna 1993, 70–96.

12. Alter 2007, 60–61

13. Psalm 19:4a developed a life of its own when Paul quoted it in Rom. 10:18 to bolster his idea that because Israel heard but did not believe or understand that Jesus was raised from the dead, God turned to the gentiles instead. In its own context, this verse is not related to Paul's concern.

The second step of the first part (19:4b–6) presses the thesis that nature sings the glory of God through the power of the sun, using the imagery of men at their strongest: a bridegroom and a skilled runner. God sets the sun to warm the earth from one end to the other and to feed its people. But God—who provides the sun to serve creation—does not stop there. He is wiser and more penetrating than any runner seeking to sprint across the racecourse could ever be (19:5). The poet undermines paganism without even naming it—so clear is God's providential control of the celestial bodies.

While speech is the dominant image for the power of the sun, the poet is also eager to portray the comprehensiveness of its reach, that is, God's reach through it. The sun reaches every corner of the globe. The word "end" or "corner" of the heaven and earth appears three times in this strophe to indicate the inescapability of the sun and its heat (19:4 and twice in 19:6).

The natural circuitry of the sun under God's control undercuts any easy distinction between a circular orientation toward time, often associated with religions of the Far East, and a linear orientation toward time, often associated with the religions of the West. God works in both formats, just as he uses different forms of discourse.

Orderly Decrees (19:7–11)

The second strophe moves from God's physical maintenance of the world to its moral maintenance. The regulation of physical cycles of the cosmos is needed for growing food, but the torah is needed to grow the soul into wisdom (19:7), enabling it to be happy and secure. The soul is exalted by living the teaching until the precepts gladden the heart and the "clear" commandments light up the eyes (19:8), making them alive to the moral goodness that God's way of life embodies. Just as day and night "speak," the precepts give clarity and light like the sun. The New Revised Standard Version translates *nizhār* in 19:11 as "is warned," but it also means "becomes radiant," a translation that is more in keeping with the surrounding thoughts of 19:10–11 that exalt the desirability of keeping the divine precepts. "Becomes radiant" is also another example of the creative use of metaphor in both strophes, making the text dance with poetic jubilation by attributing sound to the sun and light to the commandments. By reversing the sense experience of the sun and the commandments so that one "hears" the sun run its course and "sees" the light of the commandments, the poet teaches the reader that God's gifts and power are to be heard and seen at every level of life.

Together, these strophes teach that God provides for both the physical and spiritual welfare of his people through the light of the sun and torah; reveling in the commandments is the daily path of a fine life, made possible on the physical plane by the sun running its mighty course from one end of the sky to the other. As William Brown puts it, "As the sun, cast in the image of an athlete or warrior (*gibbôr*), exudes energy and strength, so *tôrâ* imparts renewed vigor. Through [divine teaching] one is rejuvenated for the tasks of obedience and empowered to follow the prescribed path of righteousness, which is cosmically forged."[14] Together the physical and moral orders provide for creation's flourishing.

Anxiety Threatens (19:12–14)

The final strophe of this psalm is a jarring departure from the jubilant tone of the preceding ones. Nothing has prepared the reader for it, least of all the celebratory tone of the second strophe. It is a candid confession of anxiety; the author longs to be able to live up to the call of the commandments but fears failing because some of his faults are hidden even from himself and because he knows himself well enough to admit that he may become impudent or be swayed, perhaps thinking that he won't comply with the commandments or will fail to try. It is an anxiety shared by Ps. 119, the greatest torah psalm, and much later by Martin Luther, who built his entire theology on that fear. Although obedience may be of lasting benefit, enacting it is a challenge for those sobered by realistic self-appraisal.

The psalmist is anxious that his devotion might not overcome his weaknesses. His fear is not that God will punish him for falling short but that he might miss the wealth and sweet life that living by the precepts promises. Despite his faults (his anxiety perhaps being one of them), he longs for innocence. In conclusion, he supplicates God with a prayer for acceptance that resounds down the generations in the mouths of those who find themselves precisely in his shoes: "Let the words of my mouth and the meditation of my heart be acceptable to you, O Lord, my rock and my redeemer" (19:14).

Theological Pedagogy

Psalm 19 hopes to attract us to the glory of God in stages. Beginning with the Creator (perhaps because contemplating God as Creator is relatively easy), the psalmist lures us to consider the wisdom of God the legislator as he carries us into deeper water. His final step is meant to stir up longing to become the beautifully pure self that God deserves from those on whom he lavishes such care and effort. God's teaching (torah) is perfect (19:7), and the speaker knows that genuine reverence for God is pure (19:9). Lured as he is, the speaker wants to be blameless, and cleansed of small hidden faults (19:12) as well as great transgressions (19:13). Psalm 19 aims for a person's best self in the hope that she will enlist as one of God's radiant servants.

As stirring as the poetry and imagery of this psalm are, perhaps its greatest appeal comes from its unfeigned candor. Moral arousal, however necessary, will not suffice. More than volunteering is needed. God must make one more push for his people—this time not in a public way, as with the heavenly bodies and the

14. Brown 2002, 93.

commandments, but on a deeply personal level. God must protect the would-be servant from going astray and accept the meditation of her heart that she might find acceptance.

The point is not, however, that one should think of oneself as a dirty mop that needs to be cleansed in a bucket of water and wrung dry of its dirt.[15] Thinking of oneself as a mop besotted with dirty water from cleaning the floor betrays both the beauty of the commandments (the water that washes us) and the beautiful self whose heart rejoices in God's ways. Psalm 19 has something else in mind. While it concludes on a suitably humble note, it calls us to envision ourselves as partakers of the glory of God—proclaimed by the sun as much as by torah—so that we might triumph as God's faithful servants.

15. Aimilianos of Simonopetra, 253–54.

PSALM 20

Canonical Context and Themes

Psalm 20 echoes themes in the beginning of Ps. 18. Dedicated to David, it attests to God's anointed in need of help, with an encouraging gesture of support for his eventual victory over military opponents. Like so many of the psalms, it proclaims confidence that God will come through. However, it departs radically from Ps. 18 by taking a pacifist stance, making it a protest against the militarism of Pss. 2 and 18.

Structure and Dynamics

This psalm continues the practice of employing various voices. It begins with a prayer in the third-person singular (20:1–4), moves to the first-person plural (20:5), then to the first-person singular (20:6), and concludes in the first-person plural (20:7–9).

May God Support You (20:1–4)

The opening strophe is an intercessory prayer on behalf of another person on a troubled day. It is intoned by an authorized minister in what seems to be a service of healing, much like those that have been revived in churches today for those seeking spiritual support in time of personal need. It encourages the suppliant to anticipate a positive response from God by engaging in prayerful worship for strengthening.

Following a different train of thought, *Midrash on Psalms* identifies Ps. 20:1, "May the LORD answer you on the day of trouble," with Ps. 91:15, "I will answer when he calls me, I am with him in trouble and I will save him and honor him"; in both verses the word *ṣārâ* (trouble or anguish) appears. Extolling God's compassion on those in anguish, the midrash elaborates the overtones of "trouble" with three examples of a woman in labor crying out in pain. In one of these,

> R. Yudan told a parable of a pregnant woman who was angry with her mother. Even as the woman was giving birth, she made her mother go into an upper chamber. And as the woman below groaned with pain, the mother above, hearing her voice, groaned with her. The neighbors asked: "What sort art thou that thou criest? Givest thou birth with her?" She replied: "My daughter, is she not in pain? How can I endure her cries? So behold me groaning with her, for my daughter's anguish is likewise mine." Just so, when the Holy Temple was destroyed, there was heard through the whole world a sound of weeping and wailing. . . . [It was God who replied to a similar question from the angels, asking,] "Is not My Temple destroyed, are not My children thrown in chains, and should I not therefore be in anguish?" Is it not written *I will be with him in anguish* (Ps. 91:1)?[1]

Perhaps even more tellingly, the story implies that God groans in pain with Israel even when spurned, just as the daughter giving birth spurns her mother, though the mother's love will not be quelled, even by the hurt that her daughter is causing her. It is worth noting that although God groans with Israel, he does not really answer the petition. God's cries of love must suffice for comfort, suggesting that God should not be expected to simply make troubles vanish the way labor pains do once the baby is born. Rather, it is God's cries that Israel carries in its heart, as the daughter carries her mother's love despite the alienation that separates them.

We Anticipate Rejoicing (20:5)

At the conclusion of the intercession, the intercessor turns to the congregation witnessing the healing service, adding them to his prayer while continuing to pray for the supplicant. This verse may be a liturgical response that is sung or recited by the group. In the first-person plural, the choir assures the supplicant that she is not alone; they are all rooting for her and will rejoice with her when she emerges from her misery. Psalm 20:5 not only expresses but also enjoins public solidarity among the people of God. When one suffers, all are affected; when one is lifted up, all will celebrate. In this way, no one is alone with her troubles or even with God. The individual is embedded in the community that stands together before God.

I Trust God (20:6)

In Ps. 20:6 the voice shifts again with the narrator jumping into the first-person singular and speaking for himself. The intercessor speaks confidently to

1. Braude 1959a, 287.

the gathered community (rather than the community speaking or the intercessor speaking to the suppliant), urging confidence that the Lord will answer his anointed. As the community leader, he needs the people to hear that he is sure in his role and calling; he can assure them that their prayers will be answered.

Calvin offers a nice note on this point. Though he is commenting on 20:9, it holds here: "And of [salvation] we shall then only become partakers when, being all gathered together into one body, under the same Head [Christ], we shall have mutual care one of another, and when none of us will have his attention so engrossed with his own advantage and individual interest, as to be indifferent to the welfare and happiness of others."[2]

Trust, Not Armaments (20:7–9)

Psalm 20:7–9 again uses the first-person plural, carrying the whole community with the speaker. These verses are strikingly out of keeping with the Older Testament's frequent reliance on the military might of David's reign as an instrument of divine rule over the earth. However, a famous departure from that strategy is the confrontation between King Hezekiah of Judah and King Sennacherib of Assyria, which is mediated by the prophet Isaiah (2 Kgs. 18:13–20:19; Isa. 36–38). Threatened by the Assyrian army, Hezekiah refuses to capitulate to Assyrian demands but also refuses to take up arms against Sennacherib, choosing rather to go into mourning and prayer, seeking support and encouragement from the prophet. Hezekiah is vindicated by God. Sennacherib's army falls dead by the hand of the angel of the Lord, and the Assyrian king is murdered by his own sons. Immediately after, Hezekiah falls deathly ill, but God revives him, granting him fifteen more years as a further sign of God's deliverance from his enemy (Hezekiah's death following close on Sennacharib's death would have been an ambiguous testimony to God's rescue of Judah) and his faithfulness to the house of David. Psalm 20 might well have this important biblical drama in mind as a further way of calling Israel to confident trust.

Psalm 20:8 proudly contrasts those (*hēmmâ*) who trust in armaments yet collapse with us (*wa'ănaḥnû*) who stand up and are encouraged by trusting in the name of the Lord God. The first-person plural carries forward the energy of 20:5 where together those gathered in prayer will rejoice in God's salvation. Again, this final strophe is probably meant to be recited by the community in a dramatic reading of the text. The dynamic brings the whole community into this pacifist position of trust, standing behind the king.

In Ps. 20 the psalmist becomes a political theologian. As Calvin observes, "There is here a comparison between the people of God and all the rest of the world. We see how natural it is to almost all men to be the more courageous and confident the more they possess of riches, power, and military forces. The people of God,

2. Calvin 1998, 343.

therefore, here protest that they do not place their hope, as is the usual way with men, in their military forces and warlike apparatus, but only in the aid of God."[3]

In the last verse (20:9) the phrase "answer us when we call [upon you, Lord]" echoes the first verse, "God will answer in the day of trouble," effectively creating poetic closure that leaves the reader with a sense of satisfaction at having moved from plaint to platform.

Theological Pedagogy

The psalmist's first goal is to instill confidence in God when confidence is not easy to come by, which is standard psalmic theology. The authorized ecclesiastical leader means to gather the community around someone needing help and to have everyone beseech God on that person's behalf. The setting is public worship, yet the scene also conveys intimacy.

The leader, however, is interested in more than the specific day of difficulty. His further goal is to infuse Israel with distaste for war. Perhaps he is war-weary. Whatever the source of the text, it supports public worship, political theology, and personal supplication in nine compact verses. As we have it, this song challenges current thinking that would house these three pursuits in different camps guarding different (even opposing) interests: one on behalf of institutional religion, another promoting a political platform, and a third advocating individual spirituality. This poem points out that such divisions defeat one another; only interlinked do they advance the poet's hope for the people of God.

3. Calvin 1998, 340.

PSALM 21

Canonical Context and Themes

Dedicated to "the victor, a song to David," Ps. 21 is not a particularly beloved psalm, and it does not appear in the Revised Common Lectionary. It proposes no particular historical context, although Theodoret picks up where the previous psalm left off, linking it to the story of Hezekiah's recovery from illness. This interpretation is probably based on 21:4, which says that God granted the king's petition for life.[1] Psalm 21 continues the theme of Ps. 18, which extols the king's trust that God will rescue him by defeating his enemies. It is a public song that exuberantly celebrates what God has done and will do, singing of the king's confidence in God to destroy his enemies mercilessly. Presumably, God's enemies are also the king's enemies, and presumably the king's enemies—be they rebellious kings, foreign aggressors, or contenders to the throne—are also Israel's enemies. As John Goldingay notes, Ps. 21 shows how important the deliverance of leaders is for the well-being of the community, especially in a society that lacks governmental structures that keep leaders accountable to the people and provide for the orderly transmission of authorized power.[2]

Structure and Dynamics

The narrator in Ps. 21 speaks in the second person throughout most of the poem. Psalm 21:1–6 reviews blessings that God has bestowed upon the king. Thereupon follows 21:7 in the third-person singular, which is addressed to the audience. It sums up the preceding recitation and concludes the first half of the poem with a statement of the king's unshakable trust in God. Psalm 21:8–12 shifts from past to

1. Theodoret 2000, 141.
2. Goldingay 2006, 318.

future tense to detail the content of that trust in terms of what the king expects from God in the future. Psalm 21:13 is a rallying cry to encourage God in these works, and in the last verse it shifts into the first-person plural in a communal exaltation.

God Blesses the King (21:1–6)

Addressed to God, the opening segment reminds the community of the extraordinary blessing God has bestowed upon the king. One must assume that God has not forgotten these blessings, nor does he need to be fawned over for them. No, the true audience for the recitation is the Israelite, later Jewish, and eventually Christian audience hearing or singing the song. Most of the gifts are quite general. God has given the king his heart's desire, rich blessings, a crown of pure gold, glory, and majesty. Only one specific request of the king is mentioned: life. This request has been granted as long life—indeed, it has been granted forever (21:4). Further, all these blessings will last forever (21:6), with "forever" being a hyperbolic hope for the endurance of the Davidic dynasty, or perhaps for its postexilic reestablishment. The king is naturally delighted both with the gifts and with the prospect of dynastic longevity.

Immovable Trust (21:7)

At this point, the narrator turns to his audience to be sure that they grasp that the king's unshakable trust in God is based on God's prior performance and not on wishful thinking. Blessings from God earn the king's gratitude, and the lesson should not be lost on later hearers and singers of the song. Christian piety, especially in Reformed theology, highlights gratitude as the proper response to God's gifts and promise of salvation. The first half of Ps. 21 lays the foundation for that piety. Christianity takes Christ to be the final and permanent occupant of the Davidic throne. His resurrection presages his eternal reign, forever fulfilling the promises to the king in 21:4 and 6. Hebrews 1:8 and 12 echo the theme of an eternal reign associated with the anointed son of Ps. 2:7, who now is seated on the throne of God (Heb. 1:8). Gratitude for that work of God is the pious Christian posture.

Augustine interprets this psalm christologically. The king's glory and majesty are exemplified by Christ's resurrection, ascension, and session at the right hand of the Father in heaven, which are God's eternal blessings.[3] Jewish commentators interpret the text differently. *Midrash on Psalms*, perhaps innocent of christological interpretation, reads the text messianically to promote Jewish hope that the nation would be liberated from Roman oppression represented by Edom. It goes so far as to say that "all the nations shall bless themselves in the king Messiah."[4] Rashi, chafing under Christian domination, certainly had the *Midrash on Psalms* in view and mentions its reference to the king messiah, but he reads the psalm as

3. Augustine 2000a, 218–19.
4. Braude 1959a, 296.

pertaining to David in order to protect his Jewish readers from a christological interpretation, even referring to the enemies of 21:11 that God would destroy as the offspring of Esau, who perhaps symbolizes Christians.[5]

God Destroys His Enemies (21:8–12)

What the king expects from God in the future is based on God's proven track record. He assumes that God will act in the future as he has in the past. Resuming direct address to God in the second-person singular, this strophe takes up the central psalmic theme of defeat of enemies. Assuming that God is the addressee, the poet employs a particularly violent portrayal of God as a warrior who seeks out enemies—those who hate God (21:8)—and swallows them in a blazing furnace kindled by divine anger (21:9). Not only God's enemies but also their children will be wiped off the earth (21:10). It is the psalmist's final solution to the problem of those who hate God. The narrator adds that this will prevent them from plotting against God and from attempting to execute any nefarious plans (21:11). The strophe concludes with a particularly gruesome image. Even as the enemies flee in terror, the psalmist hopes that God will pursue them, aiming his arrow at their faces (21:12).

While often taking psalmic imagery such as this out of the realm of physical military battle, Christian theology not only spiritualized but also eschatologized it; as both a deterrent and a motivation to piety, the fiery furnace of divine wrath was interpreted as a literal hell. Reading within the framework of medieval eschatology after Dante, Calvin interprets the enemies as a metaphor for the enemies of Christ and the church. He is inspired by the psalm's theology of divine judgment and comforts the righteous with the thought of the destruction of God's enemies. He uses the passage to teach patience when God's judgment of the wicked seems to be delayed:

> It was of importance . . . to arouse from their torpor those who, unapprehensive of danger, boldly despise all the threatenings of God. Besides, this serves not a little for the consolation of the righteous. . . . The expression, *In the time of thy wrath*, admonishes us that we ought patiently to bear the cross as long as it shall please the Lord to exercise and humble us under it. If, therefore, he does not immediately put forth his power to destroy the ungodly, let us learn to extend our hope to the time [at] which our heavenly Father . . . will come forth to execute vengeance.[6]

Psalm 21's depiction of the king (who represents those favored by God) set over against the enemies of God accurately captures the gist of the later western

---

5. Rashi, 2004, 254. The medieval Jewish portrayal of Esau as the symbol of the Christian church would constitute a polemical retort to the Pauline-Augustinian inversion of the biblical text, beginning with Rom. 9 that takes Jacob to represent the gentiles gathered into the church and Esau to represent the Jewish people.

6. Calvin 1998, 352.

Christian doctrine of election. Calvin's approval of divine vengeance reflects a central theme of western Christian eschatology. It is the idea that all persons are the enemies of God and deserve death just for being human, which is an elaboration of Augustine's reading of Rom. 9. That God should be merciful to anyone—be it the king, Israel, or the faithful—is a great gift of undeserved grace that should bring all to their knees; those blessed with the reprieve can be grateful for a gift they do not deserve, and those condemned can experience humble gratitude for receiving the treatment they do deserve. Since one cannot discern by sight, smell, or hearing who will be among the saved and who among the damned, the most one can do is hope to be among the favored few.

We Sing to God's Strength and Power (21:13)

Psalm 21:13 stands alone (as does the last verse in Ps. 20) as a rallying cry for the people instructed by this psalm to join the narrator in praising God. This follows the doxological pattern of the conclusion of Pss. 3, 7, 19, and 20. Like Ps. 20, it gathers up the community in exhilaration by speaking in the first-person plural.

Theological Pedagogy

Despite the longevity of Ps. 21's theology in Christian piety, the celebration of God's destruction of enemies leaves a bad taste in the mouth of those who try to take to heart Jesus's injunction to love one's enemies. The portrayal of God's vicious treatment of those who hate him sets a precedent for social behavior that invites similar conduct, condoning tribal warfare and the cycle of vendettas with no rule of law to disrupt it. Indeed, Christian theology teaches Christians to long for God's loving mercy, instantiated in the amazing dynamic of Christ's death and resurrection—first death, then life. While useful to Calvin's way of thinking, Ps. 21's want of mercy to the point of destroying the progeny of God's enemies (21:10) fails to encourage repentance and conversion from the rebellious behavior that constitutes enmity with God. Further, should one piously count oneself among God's enemies, as the Augustinian-Calvinist tradition encourages everyone to do, the outlook is bleak.

Setting the second half of Ps. 21 against the first half, however, gives a more balanced picture of God. Here one sees God's steadfast love arrayed at its most opulent. God lavishes gifts and honors upon the king, who gains his heart's desire. The psalmist depicts God in extreme terms.

While the enemy's fault is named as hating God, begetting God's animosity in return, no virtue of the king is mentioned. As depicted in Augustinian thought, God's election of the king is gratuitous, as is the selection of David in the narrative in 1 Sam. 16—a central theme in western theology. While one can do nothing to merit divine favor, rebelling against God is named as our common heritage.

In sum, the message of the psalm—to rely entirely on the utterly free grace of God, who showers gifts on those he loves—perfectly and succinctly sets forth the theological mainstay of western theology.

While this poem captures the core of later theological developments, the portrait of God that it advances is harsh, and the message it sends leaves no room for ambiguity; people who experience their lives as blessed in some ways or at some times and cursed at others are uncertain how to proceed. God seems to be engaged with people in a zero-sum game. There is no middle ground between God's love and anger, no underlying compassion waiting in the wings, no encouragement for people to become their best selves. Perhaps most poignantly, Ps. 21 offers no basis for approaching God in prayer. God's chosen pedagogical instrument is raw fear. Perhaps in spite of himself, the poet invites his readers to ask whether posing such stark alternatives is the best way to teach people about God or motivate them to righteousness.

PSALM 22

Canonical Context and Themes

It is often noted that both Abraham and Moses argued with God to save people from God's wrath. It is less frequently noted that the psalmists often do the same; at an individual level, Ps. 22 does just that. Like Pss. 7 and 13, this poem laments God's absence and then celebrates rescue to reassure the community that God's love and power are active. Like Ps. 9, it is evangelistic. After pleading for help for twenty-one verses, it suddenly bursts into exultant praise of God without explaining anything, except perhaps (according to some readings of 22:21b) that the petition was answered. At this good news, the psalmist says that the community will celebrate, broadcasting knowledge of who God is and what God has done for the suppliant across the world; the nations and their posterity will know that the God of Israel lives and will "turn to the LORD" (22:27). The lament is instrumental to the spread of the good news of God and the establishment of his universal rule.

Although dedicated to David, Ps. 22 has inspired some commentators to associate it with other biblical figures. While Theodore of Mopsuestia, Abraham Ibn Ezra, and Calvin associate it with David, *Midrash on Psalms* associates its most poignant phrases with Esther in her days of fasting before seeing the king, and many Christian commentators associate it with Jesus (Theodoret of Cyrus, Augustine, Patrick Henry Reardon, and Goldingay, who uses the association to better understand Jesus, not the psalm).[1] Wholesale association with Jesus is encouraged by the fact that Matthew and Mark have Jesus speaking the first verse of this psalm on the cross; Mark incorporates 22:7–8, and Mark, Luke, and John cite 22:18 at the crucifixion.[2]

---

1. Goldingay 2006, 342–43.
2. Augustine is the most brilliant of the christological interpreters. He comments twice on Ps. 22, once with a running commentary and once in a long and exhaustive sermon. He is persuaded both that

Structure and Dynamics

The bedraggled suppliant is desperate (22:1–21) and, in typical fashion, addresses God directly, adducing all sorts of reasons why God should hurry to his rescue. In unexplained succession, Ps. 22:21 is a final plea for rescue as well as a dramatic and sudden announcement of it.[3] With the abrupt shift from imploring God in the imperative mood to proclaiming God's answer in the perfect tense, the poem segues into public worship and praise (22:21b–26), moving outward to "the ends of the earth" and into the future (22:27–31).

The dynamic is typically expansive. It begins with personal distress, which is likely to arouse the hearer's sympathy, then turns outward—first in communal praise of God and then to the global conversion of those who learn of God's wonderful work for the suppliant from the lauding congregation. The rescue of one is for the expansion of God's reign beyond Israel, enabling Ps. 22 to resonate deeply with the evangelistic commitment of the Christian gospel.

I Am a Mess! (22:1–21)

In the long lament, the speaker complains of feeling abandoned by both God (22:1–5) and other people (22:6–8). Despite being *in extremis* he cannot bring himself to abandon God. Groveling, he turns back to God and pleads for rescue from the enemies depicted as a variety of wild beasts. On account of both the longstanding intimate relationship he has with God (22:9–11) and the dire straits in which he finds himself (22:12–21), he thinks his prayer will surely rouse God to action.

WHERE ARE YOU, GOD? (22:1–5)

The sufferer finds no reason why God has not acted given the sufferer's constant imploring.[4] He is exhausted by the intensity of his own prayers (22:2). As

---

the speaker is Christ and that the poem is written to the church catholic against the Donatist church that he was fighting at the time. A vivid reading of the psalm enables one to read personal suffering through Christ's suffering on the cross, realizing "that God is a doctor, and that our troubles are a medicine bringing us to salvation, not a punishment leading to damnation. Under medical treatment you undergo cautery, or the knife, and you scream with pain. The doctor does not listen when you beg him to stop, but he does listen to your need for healing" (2000a, 230).

3. Both Ḥakham and Goldingay hold the clauses of 22:21 together by interpreting the second verb, *'ănîtānî*, to be in the precative mood (indicating a request) rather than in the past tense as the NRSV and Alter interpret it because, as Goldingay says, the shift within one verse from the imperative to the past tense "seems artificial" (Ḥakham 2003, 164; Goldingay 2006, 335). Alter points to this second clause of 22:21 as the turning point of the psalm precisely because it accounts for the next and concluding segment that bursts into praise by stating that God has indeed answered, rescuing the complainant from the horns of wild oxen (Alter 2007, 75). Reading this verb as a precative, however, is even more jarring than reading it as a past tense because that leaves no point at which the complainant receives an answer.

4. Psalm 22:1 gained special notoriety because, according to Matt. 27:46, Jesus speaks the first clause after the superscription from the cross. This causes some consternation in Christian circles since, being

a reason for God to awaken to his cries, the sufferer appeals to the faithfulness of Israel's patriarchs who trusted and were released from their suffering without reproach. Appealing to the ancestors suggests that the current generation is not as worthy, perhaps not as faithful, as in ancient times; God must be relied upon to act mercifully on account of the past praises of Israel rather than those of the present generation. As a result of the dramatic reversal of the speaker's circumstance, the author is inviting the congregation back into those very praises by the end of the poem. He is reminding his congregation of the standard of piety they are called to as much as he is reminding God of the piety of Israel's ancestors who set the standard for Israel's piety. That is, the poet calls Israel to faithfulness indirectly, not haranguing or scolding, but inviting them to honor their heritage and live into the strength of that identity.

I Am Mocked (22:6–8)

Following his attention to Israel's noble past, the complainant turns to his personal circumstance, offering a second reason God should act decisively. He feels like a worm from the shame he is suffering and mentions both the nonverbal and verbal forms of contempt he experiences (22:6); he reads contempt in people's facial gestures (22:7). While the Rule of Benedict appreciates the power of the worm analogy to cultivate monastic humility, other commentators were arrested by such a negative metaphor and sought to turn it to good effect.[5] *Midrash on Psalms* uses it to comfort: "Like a worm whose only resource is its mouth, so the children of Israel have no resource other than the prayers of their mouths. Like a worm which roots out a tree with its mouth, so the children of Israel with the prayers of their mouths root out the evil decrees which [hostile] nations of the earth devise against them."[6] Even Calvin, who does not usually shy away from using discouraging imagery to remind his readers of their lowliness, finds the worm image too strong: "This, it is true, seems at first sight to have a tendency to discourage the mind, or rather to destroy faith; but it will appear more clearly from the sequel, that so far from this being the case, David declares how miserable his condition is, that by this means he may encourage himself in the hope of obtaining relief."[7]

God, Jesus could not abandon himself! Relying on the orthodox two-natures Christology that had been worked out by the mid-fifth century, the remark was often attributed to Christ's human nature in order to protect involvement of the divine nature. For example, Theodoret says that the abandonment does not suggest separation from his divine nature but "the permission given for the Passion: the divinity was present to the form of a slave in his suffering and permitted him to suffer so as to procure salvation for the whole of nature. Of course, it was not affected by suffering from that source: how could the impassible nature suffer? It is Christ the Lord as man, on the contrary, who speaks these words, and since he was the first fruits of human nature, it is on behalf of all of nature that he utters the words in what follows: *The words of my failings are far from saving me*" (2000, 146).

5. Benedict 1981, 199.
6. Braude 1959a, 315–16.
7. Calvin (1854) 1998, 365.

The verbal taunt of 22:8 both takes one back to the struggle played out in Pss. 10:4 and 14:1, where the suppliant finds his faith challenged by disbelief, and ahead to Jesus on the cross, where his messianic pretensions are ridiculed with these same words (Matt. 27:43). Sarcasm is the voice of cynicism, and it is easily arrayed against anyone who suffers willingly or even dies for the integrity of earnest conviction. When the stakes are high, the skeptic hides from becoming embroiled in the struggle for the common good, feeling prudent for having avoided risk. The thwarted risk-taker looks foolish by comparison, at least in the short run.

COME TO ME (22:9–11)

This strophe offers God another reason to help the afflicted one: it is God's job. God has been taking care of the sufferer since the womb; why would he stay away now, when no one else can help? God assumed responsibility for people's well-being by creating them and until now has stayed faithfully at his post. The pleader knows himself to have been cared for by God all his life. The complaint is that God is now shirking the responsibility that he took on at the onset of human life itself. The suppliant is not pointing to any virtue or merit of his own but to God's role as giver and provider of life. The assumption is that God has no right to "slumber or sleep," as Ps. 121:4 puts it. His watch does not end at midnight or at dawn. The poet reminds God that caring for people is a full-time job. Again one can see theism hiding behind the translucent curtain of theodicy.

The theology presented here is the precise opposite of the idea that suffering is punishment for sin or that God is angry and justly punishes in order to humble rebellious people. On the contrary, God is responsible for failing to alleviate the suffering. His love for the sufferer is so obvious to both the speaker and the human audience that it does not need to be stated but can be called upon to embarrass God into acting. The deep trust in God's providential care attests palpably to the inability of the speaker to actually believe the words he spoke in 22:1. He cannot believe that God has or even could abandon him. The opening verse is an attention-getting device set against the deeper revelation that the speaker cannot abandon God, believe that God has abandoned him, or embrace the skeptical alternative.

In contrast to much Christian psychology, which holds that suffering should stimulate introspection on one's sinfulness to generate humility and a turn to God in self-despair, the poet believes that celebrating God's powerful deeds of rescue in the past will arouse confident devotion whatever one's personal circumstance. The psalmist's interest is not in fostering humility but in energizing devotion and praise. In a striking essay on Ps. 22, Ellen Davis argues that it is fundamentally a psalm of praise. The old *mythos* of salvation—that God will simply make bad circumstances go away—lies in the dust. It has been supplanted by a stronger re-symbolization facilitated by poetic language that enables faithful suffering even in the absence of material rescue.[8] Surely one need not be forced to choose; humility and praise will both speak their own word in due season.

I Am Perishing (22:12–21)

God's faithfulness throughout the speaker's life and in the past life of Israel sets the stage for the next reason he offers God in his argument for immediate rescue: his suffering is acute. The heart of the lament analogizes the vicious oppressors to wild beasts: bulls, stallions, lions, wild dogs, and wild oxen. The images aggregate to depict the suppliant surrounded by feral forces that are not subject to reason and will not be assuaged until the victim is done away with. Psalm 22:18, famously quoted by all four evangelists at the crucifixion of Jesus, depicts both enemies and cynical bystanders unable to restrain their crude urge to seize the victim's clothes even before he is dead! Psalm 22:6 depicts the speaker feeling like an innocent and vulnerable worm whose pursuers are vicious brutes who would crush a worm without batting an eye.

One of the most arresting features of this poem is its graphic portrayal of the psychosomatic effects of the experience of rejection and persecution by these "animals." The speaker tells us what he feels. He is poured out like water; his bones are collapsing, and his insides are melting like wax (22:14). His whole body is dried out so that his tongue sticks with aphasia (22:15), and his limbs falter from constriction (22:16). Anxiety/depression is in full array.

No conversation passes between victim and persecutors. There is nothing to say. It is too late for words, for each side has dug in its heels. His pursuers look at and stare right through him as he struggles to "count his bones" and pull himself up to whatever dignity he can muster (22:17) as he feels his life in peril at sword-point (22:20). With one last plea for salvation from the lion (22:21a), the second half of 22:21 suddenly catapults to "from the horns of wild oxen you answered me."[9]

The Community Celebrates (22:22–26)

Regardless of whether 22:21b pleads for deliverance or announces it, the following strophe finds the speaker publically celebrating good news that cannot be suppressed (22:22), even if it is no more than the personal news that he has the strength to praise God amid suffering without rescue, as Ellen Davis suggests. However, if evidence of material rescue does exist that the psalmist does not report but celebrates, one is reminded of an antithetical situation described in the Younger Testament: the inability of recipients of Jesus's healing miracles not to tell everyone what they had seen, despite Jesus imploring them not to do so (Mark 1:44–45//Luke 5:14–15 and Mark 7:36). In all cases, however, word of mouth (or now social media) is the way the good news of God spreads.

8. Davis 1992.
9. See note 3 above.

In Ps. 22, the victim calls those who revere the Lord—indeed, every single Israelite—to praise, honor, and admire God, even if they have not been lifted from their suffering (although it makes one swallow hard at the thought). If that is the case, the complainant is certainly leading Israel to praise God even amid spiritual and psychological death. Whether rescue happened "onstage" in 22:21b, "offstage" in some other unmentioned moment, or not at all remains unclear. But by 22:24 something seems to have been accomplished, and the speaker is at least rescued from the despair of spiritual and psychological death, if not from the actual circumstances that cause it. The bottom line is that God is not preoccupied with rich and famous characters who act brutally against the weak but with the weak and lowly who experience themselves as vulnerable worms. God not only listens but also acts—either by physically rescuing his people or at least by rescuing them from the despair in which they languish unable to abandon him.

If it is the latter, as Davis suggests, her interpretation abets the Augustinian-Calvinist doctrine of election that works from Rom. 9:15, which in turn works from Exod. 33:19: "I will be gracious to whom I will be gracious, and I will show mercy on whom I will show mercy." Davis's model of faithful suffering—praise of God when suffering—is central to Calvinism's high doctrine of divine sovereignty, which regularly appeals to the inscrutable divine will in the face of divine arbitrariness. Augustine set this train in motion with his insistence that since all deserve the wrath of God, those who are exempt and actually saved (the minority to be sure) are reminded that they are no better than the lost who should also praise God, knowing that they deserve no better.[10]

Psalm 22:25 of this strophe begins with an odd phrase. It reads literally "my praise is from you (*mēʾittĕkā*)" and is usually translated that way.[11] Perhaps the fuller thought of 22:25, in keeping with the preceding verses, is that the transformation from pleading to public praise is "from God" in the sense that praise results from what God has done. The public testimony has cash value too; the celebrant offers to keep his vows with total disclosure. While here the fulfillment of vows—perhaps a sacrifice of thanksgiving—is spontaneous, Jesus commends the same practice when, after healing a leper, he prods the man to go to the priest and offer sacrifice "as a testimony to them" (Mark 1:44 NRSV).[12] The experience of release from suffering is not a private exchange between God and an individual but an opportunity to strengthen the community spiritually and materially through various expressions of gratitude, which lies at the heart of testimony.

At this point, the celebrant's personal victory gives way to the larger point God is making though him. He is not as important as the possibility and hope that his

10. Charry 2012.

11. To avoid the awkwardness, Alter translates it "for you" (2007, 75).

12. Jesus's instructions to the healed man not to tell anyone what had happened and yet to go directly to the priest to offer sacrifice as a public testimony seem a bit odd, if not disingenuous, since telling the priest is a sure way to publicize the healing.

rescue opens up for others. The poor will eat their fill and, like the speaker, praise the Lord. Now the singer sings with doubled joy. Not only is he experiencing his own rescue, but he is also able to bring the good news of God to the poor everywhere so that those who seek God may join his thanksgiving. The strophe ends with a rousing cheer: "May you be enlivened forever!"

Everyone Will Worship God (22:27–31)

By this time, the reader has traveled from anguished despair to public celebration and thence to far-ranging hope. Now the poet carries that hope in yet another outward-streaming direction. Psalm 22:27–31 reaches to the ends of the earth to gather all the families of the gentiles to worship God. The phrase "all the families" immediately calls to mind Gen. 12:3, of which Paul makes much ado. This single rescue operation—although it occurred in Israel—constitutes proof that extends far beyond this people. The psalmist concurs with the conviction of Isa. 2:2–4: God's reign extends to gentiles. With this dynamic, the rescue of this one Israelite is also a model for that later Jew, Jesus, whose death and reported resurrection finally succeeded in bringing masses of gentiles to the God of Israel, which perhaps the poet envisioned but did not witness. This vision of the universal scope of God's reign is not a prediction of the events in the first Christian century that were interpreted in these earlier terms. Indeed, this poem authenticates the theological continuity of the latter events not only with scripture but also with the sensibility of the community shaped by many experiences of deliverance, the example in Ps. 22 being but one of them.

While 22:30 transposes this eschatological vision of God's global reign into temporal terms—God's reign is not only geographically but also temporally extended—22:29 offers a perspective that is out of keeping with other expressions of psalmic theology. Taken at face value, it suggests that God will be worshiped not only across the world (22:27–28) and on into posterity (22:30) but also by the dead. That the dead are in some sense conscious and able to worship God may resonate with later Christian eschatology that portrays souls distributed in various locales awaiting reunion with their bodies. However, the psalms are usually quite clear that the dead do not praise God (Pss. 6:5; 88:10; 115:17), and they use that belief to rouse God to action on behalf of the living.[13] If 22:29 is the psalmist's distinctive theology, he employs it to offer a grand vision of the triumph of God's reign that emerges from one Israelite and continues to all Israel, all those who dwell on earth, all those who have passed on, and finally all those yet to be born (22:30–31).

13. Ibn Ezra was understandably uncomfortable with the idea that the dead worship God; it is not a Jewish idea. He interprets *dišnê-'ereṣ* (those who sleep in the ground) as "fat ones of the earth . . . who enjoy themselves in this world. They eat all kinds of fat food. *The fat ones* are the opposite of *the humble* [of 22:27]. . . . If the fat ones enjoy themselves in this world, they will ultimately bow to God who gathers their spirit at the end of their lives" (2009, 271).

Theological Pedagogy

The poet is a deft pastor. He has been quite busy, gently and indirectly leading Israel to rely unflinchingly on God even as it is tempted to be skeptical in the face of God's seeming absence from those who cling to him. While the psalmist depicts his enemies as vicious animals, he allies his auditors with his own situation, calling forth their sympathy, compassion, and support even as they realize that someday they could be in his place. He works two fronts simultaneously, teaching compassion for the suffering and the poor while binding the community together in mutual support of those who revere God and nourish community morale and well-being. He lays a third responsibility on the shoulders of his hearers. By their compassion, mutual support, celebratory worship, and devotion to God they extend the reign of God in both space and time.

While this psalm covers many bases, above all it is about Israel's responsibility for its own well-being and the well-being of gentiles who are to be ushered into God's reign. All of this is without a harsh word, without threat, and without embarrassing his audience. The writer trusts his hearers to take up the challenges he lays before them because he and they are fundamentally of one accord—or so he treats them. That is, his theology and his call dignify his hearers as the Israel of God, elected for the great and noble purposes to which he lifts them.

PSALM 23

Canonical Context and Themes

In a scant fifty-five words, the psalmist brings us the most beloved text of the Bible. We cling to life through it when the angel of death stalks our path. We recite it to face down danger and fear when they lunge out in the dark. We sing it as we long to live the mercy that we need to dwell in the house of the Lord every day of our life. Such is the comforting eloquence of the Twenty-Third Psalm.

Augustine's most famous sentence is that our hearts are restless until we rest in God.[1] Psalm 23 transforms that longing into a lush landscape of secure peace, safety, and strength. Here our steps are sure, our hearts steady, and our minds serene amid struggles because we follow the shepherd who guards his charges as they graze, safely protected from the salivating jaws of the wolf who is now stayed. Patrick Miller notes Ps. 23's sequential relationship to its predecessor. It is the answering word of deliverance to the mournful cry of distress in Ps. 22.[2]

Structure and Dynamics

While this brief poem is usually treated in two parts (23:1–4 and 23:5–6), based on the assumed transition from metaphor to realistic language,[3] I treat it in three parts,

---

1. Augustine 1991, 1.1.
2. Miller 1986, 118.
3. Dividing the psalm after 23:4 is not necessarily warranted. It is based on the occurrence of the phrase "rod and staff" that sustains the shepherding metaphor. But the transition to a human referent begins in 23:3, which introduces human emotions that sheep do not possess; God refreshes the speaker's life. Emotion is also brought in at 23:4 with the calming of fear. One of scripture's observations about sheep is that they do not sense approaching danger and lack the adaptive mechanism of fear. So while rod and staff do sustain the shepherding metaphor, a gradual shift to the human plane certainly takes place.

following the grammatical person used by the psalmist. Unlike many of the laments that begin by addressing God directly in the second person and later move to the third or the first person, this song begins in the third-person singular (23:1–3) and moves to directly address God (23:4–5) before concluding with a confident one-sentence soliloquy (23:6). Despite the shifts of grammatical person, the whole psalm speaks in very personal terms. Everything that God does for the singer is personal, and the singer relates it all to himself. He invites his readers into his emotional life that they might share both his vulnerability and his confident contentment.

Sheep and Their Shepherd (23:1–3)

The metaphor of shepherding is plentiful in the Bible, appearing in fully half the books of Christian scripture.[4] Ezekiel 34 and John 10 are built entirely upon this metaphor. While "sheep" represent the people of God, the "shepherds" can be duly appointed leaders of the people (Saul, 2 Sam. 5:2; David, Ezek. 34:23; Cyrus, Isa. 44:28), various tribal and nonroyal leaders (2 Sam. 7:7), or God (and Jesus).

Metaphorical sheep appear as hapless dolts in many scriptural references. They are stupid, helpless animals and the most easily domesticated for food, especially since they are relatively small and easily managed. They are unable to sense danger to protect themselves (Ps. 44:11, 22 [quoted in Rom. 8:36]; Isa. 53:7 [quoted in Acts 8:32]; Jer. 12:3) or care for themselves very well (Jer. 43:12) and need someone to guide them, as the refrain "like sheep without a shepherd" makes plain (Num. 27:17; 1 Kgs. 22:17; 2 Chr. 18:16; Matt. 9:36; Mark 6:34). Being herbivores, sheep are innocent of blood and are vulnerable to beasts of prey (Ezek. 34:8; Matt. 10:16). That is to say, sheep need a shepherd. The ubiquitous use of this pastoral image throughout scripture is more than a ready-to-hand image in a seminomadic culture. It is a teaching device to instill in readers and hearers of the texts a particular self-concept as one needing to be led, cared for, and helped by someone more intelligent, able, and sophisticated than oneself.

The Bible portrays God's people as defenseless sheep, readily getting lost (Ps. 119:176; Isa. 53:6; Jer. 50:6; Zech. 10:2; Matt. 10:6) and needing their shepherd to search for them (Ezek. 34:8, 11; Matt. 18:12; Luke 15:4, 6), gathering them back when they scatter (Ezek. 34:5–6, 12) lest they become food for wild animals. This vision contrasts sharply with the later Christian portrayal of people as sinful, conniving for their own advancement, arrogant, and rebellious against their "shepherd." The purity of the ingenuous sheep heard in the haunting boy-soprano solo so masterfully created by Leonard Bernstein in his *Chichester Psalms* is true to the biblical portrait.

Shepherds, on the contrary, are not always innocent. The prophets rail against bad shepherds who, though duly appointed, shirk their responsibilities (Jer. 23:1–2; 50:6; Ezek. 34:2–3, 6, 10), even deserting their charges (Zech. 11:17). Against

4. To appreciate the resonances of the theology of this psalm, the Younger Testament is relevant, and it is not known precisely which other Hebrew scriptures would have been known to the author or his audience. For the purposes of current readers, however, I identify resonances throughout the Christian Bible.

this background, Jesus rehabilitates Peter at the end of the Gospel of John, making him the shepherd of his flock. Jesus adjures Peter to be a good shepherd (as Jesus is), imploring Peter to feed his sheep, now their common responsibility (John 21:15–17). In deputizing Peter, Jesus follows the precedent of scripture whereby God regularly appoints human shepherds to care for Israel.

The message of Ps. 23, followed later by John 10, is that God is the consummate good shepherd, and the psalmist's audience presumably read this psalm with many of these passages ringing in its ears. Undoubtedly, some recalled that Jacob/Israel was the first to call God his shepherd when he blessed his grandchildren (Gen. 48:15)—as did R. Jose bar Hanina in *Midrash on Psalms*—and recognized that the psalmist was inviting them back into that framework to receive Israel's blessing by extension.[5] Furthermore, they were personally acquainted with livestock handling and could distinguish a good shepherd from a bad one.

The poet begins by telling what God is doing for him. Note that 23:1–3 is not a historical recounting of God's care for people in the past, as I have pointed out in several other psalms. The speaker narrates his personal experience. From the opening verse, the reader learns that the shepherd takes care of all his needs. With John 10 resounding in their ears, it is little wonder that Theodoret and Augustine assumed that the shepherd is Christ. All the things that the shepherd does for this particular sheep, Christ does for the church. The restful waters of 23:2, for example, distantly recall the waters of baptism "in which the baptized person longs for grace and sheds the old age of sin and is made young instead of being old," restoring the soul.[6]

The phrase "restores my soul" in 23:3 takes the song out of the metaphorical realm of animal husbandry and into a clearly human arena, blurring the traditional division of Ps. 23 into two parts. The rabbis of the midrash believe that torah restores the soul,[7] while Theodoret, making a similar point, associates the phrase with being freed from error by Christ to go the right way.[8]

The phrase "for the sake of his name" suggests that the gracious gifts with which God shepherds the people benefit him, because by leading them where they need to go they reflect well on him (God) and his leadership. It is in God's own best interest that the sheep flourish under his auspices. As numerous other psalms show, when the people flourish and praise God, they celebrate and broadcast God's goodness and extend the scope of his reign.

Discipline as Comfort (23:4–5)

Psalm 23:4–5 speaks in the first person and addresses God directly. The tranquility of the first strophe prepares for the dangers that beset even those who are

5. Braude 1959a, 327.
6. Theodoret 2000, 156.
7. Braude 1959a, 331.
8. Theodoret 2000, 157.

at peace with themselves and whose lives are rightly directed. The phrase "your rod and your staff" (the equipment associated with shepherding) extends the shepherding metaphor, though 23:3 has already introduced the human subject. The rod of a shepherd is a long thin pole used to reach into the middle of the flock to tap the sheep to get them to go in a certain direction or to lie down, as 23:2–3 suggests. Yet the bishop's crook is also the shepherd's staff that reins in straying "sheep." The verb suggests gentle prodding in one way or another, which is needed for the sheep to remain on the right path. The verb *yarbîṣēnî* in 23:2 means both "to cause to lie down" and "to beat." The rod conjures up images of the discipline and correction needed to remain on the right path. The rabbis of the *Midrash on Psalms* associate this with the afflictions of exile,[9] and Rashi associates it with the suffering that atones for sin.[10] The staff is the means of comfort and support even as the associative affliction bears out its good intention. Discipline comforts, for it enables one to go the way one deeply desires to go.

While theology has tended to view discipline and encouragement as opposites, both Jewish and Christian premodern exegetes held discipline and encouragement not as antithetical approaches but as two forms of encouragement. Theodoret has a creative read of these two images: "This is the meaning of *your rod and your staff comforted me*: the cross is assembled from two rods, with the upright staff confirming and directing those who believe in him and strengthening those who are weak, and using the crossbar as a rod against the demons."[11] Augustine is of the same mind: "Your discipline is like a rod used on a flock of sheep, and like a staff used to support older children as they grow from sensuous to spiritual life. They have done me no harm; rather they encouraged me, because you are mindful of me."[12] One does not correct those about whom one does not care.

The second verse of this strophe (23:5) details the comfort provided by the rod and staff. Despite the threat of those who keep him tied up in fear, threatening to undo the secure experience of being led by the good shepherd, the speaker experiences God as setting him at a feast flowing richly with oil and wine. The preposition *neged* is intriguing here. Prepositions often invite speculation. It could be that the threatening forces watch the feasting either from a distance or from a nearby post. Alternatively, the preposition may suggest that the singer enjoys this feast even though he has been assailed by foes so that God's support truly enables him to stand against them. A third possibility is that the enemies are reconciled with the speaker at the table. Whatever the case, a picture emerges of a person secure in himself because he is nourished by God in the face of life's inevitable contingencies and vicissitudes.

The prepared table has sacramental associations for Christians who come to the altar to feast on Christ himself. Augustine comes to the sacramental table for

9. Braude 1959a, 334.
10. Rashi 2004, 263–64.
11. Theodoret 2000, 157.
12. Augustine 2000a, 244.

strength to withstand assaults of oppressors. Calvin views the overflowing oil and cup as cause for great gratitude for the benefits God bestows upon us. In truth, the sacramental table dispenses strength, blessings, and solace when strength is elusive. The Episcopal *Book of Common Prayer* captures the thought beautifully: "Deliver us from the presumption of coming to this Table for solace only, and not for strength; for pardon only, and not for renewal. Let the grace of this Holy Communion make us one body, one spirit in Christ, that we may worthily serve the world in his name."[13]

I Am Strong (23:6)

Having impressed upon the reader how protected and well provided for he is, the singer concludes with a soliloquy that looks ahead confidently in both clauses of 23:6. He is sure that he will not only continue to experience goodness and grace but also be actively pursued by them all his life.[14] That is, he is destined to dwell in God's "house." This is not a naïve hope that no evil will befall him. He has told us that he fears no harm even in the darkest moments of life. That he expects his entire life to be beset by goodness and grace casts additional light on 23:3–4. This is a poet who understands the inevitability of suffering in life, even disaster, as John Goldingay translates *rā'* in 23:4.[15] Psalm 23:3 prefaces the fearsome threat of 24:4 by saying that he is being led in paths of righteousness. The just way of life that God extends for his own sake is the protection from the harm that injury might otherwise bestow. Even in the face of hardship and evil, the paths of righteousness in which the psalmist walks and that have refreshed his life make his adversaries look on incredulously; the threat of death itself may destroy him physically, but it cannot harm him morally or spiritually.

Theological Pedagogy

Just as Ps. 8 is an oasis amid laments that focuses our attention on the glorious creation, so Ps. 23 is another oasis focusing our attention on the paths of righteousness that are the goodness and grace of God, which cannot be broken through by adversity. This perspective casts further light on the ambiguous preposition *neged* of 23:5. If the oil and wine of the table prepared is the righteous path of life that God lays down for the sake of his name, *neged* truly means "against" the adversary of fear—that is, against the fear of losing one's moral and spiritual grounding in the face of adversity. This is the fear that is stilled by the care-taking shepherd. The "sheep" lack nothing (23:1) because God supplies the need that

13. *Book of Common Prayer* 1979, 372.
14. Most translations fail to note this, suggesting instead that God has replaced the enemies who are in hot pursuit of the speaker.
15. Goldingay 2006, 344.

truly enables them to dwell in his house throughout their lives. The tracks for a morally strong life are secure. This reading carries us back to Ps. 1 that links happiness to God's teaching. Considered in light of Ps. 23, that happiness is the freedom from the fear that one might become one of the evil ones whose deeds and malevolent aspirations haunt the lament psalms.

PSALM 24

Canonical Context and Themes

This rousing hymn exhorts people to confess God's sovereign ownership of both the world and themselves and to live a holy life because of that knowledge. It is thought to have been a hymn sung as the temple clergy and musicians processed into the designated worship space. However, its distinctive question and answer structure suggests a less formal and more intimate setting, although those elements might have been incorporated into a liturgical structure. The antiphonal call-and-response format is similar to catechetical questions in which the catechist poses theological questions and the responders give back acceptable answers, showing that they have grasped essentials of the faith. The content of the questions involves the identity of God and the character of those who are answering. Those giving answer are learning as they sing.

Structure and Dynamics

The psalm's opening two verses state what modern theology calls a doctrine of divine sovereignty. Psalm 24:3–6 asks and answers the first of three questions, all beginning with the word "who." The first question (24:3) is about the character of the pious. Psalm 24:7–10 is two sets of verses, each asking the second and third questions—which are the same question (about the identity of God)—and give variations of the same answer.

The World Is God's (24:1–2)

Hearkening back to Gen. 1, Ps. 24 opens with a strong statement about the creative power of God. It envisions the world floating on bodies of water, yet stably built. The world and all its inhabitants belong to God. The message here is that God is in control of the world, implying that humanity's role in its governance is peripheral. The global vantage point casts human life as a small part in the great scheme of things that God has wrought.

Paul cites 24:1 as justification for followers of Jesus to eat meat sacrificed to idols because nothing is outside the goodness of God's creation (1 Cor. 10:26). This contrasts greatly with Pharisaic Judaism, which forbade partaking of such impurities. For Paul, even idolatrized meat belongs to God. Paul's theology contrasts with later Jewish interpretations of this verse that identify "the earth" of the first clause as the land of Israel, which possesses a special holiness, and "the world" of the second clause as the rest of the world.

It is worth pausing over the two theologies expressed in both Jewish and Christian interpretations of this verse. The rabbis and Rashi follow the Jewish (i.e., Pharisaic) principle that Israel as a people and its land are sacred to God—sacralized by God's special affection for them. Holy things are set apart from profane things in order to identify and protect them. Similarly, Judaism distinguishes holy from profane time, for example, in separating the Sabbath and other holy days from the workweek.

Paul's theology is the precise opposite of this Pharisaic orientation. Undermining the very core of the Jewish commitment to a people set apart for God, Paul teaches that not only pagan food but also pagans themselves are redeemable. Foreign things are not to be avoided because they defile holy things but are to be embraced in order to sanctify them. Paul's principle is clearest perhaps in his tolerant attitude toward intermarriage (1 Cor. 7:12–14). Association with pure people and things purifies impure people and things. There is no need then to fear that pure things will be polluted by contact with impure things; there is no need to keep apart from the larger world. Paul's perspective contrasts sharply with the enforced divorce of foreign wives in Ezra 10 designed to purify Israelite worship. This notion of purity may have arisen against the history of Solomon's importation of foreign wives as instrumental in forging political and military alliances.

Martin Luther applied Paul's purification principle to ingesting the communion elements: "It is as if a wolf devoured a sheep and the sheep . . . transformed the wolf . . . into a sheep. So, when we eat Christ's flesh physically and spiritually, the food is so powerful that it transforms us into itself and out of fleshly, sinful, moral men makes spiritual, holy, living men."[1] Perhaps the underlying theological difference between Paul, who embraces impurity to purify it, and Pharisaism, which rigorously separates pure things from impure things in order to protect them from idolatrous "infection," is that Paul believes that pure things are more powerful to purify impure things than to be desecrated by them. The Pharisaic principle is that pure things are delicate and fragile and vulnerable to desecration. For Paul, touch does not desecrate; attitude and actions do.

1. Luther (1527) 1961, 101.

For him, people are defiled by their behavior, not by their associations. The Pharisaic/rabbinic view is that proximity to defiling things is contagious. It is better to avoid them altogether.

Who Dwells with God? (24:3–6)

The Psalter repeatedly asks this question: Who will endure in the house of the Lord? Who will come or be in the courts or the tent of the Lord; who will be on God's holy hill or mountain? Despite the spatial exaggeration of the locale—be it house, tent, hill, or mountain—the issue does not involve making physical pilgrimage to a distant place. God dwells in people who lead holy lives. This same question appears in Ps. 15, where a similar answer is received. Moreover, the same answer is given in Ps. 23:6, although the question is not raised.

To the pointed question "Who ascends to holiness?" 24:4 answers plainly: he who is pure in thought, intention, and action (especially in legal matters) ascends to the divine dwelling. Later Christian thought might be tempted to read Neo-platonism into the soteriological sense of ascent, but, of course, no such notion existed when this poem was penned.

Rather, Ps. 24 provides another reverberation of Ps. 1's insistence that happiness and prosperity belong to the righteous. They carry the blessing of justice from the God who saves them. Psalm 24:6 interrupts the progression of the poem to offer a comment on the preceding definition of a holy person as one who bears righteousness in herself, in case the message might not be clear to the singers or their audience. The poet adds, "This is the company of those who seek your face, Jacob, selâ" (24:6). The poet is generalizing the definition of a righteous person, which is presented in the singular, as that which characterizes all those who seek God. The syntax in the Hebrew is ambiguous, but it is possible that these God-seekers comprise normative Jacob/Israel—that is, an ideal community of mutual support based on shared aspirations, attitudes, and an approach to life grounded in divine guidance.

God Is King (24:7–10)

The final four-verse unit of this psalm consists of a two-verse couplet repeated with minor changes that express parallel thoughts. It introduces a wholly new theme into Ps. 24, confusing things both because there is no transition to the new topic and because the language is metaphorical and lacks a key referent by which to decode it. The point of the repeated couplet is to open doors to let the glorious king enter some place, perhaps the sanctuary. The command "heads up," which in current English parlance signals a warning that some unexpected object is approaching, may not be an inappropriate interpretation here. "Pay attention," the first verse of the couplet (24:7) cries out. The gates of eternity are opening, and a glorious king is approaching. At this public announcement, one can imagine people turning to one another and asking the second (and third) question of this psalm, perhaps with uncertainty or dismay: "Who is this glorious king?" as if to say, "What is happening?" While Ps. 24 is dedicated or ascribed to David, presumably he is not announcing his own arrival. No, this glorious king is someone else. He is, of course, the Lord God, depicted here as a brave general commanding his troops, an image that appears in Pss. 7 and 21. Indeed, the gates must be thrust open wide to accommodate his arrival with his retinue.

Theodoret reads the rhetorical question repeated in 24:8 and 24:10 through the two questions of 24:3, which concern who will ascend to God's holiness. The speakers of these verses know the correct answers, and Theodoret urges his own readers to believe that the questioners "are not speaking in ignorance, but through this proclamation of the one ascending are teaching all human beings his lordship. Hence the powers in reply say he is king of glory in that he receives glory from all and has the true and lasting kingship."[2] In case there is any confusion about where to point one's life, the antiphonal rhetorical question and answer repeated in this strophe assure the reader that the audience of this text has no doubt about whose lordship is being pointed to. Theodoret teaches that the king of glory receives that splendor from the admirable lives depicted in 24:4. It is not simply words but a particular way of life that glorifies God, who must be let into the "gates" of one's life.

> Now, they call him also *a Lord mighty and powerful in war*: he destroyed the harsh tyranny of the devil and dissipated the deceit of the demons who are subject to him. *Eternal gates* are bidden open up as though never admitting human nature before. In fact, no human being had ever passed through them; but when God the Word became human and took up our firstfruits, he both led the way up to heaven and took his place at the right hand of majesty in the highest places, above every principality, authority, dominion, and every name that is named, not only in this age, but in the age to come.[3]

Augustine interprets this psalm through the resurrection of Christ that is the gateway to eternal life. People erect barriers of greed and fear that block the way of Christ, who nevertheless will enter into the souls of those who seek God. "*But you, everlasting gates, lift yourselves up!* You gates to eternal life, gates of renunciation of this world and conversion to God, open up, *and the King of glory will enter.* The King will make his entrance; let us boast of him without fear or pride, for he overthrew the gates of mortality and flung open before him the gates of heaven, making good his claim, *Be glad, for I have overcome the world* (John 16:33)."[4]

2. Theodoret 2000, 162.
3. Ibid., 162.
4. Augustine 2000a, 247.

Theological Pedagogy

While it opens proposing a grand view of divine sovereignty, Ps. 24 sets aside the view of God as distant as it moves quickly to moral exhortation with the explanation that abiding in God is not the side effect or reward for the pursuit of a pure way of life but is the ascent to that holy dwelling of God. God's power in establishing the cosmos may make him seem distant, but an excellent life will enable those who desire God to experience him as nearby. By drawing near to God, those who seek him will be blessed, and that blessing will infuse community life by their participation in it.

For the distant God of creation to enter the human heart as more than the idea of majestic power, heads must lift and gates of the hearts must open to make room for God to enter one's life. Taken together then, the questions posed in Ps. 24 can be reduced to the question of how the transcendent creator who is also the commander in chief of armed battalions finds his way into human lives to lift them to himself.

Theodoret and Augustine read the upward-turning images in this psalm in terms of the ascension and resurrection of Christ. For us, "up" is moral-spiritual improvement. The exhortation of the psalmist and later Christian interpreters adjure readers to lift their sights to morally uplifted lives. It is a poem of possibility and encouragement. For the Christian writers, to look up is to be brought near to God by the incarnate one who leads by going on ahead, first in resurrection and then in ascent to God. Both the psalmist and his Christian readers want to expand the self upward, thus giving hope.

PSALM 25

Canonical Context and Themes

Psalms 23 and 24 introduce a more confident and secure tone into the Psalter. With Ps. 25, the cry of personal anguish that dominates the first half of the canonized collection returns. The canonical arrangement defies assigning it a pastoral pattern of development. Perhaps its final editor(s) thought that beginning with despair and moving gradually into hope, confidence, and the triumph of the creation itself, which appear in the later psalms of thanksgiving and those that celebrate the history of Israel, Torah, and creation, would lift readers emotionally into the great concluding hallelujah at the end. Nevertheless, Ps. 25 continues to lament the circumstance of the distressed complainant whose life is in disarray, although the reader is not privy to the particulars.

The standard theme of the languishing suppliant appears again, augmented by two subthemes. The suppliant waits restively for God to rescue him, basing his hope on God's steadfast love (25:6–7, 10). God's forgiveness of sinners is an expression of that love as he teaches them a better way to live (25:4–5, 8–9, 12, 14). Those who are lost because they are ashamed of their sins need God to instruct them in another life path, that path being the way of the covenant (25:14). The suppliant does not plea for God to make things better by fiat but requests concrete help to do better at his life in order to escape the taunts of watchful enemies. Psalm 25 adds both accountability and repentance to the genre of lament.

Structure and Dynamics

Psalm 25 is an imperfect acrostic poem with two letters of the alphabet missing. Taking the form of a penitential prayer, it is interrupted by a teaching about God's character and activities. Following the practice of segmenting the psalms by grammatical person, I have divided Ps. 25 into three strophes. Psalm 25:1–7, 11 opens the prayer in the second person, addressing God directly, while 25:8–10, 12–15 is in the third person. That is, 25:11 belongs with the first rather than the second segment of the psalm, which moves from directly addressing God to instructing the speaker's hearers about God. Psalm 25:16–21 continues and completes the prayer. Like Pss. 3 and 5, Ps. 25 moves from individual to corporate concern at the very end, effectively enabling the pray-er and his personal prayer to become the prayer of the whole people of God (25:22).

Guide Me! Teach Me! (25:1–7, 11)

The prayer begins with the lamenter lifting his life to God. The rabbis' corporate commentary (*Midrash on Psalms*) links this act with the daily cycle of sleeping and waking. Perhaps the writer is mindful of the prayer of thanksgiving said upon regaining consciousness in the morning: "Living and everlasting king, I stand before you grateful that in your great faithfulness you mercifully returned my life to me."[1] The *Midrash* associates the verse with Ps. 31:6 ("into your hands I commend my spirit"), relating it not to death, as the Christian committal in the burial rite does, but to the revivification of the body from sleep: "Things worn and used are left with Him for safekeeping, and He returns them new. You can see for yourself that this is true. For the worker labors the whole day, and his spirit within him becomes weary and worn, so that he is tired when he goes to sleep. But his spirit is at peace, for it is in the safekeeping of the Holy One, blessed be He, and at dawn it returns, a new creation, to his body."[2]

The psalmist, however, seems to be experiencing a good deal of anxiety over sins committed in his youth (25:7) that perhaps have become known (or are becoming known) and now haunt him. In Ps. 25, four verses refer to sins: three to the speaker's own past sins (25:7, 11, 18) and one to God's general instruction of sinners (25:8).[3] The protagonist is terrified of public shame and begs God not to allow him to be publically humiliated by whatever it is that weighs heavily on his heart (25:2–3, 20). Psalm 25 is a good example of "biblical anxiety management."[4] The turn to God, not only for pardon (25:11) but also for guidance, is penitential because the protagonist now realizes that not following God's ways has not served him well; he begs to be spared further public shame and for guidance and teaching (25:4–5). Calvin, himself no stranger to anxiety, remarks:

> There is an allusion to those sudden and irregular emotions which arise in our minds when we are tossed by adversity, and by which we are precipitated into the

1. Birnbaum 1949, 1 (author's translation).
2. Braude 1959a, 348.
3. It is noteworthy that the poet portrays God instructing sinners in another way rather than punishing them, as much later Christian theology would expect.
4. The phrase is from Jeffrey Thompson in private correspondence.

devious and deceitful paths of error, till they are in due time subdued or allayed by the word of God. Thus the meaning is . . . let thy truth preserve me in a state of quiet repose and peace, by an humble submission to it. . . . every one knows from his own experience how difficult a thing it is, while these clouds of darkness continue, to discern in what way we ought to walk. . . . what shall become of us if, in our afflictions, God dispel not from our minds those clouds of darkness which prevent us from seeing his light?[5]

Calvin empathizes with the speaker, who is not yet tranquil. Though distressed, he displays emotional maturity and spiritual strength in asking for both protection from public shame and guidance. Shame is awkward and deeply discomfiting, but when done in a mild and discerning way, it can be therapeutic if it enables people to come to terms with their misdeeds. Ridicule, however, is not well-ordered shaming, and the speaker is understandably frightened at the prospect. He does not need public shaming, for he has already benefited from reflecting on past missteps (25:7). Rather than defensiveness, he exhibits a mature acknowledgment of wrongdoing and recognition of the need to change course. Being further from the events, he is calmer and perhaps less defensive and more humble than he would have been at a younger age and is able to ask for help maturely. When sins are fresh, they invite defensiveness. In calmer moments, one is often more teachable and able to benefit from both judicious admonition and self-reflection.

Ibn Ezra associates the admission of sin and desire for guidance with David, who means by it, "You save me from all things that hinder me from walking in the path of truth, for I have no one to wait for but you."[6] "David" bases his appeal on God's grace and mercy (25:6–7), reminding God that forgetting sins has always been consistent with the dignity of the divine character.

In response to 25:7b, which dwells on the generosity and goodness of God, the rabbis of the *Midrash* observe that God wants good for us. *Midrash on Psalms* likens God to a king who invited people to a banquet, and although they arrived late, he was grateful that they had come so that the food would not be wasted. Similarly, "Even so, the Holy One, blessed be He, says to the righteous: I consider this a great favor on your part, for I created My world because of you; and were it not for you, all the goodness which I have prepared for the future, of which it is said *Oh how abundant is Thy goodness, which Thou hast laid up for them that fear Thee* [Ps. 31:20], to whom could I give it?"[7]

Attend to My Experience! (25:8–10, 12–15)

The penitential prayer is interrupted abruptly as the speaker turns to his audience in an aside to explain more about God and why he is to be trusted. Despite

5. Calvin 1996, 417.
6. Ibn Ezra 2006, 290.
7. Braude 1959a, 352.

their sins, God lovingly informs people for transformation through the covenantal precepts, and as the first strophe suggests, perhaps those slowed down by knowledge of their sins are God's more attentive patrons. These are the 'ănāwîm of 25:9. They need to understand that divine instruction expresses divine goodness, which lures those appropriately humbled into paths of loving-kindness and truth. Theodoret notes that "employing goodness [God] does not immediately punish sinners, but both gives them a glimpse of the right way and also teaches them the law of repentance; and those practicing gentleness and simplicity he teaches to discern the nature of things, and causes them to know all his dispensations lest their simplicity prove an occasion of ignorance and cause them great harm."[8]

Augustine reads "all of God's paths are loving-kindness (ḥesed) and truth ('ĕmet)" (25:10) to mean life lived between the incarnation (ḥesed) and the second coming of Christ for the final judgment ('ĕmet). "What *ways* will he teach them, other than the *steadfast love* which makes him ready to be appeased, and the *truth* which renders him incorrupt? The first of these he has demonstrated by forgiving sins, the second by judging merits. This is why the psalm speaks of *all the Lord's ways*, meaning the two comings of the Son of God, one in mercy, the other in judgment."[9] Christ both teaches God's ways lovingly and judges righteously.

Those humbled by their sins revere the Lord (25:12, 14). They benefit from knowing the covenant and its statutes and by choosing God's ways (25:12); furthermore, they will prosper from this closeness with God, and their children will inherit the land (25:13).[10] This complete orientation toward the Lord and the new way of life it yields draws the speaker out of the tangle in which he has been mired (25:15).

God here is no deus ex machina. He does not bail people out of trouble by simply making their enemies vanish suddenly. Rather, the way forward is to be carved out via divine guidance and teaching that is close to hand in scriptural precepts that constitute God's covenant with Israel. The way to success is published in *tôrâ*.[11]

Hatred Abounds but God Redeems (25:16–21)

The final strophe of this psalm returns to the prayer format, picking up from 25:11. It addresses God directly, pleading for mercy in the accustomed vein. Sinking back into the complaint genre, the distressed protagonist asks God to turn and see his affliction and isolation, with special pleading for his troubled situation. Again, the anxiety level rises to great heights; enemies violently pursue the speaker's life, though perhaps in a metaphorical sense. The fear of shame at

8. Theodoret 2000, 165.

9. Augustine 2000a, 250–51.

10. The phrase "inherit the land" reappears in Ps. 37:9 (also an acrostic) and more familiarly as one of the beatitudes in Matt. 5:5.

11. Although the noun *tôrâ* does not appear in Ps. 25, its presence is palpable. The word appears in verbal form in 25:8, 12.

past sins recurs, and he feels himself confronted by baseless hatred (*śin'at ḥāmās śĕnē'ûnî*).

Although feeling overwhelmed by adversaries, the speaker calls upon his strengths. Having taken refuge in God, he operates with some degree of security (25:20). He is where he needs to be. Knowing that he has done the right thing now, he has the strength of his integrity, even as he regrets past sins. His spiritual location has changed. On this basis, he believes that he can call upon God's compassion.

A Bigger Picture (25:22)

The psalmist concludes the poem by zooming back (as he often does) from the particular straits of the speaker to God's compassionate power to redeem Israel from any difficulty. In this way, he both draws his hearers into the experience of the complainant and sensitizes them to the broader implications of God's redeeming power.

Theological Pedagogy

Grammatically speaking, two psalms emerge here. One is a typical lament that complains to God of external foes who cause anxiety, worry, and perhaps even depression (25:1–7, 11, 16–21). The other is didactic instruction; God teaches a way to a productive life, offering concrete precepts that the humble can make their own (25:8–10, 12–15). This interweaving of personal address to God with third-person speech to the community about how they should think about God is commonplace in the psalmist's rhetorical style; he invites his hearers both to empathize with the speaker and to align themselves with the destiny of Israel as God's own people.

Theologically speaking, two orientations to suffering surface here, which are more difficult to tease apart linguistically. One bemoans the speaker's isolation and persecution by enemies who are incensed with what he experiences as baseless hatred that beats him down. Responding to this isolation with self-pity, the victim pleads for rescue. The other orientation to suffering engages in self-examination based on regret for past actions. It seeks forgiveness for youthful wrongs and wants to move ahead by relying on divine guidance garnered from the precepts of torah.

While the interplay between the two grammatical formats is easy to map, the two theological orientations of complaint and self-examination are not easily separated into discrete segments of the poem. The same can be said of personal reality. Psychologically, we move back and forth between special pleading and calling ourselves to accountable self-examination. We engage in self-pity but press on to find a way beyond it that we might learn from past errors and chart a fresh path for our life. At one moment we seek comfort, while at another we accept the challenge of rising to moral heights we have not previously scaled.

PSALM 26

Canonical Context and Themes

In Ps. 25, the suppliant fumbles between engaging in self-pity and mustering the strength to engage in critical self-examination. In light of that tentative forward movement, Ps. 26 sings of the comfort he has found in conscious ingenuousness (*bĕtummî*, 26:1, 11) once he forged a better foundation for an intentional life. Psalm 26 offers the tranquility that Ps. 25 seeks. Because Ps. 26 exudes self-assurance in living an ingenuous life, it has troubled Christian commentators who fear that readers may misuse the psalm by reading it as grounds for self-righteousness, distracting them from putting their confidence in God. That fear may, however, be unwarranted because the basis of confidence is God's love and truth (as Augustine reads it).[1]

Structure and Dynamics

Psalm 26 is a direct address to God, with the exception of 26:1b that refers to God in the third person. It can be divided into three segments. Psalm 26:1–3 invites God to judge the protagonist on the grounds that he has been guided by God's loving-kindness and truth. Following this, 26:4–8 offers concrete evidence for the confident invitation of 26:3, and 26:9–11 petitions God for gracious treatment. As usual, the last verse (26:12) carries the personal hope of vindication into the public realm with the promise that the speaker will bless God when the community assembles.

1. Augustine 2000a, 254.

Inviting God's Judgment (26:1–3)

Psalm 26 opens boldly with the singer inviting God to examine the integrity that directs his life. He asks to be judged, tested, tried, and refined as if he were a precious metal. He has no fear of divine examination and tells the reader why: his life is whole—or perhaps better, wholesome—for he trusts God and has betaken himself to the loving-kindness and the truth of God. Seeing Ps. 26 as a follow-up to Ps. 25 is particularly warranted by 26:3, which mentions the loving-kindness and the truth of God. Both appear in Ps. 25:5–7 (in 25:5 the speaker asks to be directed by God's truth), and 25:10 mentions loving-kindness and truth together; in 26:3 they appear together and in the same order.[2] As I mentioned earlier, Augustine interprets divine loving-kindness as the incarnation and God's truth as divine judgment. Here, the two divine attributes appear as poles around which the singer has wrapped his life in deliberate integrity, rendering him trustworthy.

Being uncomfortable with the possibility that some might interpret the speaker as referring to his own sinlessness, both Theodoret and Theodore interpret the openness to judgment to be about God taking up David's cause and judging others for their unwarranted actions against him, rather than God judging David. His innocence is not innocence before God but before malicious accusers. As already noted, Augustine finds the invitation to judgment warranted because "thanks to the mercy with which you forestalled me, I have some entitlement from my innocence, and have kept to that path. *With my hope set on the Lord I shall not be moved.* But I do not on that score hope in myself; rather it is by trusting in the Lord that I shall abide in him."[3] Calvin, having experienced opposition and persecution himself, defends David more in line with the earlier Greek commentators. David's claim to innocence is warranted because "it was the wickedness of his enemies which forced him to commend himself so much. Had he not been unjustly condemned by men, he would have humbly deprecated such an examination, as he well knew, notwithstanding his zeal to act aright, that he was far from perfection."[4]

The Septuagint translates *bĕtummî* in 26:1 as *akakia mou*, which Greek-speaking theologians may have read as "innocence" in the sense of "guiltlessness." Jerome translates it as *salutare meum*, certainly implying "guiltlessness." The New Revised Standard Version better translates it as "in my integrity." I translate it "in my guilelessness"—innocence in the sense of integrity of character, not success in avoiding bad behavior. What a difference a *t* makes! Perhaps some Christian anxiety over this confident psalm is due to the fact that the innocence the speaker proclaims is often thought to be a behavioral assertion. Evidence for the translation of *bĕtummî* as "in my guilelessness" can be found in 26:4–8.

2. One is tempted here to suppose a single author for these two songs.
3. Augustine 2000a, 254.
4. Calvin 1998, 439.

Evidence of Guilelessness (26:4–8)

The next strophe ticks off evidence behind the speaker's confidence in his integrity. He avoids companions of ill repute assiduously (26:5). Instead, he keeps his hands clean by remaining steadfast in worship and prayer, "circling the altar," singing and proclaiming God's wonders. The idea anticipates the Christian injunction to "pray without ceasing" (1 Thess. 5:17). The phrase "circling the altar" may refer to the practice of censing the altar in the Jerusalem Temple, which is still practiced at the high mass. Just as the previous strophe concludes with the speaker's rationale for his guilelessness, this one concludes with an exclamation about the speaker's love of God's home and the place where God's glory dwells (26:8). In a typically allegorical vein, Augustine reads these verses as signifying spiritual realities. The altar is the pure conscience; the beauty of God's house is the beauty of the saints, and the house where God's glory dwells is wherever people glorify God, not themselves. Thus the boasting of the protagonist is acceptable because he glorifies God.

The evidence for the speaker's integrity points to a strategy of separation. He guards his purity by avoiding bad influences—an approach that I have already noted. It is not an evangelistic but a Pharisaic principle. The speaker is not out to purify the world but to avoid being harmed by its impure elements. Although Christians have generally embraced evangelism and excoriated Pharisaism, the principles at work behind each perspective (which oppose each other) are perhaps best considered in relation to particular challenges. In certain times and settings, each approach commends itself: the wise and discerning will consider carefully when protecting themselves from harm is warranted and when risking themselves for the kingdom is necessary.

Perhaps predictably, Calvin castigates the desire to protect oneself from desecration, a desire that appeared in his day as schismatic. That being said, the fact that Protestants were schismatic from the Roman perspective did not prevent Calvin from similarly impugning Anabaptists.

> Many err in this way grievously; imagining when they see the evil mingled with the good, that they will be infected with pollution, unless they immediately withdraw themselves from the whole congregation. This preciseness drove the Donatists of old, and prior to them the Cathari and the Novatians, into mischievous schisms. In our own times, too, the Anabaptists, from a similar conceit, have separated themselves from the sacred assemblies, because they reckoned them not so free from all defilement as could have been wished.[5]

On a more sympathetic Pharisaic note, John Goldingay remarks that "Psalm 26 reminds us that, ideally, people who pray need to be able to claim moral integrity and religious commitment, and must dissociate themselves from the faithless."[6]

5. Calvin (1854) 1998, 442.
6. Goldingay 2006, 388.

Petitioning Purity (26:9–11)

The passage laying out the speaker's justification leads into a plea to God to preserve the speaker's clean hands from those whose hands are soaked in lewdness and shame as a result of taking bribes. He begs not to be gathered up in a heap of sinners whom he calls "people of blood." He pleads for redeeming grace because integrity has been the main support of his life.

Here I Stand (26:12)

The protagonist is steadfast. He has dug in his heels, pointing to the uprightness of his theological integrity. On that basis he will bless the Lord publicly. As with all the psalms that conclude by publicizing the faithfulness or redemptive power of God, the conclusion to Ps. 26 is proclamatory and, in that sense, evangelical. It seeks to bring others into the appreciation of God's goodness and thereby away from the company of sarcastic skeptics.

Theological Pedagogy

The pedagogy here flows down from God into the speaker and from there out into the community. It begins with the steadfast loving-kindness and truth of God that the speaker resolutely makes his own. That is, he constructs his personality from the divine attributes that he admires. He receives God's integrity as his own and offers himself as a model to others based on his experience. Although it is a bit immodest to proclaim one's integrity rather than allow it to be noted by others, the psalmist sees fit here to speak forthrightly so that there can be no doubt in the minds of his flock. A sentence from the "Morning Resolve" of the *Forward Day by Day* meditation booklet captures the spirit of this poem: "Help me to keep my heart clean, and to live so honestly and fearlessly that no outward failure can dishearten me or take away the joy of conscious integrity."[7]

As a teacher, the poet is not lecturing the congregation about how to think about God or moralizing about what they should do, though he does carefully point out behavior to avoid. Nevertheless, he uses himself as an example of what the congregation might become in God. Paul also does this, inviting the Corinthians to imitate him as he imitates Christ (1 Cor. 4:16; 11:1). Seen in this light, Christians have scant reason to be uncomfortable with this psalm. On the contrary, to live from the integrity of the psalmist is a central goal of Christian preaching and teaching. Taking on the guise of a simple suppliant, perhaps the psalmist leads the people of God by appealing to his auditors to empathize first with his desire to be tested and found ingenuous and later with his desire to avoid being gathered up with sinners.

7. *Forward Day by Day.*

Therefore, while he strategically isolates himself from evildoers (in what Calvin takes to be a schismatic move), he does it to build up the whole community, which he enlists in the same project until, ideally, the class of evildoers becomes null. Hence, this psalm is a homily. The poet wants everyone to want to be searched and tested by God and to be able to sing about it joyfully.

PSALM 27

Canonical Context and Themes

Psalm 25 remorsefully pleads for forgiveness and rescue from the hatred of enemies, perhaps those the speaker wronged in the past. Psalm 26 proclaims that the speaker has relocated himself in the "clean" place where God is glorified; Ps. 27 takes the protagonist's reconstruction of his life a step further. These three psalms provide snapshots of progress in the spiritual renewal of life. The third step in the speaker's healing is a strong statement of triumphant confidence that God will save him from whatever may befall. He fears nothing that life's contingencies may impose now that he is thoroughly embedded in the Lord or, as Augustine puts it, that God is embedded in him.[1]

Psalm 27 is dearly beloved by both Jewish and Christian commentators, perhaps because it so strongly expresses the psychological security they both long for and regularly commend to those for whom they have pastoral responsibility. Interestingly, although it is not a "penitential" psalm, it became the signature psalm of the Jewish penitential month of Elul, to be recited daily in the days leading up to the High Holy Days. Perhaps the liturgists expected the psalmist's insistence on the absence of fear in those who trust God utterly to fortify people going into the annual ten Days of Awe (from Rosh Hashanah to Yom Kippur)—a time in which their fate was sealed for another year of life or death, prosperity or adversity. The Jewish commentators all associate Ps. 27 with this liturgical season.

Structure and Dynamics

As with so many psalms, the speaker moves rapidly back and forth between his local hearers and God so that one senses that the speaker and both audiences are

---

1. Augustine 2000a, 276.

in close proximity. Psalm 27 begins with an extended statement of confidence in God, which is addressed to the speaker's human auditors and explains that he is protected from all adversity, especially enemies (27:1–6). At 27:7, the speaker turns from his hearers to address God, beseeching him to follow through on what he has just told his human audience to expect: God will save him from trouble (27:7–9). Psalm 27:10 briefly turns back to his local audience, adding a worst-case scenario to what he told them in his opening segment. He immediately returns briefly to his plea for rescue from adversaries (27:11–12) and then turns back to his listeners, concluding with a very brief confession of trust in the Lord and commendation that his local audience should follow his lead (27:13–14). The speaker busily moves back and forth from explanation to prayer, back to explanation, back to prayer, and ends with exhortation. One can almost see his human audience watching expectantly as he turns his body now toward them, now away from them, toward God, and back to them again. The rapid movements effectively impress upon the auditors how nearby God is and how easily beseeched.

Seek, Shout, and Sing (27:1–6)

The singer is fearless in any situation—even an army encamped against him—confident that God will shelter him from trouble when and wherever it may strike. This song pointedly says that the speaker asks but one thing of God and has considered carefully before speaking. That one thing is the most important and poignant request he could make, and it models piety for everyone: he asks to dwell in God's house and to envision the loveliness of the Lord all his life by remaining in God's temple. A similar thought appears in Pss. 15:1; 23:6; and 24:3; it will recur in Pss. 61:4 and 92:13. Excellent people remain near God, and the poet sings joyously of transcending the power of his enemies, spiritually if not physically.

Augustine preached eloquently on this passage, not in the context of physical danger which threatens the speaker according to the text, but in terms of spiritual enemies that threaten the speaker's moral well-being. Taking his cue from 1 Cor. 3:16–17, he interprets the Lord's dwelling place as the believer who is made beautiful by being inhabited by God in her innermost self. The psalmist wants to live forever with God, to contemplate God's goodness perfectly, and to *be* God's temple; he wants to become divine goodness. Augustine longs

> to contemplate him always, with no misfortune to threaten me as I do so, no temptation to distract me, no one's power to sweep me away, no enemy to suffer from as I contemplate him, so that I may enjoy that bliss to the full with no worries, the bliss that is the Lord my God himself. What must happen to me if this is to be? He himself will protect me. Not only do I wish to see the delight of the Lord; I also want "his temple to be protected." I will be his temple, so that he may protect his temple, may protect me. . . . To these two aspects correspond the two assertions with which the psalm began: *The Lord is my light and my salvation, whom shall I*

fear? I shall contemplate the Lord's joy, and so he is my light; he will protect me, his temple, and so he is my salvation.[2]

Do Not Leave Me! (27:7–9)

Rather than proclaiming that he has God in his pocket—that he is confident in God's commitment to rescue him from danger—the speaker turns to God and pleads for precisely what he has just told his local hearers that he is sure of: God's protection. Suddenly, he assumes a begging posture akin to that of numerous psalms previously commented upon. He fears that God might cast him off and abandon him in anger. The protagonist is apparently not as confident when he is alone with God as he appears to be when he stands in front of his human audience. The public and the private face of the singer seem disconnected.

Augustine is undaunted by the way in which the speaker takes refuge in a secret place where he reveals his fears to God. Maybe this vacillation between confidence and fear was Augustine's personal experience. He writes: "I have not paraded myself before other men and women, but in a secret place, where you alone can hear, my heart said to you, 'I have asked you for no reward other than yourself, but have sought only your face.' . . . for it is not any worthless thing I look for, Lord, but your countenance only, that I may love you freely. Nothing more precious than that can I find."[3] In Augustine's view, the fear is not primarily of physical enemies, as the text implies, but rather of the deeper enemy—the fear of being distant from the divine presence. God is needed not to pull the speaker out of ill straits so much as to prevent separation from God. Augustine's great fear is of being alone in the universe, and God is the only one who can allay that fear with the promise of his presence. Secure in the divine presence, Augustine believes that one can scale any height, face any war, and defeat any enemy that may challenge that security.

Confident Despite the Worst Case (27:10)

Reverting to the initial attitude of untrammeled confidence, the poet adds a worst-case scenario to press home his point about God's overarching care. Even were his parents to abandon him, he would be confident that God would take their place. The terrible thought that parents could abandon their child caught the attention of commentators. Augustine points out that natural parents die, but God never dies; therefore, people need not experience themselves as orphaned. He sees the psalmist as a child in relation to God, who functions as both father and mother: "God is our father because he created us, because he calls us, gives orders and rules us; he is our mother because he cherishes us, nourishes us, feeds us with milk, and holds us in his arms."[4]

2. Ibid., 280.
3. Ibid., 272.
4. Ibid., 285–86.

In an age when sex was approved only for conception and not for pleasure, Rashi interpreted parental abandonment to mean that David's parents were interested only in pleasure, with no thought that they might conceive him when having sex. To make up for that weakness, Rashi writes: "The Holy One Blessed be He guards the semen and forms the fetus."[5] Like Augustine, Ibn Ezra reads parental forsakenness as the death of one's parents, whereupon God takes over parental responsibility so that the person is not abandoned.[6] All the commentators are concerned with comforting the reader, assuring her that she will not be alone but will be cared for even in the worst of situations.

While 27:10 continues the confident proclamation of God's sure salvation of the first strophe, its location after the plea for God not to abandon the speaker functions to fight back the fear of God-abandonment that occurs in Ps. 22. The deep gnawing fear that God could abandon us must repeatedly be repulsed. Luther, who was thrashed by this fear in a mighty way, clung to faith in the mercy of God in Christ as the best way to stave off despair. Knowing how difficult it is to remain consoled by faith when fear worms its way back into the heart, he writes: "We know God aright when we grasp him not in his might or wisdom (for then he proves terrifying), but in his kindness and love. Then faith and confidence are able to exist, and then man is truly born anew in God."[7]

Teach Me, Lead Me (27:11–12)

These verses continue the plea of 27:7–9 with the same request that occurs in Ps. 25:4–5. The suppliant is now desperate and asks for divine teaching and guidance to maintain his equilibrium, which has been undone by the false, or at least exaggerated, accusations now apparently massed against him.

Wait! Be Strong! (27:13–14)

With a confident word, the conclusion of Ps. 27 turns once more back to the local audience. The speaker believes that he will yet be vindicated in this life. He summons hope for now—soon, not in an eschatological hereafter. As one might expect, the very last word he offers is not about himself but about God and, in this case, his listening friends. He assumes that they empathize with

---

5. Rashi 2004, 277.

6. Ibn Ezra 2006, 311.

7. Luther (1519) 1989, 171. Paul Althaus summarizes the precariousness of faith as Luther understood it in this way: "Admittedly this experience of faith is not constant. Under the pressure of suffering it may even disappear. As Christ on the cross no longer felt his own deity [alluding to Ps. 22:1], so the Christian according to his outer man may 'no longer feel the faith' through which he is God's child. At such times faith 'crawls away and hides.' Then the joy which faith gives ceases. Faith stands completely alone without experience. Nothing remains except to look to Christ on the cross. But things are not always this way. Luther knows that faith from time to time must pass through such moments of anguish, but that they in turn will pass and the experience of the joy of faith will return" (Althaus 1966, 61).

him and join in his plea for rescue, perhaps having been in similar straits. He addresses them directly in the imperative, urging them to be strong and courageous and to wait for God to save them. Perhaps the counsel to wait in hope is offered against the background of psalms that utter that exasperated cry "How long, O LORD?," which occurs in Pss. 6 and 13. If so, it is noteworthy that the psalmist does not downplay the anguish of waiting and uncertainty, which can dissolve into raw fear and anger, but exposes his own anguish, mixed with his confident rallying cries.

Theological Pedagogy

Whether intentionally or not, this poem illustrates the emotional ability of the human heart struggling with conflicting emotions. The example of the speaker lurching from positive to negative feelings is all too familiar to those seeking emotional stability when under stress. In his treatise on the Psalter, Athanasius writes that "the one who hears [the psalms], in addition to learning [the commandments and prophecies of Christ], also comprehends and is taught in [the Psalter] the emotions of the soul, and, consequently, on the basis of that which affects him and by which he is constrained, he also is enabled by this book to possess the image deriving from the words. Therefore, through hearing it teaches not only not to disregard passion, but also how one must heal passion through speaking and acting."[8]

Of this particular psalm he writes, "if they savagely attack you, and the enemies become multitudinous, as rank upon rank, eyeing you with contempt, as if you have not yet been visited by grace—and on this account they wish to do battle—do not crouch in fear, but sing the twenty-sixth psalm."[9]

Athanasius agrees with the psalmist that unpleasant emotions are not to be repressed as untoward but to be healed through models that show how to handle them. Here, the psalmist gives permission to his audience to be emotionally conflicted in relation to God. He does not urge his hearers to "grin and bear it" or "put on a happy face," and he does not disparage honest fear of God-abandonment, lest it display a lack of faith in God's power or goodness.

By making his local audience privy to both his confidence and his fear, the speaker lets his supportive friends participate in the turmoil he is experiencing. By teaching his hearers to accept their emotional vicissitudes and allowing them to empathetically support him, he also teaches them to rely upon a caring community of friends in times of stress. While expressing negative emotion in a safe environment may be commonplace advice from a modern psychological perspective (though insufficient for actually succeeding in attaining equilibrium in desperate circumstances), it is a message that those who resolutely think they should "go it

8. Athanasius 1980, 108.
9. Ibid., 116.

alone" need to hear, lest isolation and fear, even of friends, exacerbate an already difficult situation.

One further consideration arises from the important role the listeners play here and in other psalms where the speaker turns to include them as active though silent participants in the drama. Although they never speak—since ostensibly the psalmist-teacher is instructing them—they act as a silent chorus of support and encouragement for him in two ways. First, they are a receptive audience. By listening to and benefiting from his teaching on how to be confident of God's power to shelter the suffering and how to raise a cry of lament, the audience provides a redeeming quality to the suffering. When the speaker's wisdom and advice can help others in the future, his own suffering and longing to behold the beauty of the Lord obtain a life beyond his own experience.

Second, the silent listeners are active by supporting the speaker in both his consolation and desolation. What are the responsibilities of those who find themselves called upon to support those in emotional turmoil? Although it carries one beyond the scope of the psalm, the skills of active listening are germane here, given the setting in which the poem is delivered.[10]

10. For the skills of active listening see "Active Listening: Hear What People Are Really Saying," Mind Tools, accessed October 27, 2014, www.mindtools.com/CommSkll/ActiveListening.htm.

PSALM 28

Canonical Context and Themes

Psalm 28 provides a stereotypical Davidic lament containing most of the elements that one finds in previous psalms of this type: personal supplication, denunciation of enemies, personal thanksgiving, confident trust, public praise, and corporate plea. For example, Ps. 3 consists primarily of personal petition and confident trust, with elements of public praise and corporate supplication at the end. Psalm 5 includes personal supplication, confident trust, a call for punishment, and public praise, while Ps. 13 encompasses personal supplication and public thanksgiving. Psalm 18 incorporates confident trust, personal supplication, personal thanksgiving, and public praise, and Ps. 22 includes personal supplication and public praise. In Ps. 28, all six elements are tightly integrated into a terse poem that enables subsequent users of the psalm to experience all of these emotions and attitudes toward God, self, and others.

Structure and Dynamics

Continuing my method of segmenting the psalms according to the grammatical form of address rather than themes, this psalm divides into three parts. Psalm 28:1–4 addresses God personally in the second person, while 28:5–8 refers to God in the third person and addresses the local (and the later) human audience. The final verse (28:9) returns to address God directly on behalf of the entire people of God rather than the speaker's own behalf.

An important feature of this psalm is that, like Pss. 6 and 22, it breaks out in doxological thanksgiving for having been rescued (28:6–7) but does not mention an intervening event. If Pss. 6, 22, and 28 did not arise from personal experience but were composed specifically for liturgical use and were later used in a liturgical context, perhaps some event or thought has intervened liturgically to shift the ground between 28:5 and 28:6, catapulting the poem into a song of exultant thanksgiving for having been rescued.

In what is by now a familiar poetic turn, 28:8 fans out from the personal experience of the speaker—be it under duress or in celebration—to proclaim God's salvation of his anointed (here the entire people of God). It concludes by deflecting to a plea for the corporate salvation of Israel, addressing God directly as in the opening strophe.

Pleading for Rescue and Revenge (28:1–4)

The opening verses voice agitation at God's silence that the speaker refers to as deafness toward the suppliant. The speaker goads God into acting—first by telling him that failure to help would "kill" him (so devastating it would be) and then by telling him that it would be like treating him as those with ill intentions, who appear to be good neighbors but harbor evil designs. That is, he advises God that people will read God's silence as condemnation, shaming him inappropriately in public. God's failure to aid the suppliant implicates God as participating in a false accusation of one who takes God as his "rock"—an act of calumny by omission. For God to be known as righteous and truthful he must not play deaf; he must attend to this situation now. It is in God's best interest to act rightly, for his reputation is on the line. The speaker experiences God's silence as betrayal. Like Ps. 7, Ps. 28 is a wake-up call to God from an impatient and needy, though stalwart, supporter.

Calvin recognized the psalmist's assumption, namely that God's answer to the cry of true believers implies that those not answered are faithless. Given the anguish that this causes the pious, added to the distress of the actual situation they are in, Calvin comments compassionately on 28:1–2, repeating that the suppliant's cry to God be heeded: "This repetition is a sign of a heart in anguish. . . . [David] means that he was so stricken with anxiety and fear, that he prayed not coldly, but with burning, vehement desire, like those who, under the pressure of grief, vehemently cry out."[1]

Augustine avoids the awkward possibility that God would calumniate innocent victims by reading Christ rather than David as the speaker here. By crying from the cross not to be separated from God (which is from his divine nature), Jesus takes the fear of abandonment into himself and away from those for whom he was crucified. To explain how faithful users of Ps. 28 are not abandoned, Augustine interprets "I reach my arms out toward your holy sanctuary" (28:2) as "I stretch them out as I am crucified, for the salvation of those who by believing become your holy temple."[2] In this way, Christ is present with believers. Relying on a Jo-

---

1. Calvin 1998, 466.
2. Augustine 2000a, 291.

hannine soteriology of being indwelt by Christ, Augustine reassures his audience that Christ unites himself with believers so that they do not feel abandoned by God when in troubled circumstances.

In the concluding verse of this segment of the complaint (28:4), the speaker turns in a divisive direction as he calls on God to avenge him by bringing down his enemies. The psalmic call for God to punish evildoers resonates with some commentators. Contrary to the later Augustinian view that divine election expresses the inscrutable will of God, which is independent of anything that one has, has not, or might do, the first Christians agreed with the psalmist's call for justice. Paul agrees with the just deserts theology of Ps. 28:4—"Deal with them according to their works"—in Rom. 2:6–8. The former reads, "For he will repay according to each one's deeds: to those who by patiently doing good seek for glory and honor and immortality, he will give eternal life; while for those who are self-seeking and who obey not the truth but wickedness, there will be wrath and fury" (NRSV). Matthew 16:27 supports the same reward system: "For the Son of Man is to come with his angels in the glory of his Father, and then he will repay everyone for what has been done" (NRSV). The same view appears in 2 Tim. 4:14, although the psalm is not cited.

Later Christian commentators are chary of allowing the sufferer to vent his anger, though the just deserts philosophy of the psalmist seems to permit it. Theodoret was disturbed by the revenge motif. "Let no one think, however, that the righteous person is cursing his enemies: the words are a mark not of cursing but of a just verdict. *Grant them their due repayment*, he says, meaning, May they fall foul of their own schemes, which they hatch against one another."[3]

Divine Justice and a Song of Rejoicing (28:5–8)

While thoughts of revenge characterize 28:4–5 (making their grouping logical), 28:4 is addressed to God, but 28:5 and the next three verses are addressed to the local audience. The condemnatory 28:5 explains to the human audience why the speaker is emboldened to ask God to avenge him. His assailants disrespect God, and in retaliation God will destroy them (*yehersēm*)—not because they harm or seek to harm the speaker necessarily, but because they do not grasp who God is. Switching from the second to the third person depersonalizes the nefarious intent of the adversaries.

Ibn Ezra notes that the "works of evil" (28:4) contrast with "the works of the LORD" (28:5). He attributes the former not to the maliciousness of the enemies but to their ignorance of the theistic sanction: "If *the workers of iniquity* would understand *the works of the Lord* they would not do evil, for they would know that God would break them down."[4] Thus Ibn Ezra protects the speaker from

3. Theodoret 2000, 179.
4. Ibn Ezra 2006, 315.

being accused of pleading for revenge on his own behalf. He is calling for God to punish only appropriately.

Calvin, however, was disturbed that David's call for revenge might countenance this ethic among those wronged by adversaries. Concerning these verses (28:4–5), he offers a practicum in anger management to set believers on another path. He is worth quoting at length since distaste for the revenge motif maintains a long life in Christian piety.

> In the first place, then, it is unquestionable, that if the flesh move us to seek revenge, the desire is wicked in the sight of God. He not only forbids us to imprecate evil upon our enemies in revenge for private injuries, but it cannot be otherwise than that all those desires which spring from hatred must be disordered. David's example, therefore, must not be alleged by those who are driven by their own intemperate passion to seek vengeance. The holy prophet is not inflamed here by his own private sorrow to devote his enemies to destruction; but laying aside the desire of the flesh, he gives judgment concerning the matter itself. Before a man can, therefore, denounce vengeance against the wicked, he must first shake himself free from all improper feelings in his own mind. In the second place, prudence must be exercised, that the heinousness of the evils which offend us drive us not to intemperate zeal, which happened even to Christ's disciples, when they desired that fire might be brought from heaven to consume those who refused to entertain their Master (Luke 9:54). They pretended, it is true, to act according to the example of Elias; but Christ severely rebuked them, and told them that they knew not by what spirit they were actuated. In particular, we must observe this general rule, that we cordially desire and labor for the welfare of the whole human race. Thus it will come to pass, that we shall not only give way to the exercise of God's mercy, but shall also wish the conversion of those who seem obstinately to rush upon their own destruction. In short, David, being free from every evil passion, and likewise endued with the spirit of discretion and judgment, pleads here not so much his own cause as the cause of God. And by this prayer, he farther reminds both himself and the faithful, that although the wicked may give themselves loose reins in the commission of every species of vice with impunity for a time, they must at length stand before the judgment-seat of God.[5]

At this point, the poet modulates abruptly from an anxious minor to a bright major key, breaking into a rousing blessing of God for a rescue about which he provides no information at all. He tells us only that God has heard him and responded appropriately. Perhaps his enemies faltered, and he reads that as his vindication by God. The opening reference to God as his "rock" proves warranted. God is the protagonist's strength and shield because he heeded the complaint and helped. The protagonist bursts out in a full-throated song of thanksgiving. He is justified.

At this point, a significant difference between the Masoretic Text and the Septuagint gave rise to Augustine's distinctive reading of these verses, for he put

5. Calvin 1998, 469–70.

great stock in the Septuagint. While the key phrase in 28:7 in the Masoretic Text, *wayya'ălōz libbî*, translates as "and my heart exults," the Septuagint translates it as *kai anethalen hē sarx mou*, "and my flesh revived." From this, Augustine reads the hope of resurrection. Since he holds Christ to be the speaker of the psalm, he offers what sounds like a Lutheran reading of the text: "Now that the fear of death has been done away with, those who believe in me will confess to him, not constrained by fear under the law, but freely and in harmony with the law. And since I am in them, I shall confess to him."[6] Christ is singing this song, and since Christ is in the hearts of the faithful, he is singing this song in them.

This middle section of Ps. 28 concludes by applying the personal experience of the speaker to the entire people of God. Just as the Lord is the speaker's personal rock, strength, and shield, he is the strength and refuge of his anointed (28:8). The parallelism of the verse indicates that "his anointed" refers to Israel and not to an individual, as Pss. 2, 18, and possibly 20 might suggest.

Save Your People (28:9)

While the final verse of Ps. 28 joins the first strophe in direct supplication, it is not on behalf of the individual complainant but on behalf of the people, as 28:8 indicates. As the Lord has proven himself faithful to one individual, so will he prove faithful to the entire nation, blessing it forever.[7]

Theological Pedagogy

The theological pedagogy of Ps. 28 is familiar at this point in our study. The psalmist seeks to shape his listeners' emotions first by drawing them into the distress of the speaker and then by having the speaker turn to them and extend God's saving grace to the whole community. The community is in solidarity with the sufferer, and the sufferer is in solidarity with his community. The lack of tension between the individual and the corporate body of the people of God demonstrates that God's love is grand enough to embrace them all. The example of one rescued Israelite stands surety for all and gives others hope throughout the ages.

6. Augustine 2000a, 292.

7. The first clause of Ps. 28:9 is enshrined in the suffrages of daily morning prayers in the *Book of Common Prayer* 1979, 98.

PSALM 29

Canonical Context and Themes

Psalm 29 develops a theme sounded in Ps. 2 that establishes God as the supreme ruler of the world; gentile kings are to subject themselves to God in the person of Israel's king, who is God's anointed. "Upping the ante," Ps. 29 takes a quite different approach to the establishment of God's universal sovereignty. Not only are the kings of the nations (and their people) subject to God's rule, but so are their gods. However, it is not military might but God's authority to control nature that subjects the nations. Psalm 29 is an energetic creation hymn honoring the Lord God, envisioned as a reigning monarch. Written to honor David, it overshadows him when compared to the power commanded by the voice of God. As Pss. 8 and 19 attest, God controls nature. Psalm 29 was probably written as a polemical rejoinder to Canaanite Baal worship as a way to persuade Canaanites (and remind Israel) that the Lord God of Israel is the one true God; he is not only more powerful than, but qualitatively different from, any personification of nature.[1]

Structure and Dynamics

Psalm 29 addresses the "children of the gods" (*běnê ʾēlîm*). Psalm 29:1–2 urges these minor deities to worship God appropriately while 29:3–9 informs them of the scope of God's powerful reach to inspire the "godlings" to awe, admiration, and respectful fear before the Lord. The penultimate verse (29:10) depicts God enthroned above all these natural forces, and 29:11 prays for peace, indicating that God controls not only nature but also history.

---

1. Pardee and Pardee 2009.

"Godlings" before the Lord (29:1–2)

This hymn begins by boldly imploring the "children of the gods" to recognize the weighty power and strength of the Lord, whose name deserves to be worshiped in sacred majesty.[2] Premodern commentators did not have the benefit of the twentieth-century discovery at Ras Shamra of the Ugaritic tablets, which suggest that the psalm polemicizes against the "godlings" of the Canaanite pantheon. *Midrash on Psalms* reads *běnê 'ēlîm* as Jews who acted as if they were deaf and dared talk back to God, while Ibn Ezra interprets them as possibly being the stars. Calvin writes that they were "stubborn and stiff-necked giants, who, if they are not struck with fear, refuse to stand in awe of any power in heaven."[3] As I point out in footnote 2, the fact that Ps. 29:1–2 was addressed to the nations in another psalm and additionally repeated elsewhere in scripture indicates the breadth of concern covered by the intense exhortation to the world beyond Israel to recognize and confess the sovereignty of the Lord God of Israel.

The Voice of the Lord (29:3–9)

The insistent repetition of the phrase "the voice of the LORD" in the midsection of Ps. 29 recalls the divine speech that brought the world into being. While in Genesis the repeated phrase attributed to God in the creative act is "and God said let there be . . ." (with analogs), in Ps. 29 divine "speech" resounds not through words that bring things into existence in an orderly manner but in the threatening harshness of nature's destructive powers, the sounds of which can strike terror in the human heart. In the post-Edenic world, nature is not benign.

Here the voice of God is not the power of order in creation but of the jarring disorder expressed through raw power, turning life-sustaining elements into death-dealing dangers. It is the voice of rushing waters and floods that sweep life away in a moment. It is so powerful that it can fell Lebanon cedar trees, coniferous evergreens growing up to 130 feet tall with trunks up to 8 feet in diameter that were used primarily for building ships but also buildings (including Solomon's Temple) in the ancient world. The image of young animals unsteady on their feet in 29:6 may suggest playfulness (along the lines of the mountains of Syria and Mt. Hermon dancing in Ps. 114:4), but given the surrounding images, it more likely refers to earthquakes, which evoke the fear of God.[4] Next, the psalmist threatens the godlings with flames of fire that when left uncontrolled devour everything in their path as they bear down on the wilderness of Kadesh, making it shake and writhe in anguish.[5] What could be more deadly than fire in the desert? Finally, the

2. Psalm 29:1–2 appears in Ps. 96:7–9 and targets the nations of the world rather than the children of the gods; it is repeated in that form at 1 Chr. 16:28–30.

3. Calvin 1998, 476.

4. For similar imagery, see Ps. 18:7; Nah. 1:5.

5. The place may be Kadesh Barnea, mentioned in Num. 20, where Miriam died and where Moses disobeyed God by striking the rock to find water for Israel.

Lord speaks, causing deer to go into labor and forests to be denuded, perhaps by disease. The psalmist sums up the message of the strophe with the word repeated in 29:1–2: everything in God's palace shouts "glory!"

The figural use of voice provides room for the imagination to play with how one might experience the voice of God. Basil suggests that "voice" is "an image formed by the mind of men whom God wishes to hear His own voice," similar to voices we hear in dreams.[6] Several Christian commentators, seeking spiritual uplift from the hymn for their Christian readers, quite ignore the dangers it evokes and use it for comfort and hope. Theodoret, for example, reads "shaking the wilderness" (29:8) in light of Isa. 35:1:

> Isaiah also prophecies about this wilderness, "Rejoice, parched desert; let the desert rejoice and flower as a lily." He calls the nations *wilderness* for being once upon a time bereft of God; but while the divinely inspired Isaiah said they would flower, blessed David said they would be in labor and give birth. . . . This is the wilderness the Lord is shaking, *shaking* suggesting God's appearance; he will cause to give birth to salvation according to the prophecy that says, "For fear of you, O Lord, we conceived, were in labor, and gave birth to a spirit of your salvation, a spirit which you wrought on the earth [Isa. 26:17–18 LXX].[7]

Indeed, the fear of the Lord that presses the birth pangs of faith may be precisely the response the psalmist is looking for from his readers.

Look to the Flood! (29:10)

Psalm 29:10 reinforces what has come before by carrying the reader's imagination back to the frightening events of Gen. 6–8. The depiction of impending havoc on earth in Ps. 29:3–9 is no idle threat. The psalmist looks back to recorded history, specifically identifying God as a king enthroned over the flood. There remains little doubt that God is the master of nature forever and will use it to punish as he sees fit. The exhortation to the godlings and their devotees is complete; the truth has been delivered without mincing words.

Look for Peace (29:11)

Tenderly, the psalmist turns back to Israel, the immediate hearers of his poem. Amid the terrors with which God threatens the earth, or at least those who do not submit to his power and authority, Israel is strong and safe. The poet offers a final note of confident comfort, invoking God's blessing of peace on his people. To Augustine, the mention of the flood recalls that ark in which Noah and his family safely rode in order to repopulate the earth. For Augustine, Noah's vessel is the church, the ship of salvation that carries God's holy ones safely through the

---

6. Basil of Caesarea 1963, 199.
7. Theodoret 2000, 185.

storms of life. He thoughtfully concludes his comment on Ps. 29 by adding that God did not promise his people peace in this world amid its squalls; rather, he grants them peace in himself. To support this interpretation, Augustine quotes John 14:27, "My peace I give to you, my peace I leave with you."

Theological Pedagogy

Like Pss. 9, 22, and 26, the polemical aim of Ps. 29 is evangelistic in service to the universality of God's authority. While the immediate target population is the Canaanites, it also targets Israel, which is constantly tempted by its neighbors' religious practices. Listening Israelites certainly know that God could at any moment unleash the violent forces of nature against them. The psalmist's strategy here is to invoke raw fear of brute power, which God is not afraid to brandish when necessary, as evidenced by the transformation of the peaceful garden into the raging flood in the first six chapters of Genesis. Order and chaos are but a hair's breadth from one another, and God controls the space between them.

Perhaps a final note on the liturgical use of this psalm would not be out of place, given the power of its message. James Mays points out that Ps. 29 is often used for the first Sunday after Epiphany, which focuses on the baptism of Jesus. Echoing Ps. 2:7b, the voice of the Lord in the thunderstorm is paired with the voice from heaven in Matt. 3:17: "This is my Son."[8] As Mays puts it, "The storm says, 'This is my cosmos'; the baptism, 'This is my Christ.' The two go inseparably together. The Christology is not adequate unless its setting in cosmology is maintained. The Old Testament doxology is necessary to the gospel."[9]

In the Jewish sources, both *Midrash on Psalms* and Rashi connect the eighteen mentions of Adonai in Ps. 29 with the eighteen benedictions of the weekday Amidah (the central prayer of Jewish liturgy); thus Ps. 29 maintains an unparalleled place of honor in the Sabbath service. It is often sung by the congregation following the recitation of Ps. 148:13–14 at the conclusion of the reading of the Torah when the scrolls are returned to the ark.

The use of Ps. 29 in Jewish liturgical practice is not as clear as the Christian church's use of it in baptism, especially when one takes into account the water imagery. Psalm 29 is not a torah psalm or even one that celebrates Israel's heritage as God's own. Perhaps the liturgical placement may be explained by the repetition of the phrase "the voice of the LORD," which points the congregation to God's instruction (torah) through the reading of the Torah that has just been completed.

Nevertheless, both Christian and Jewish appropriations of this fearsome psalm relocate it quite far from the plain meaning of the poem. In effect, both faith communities transform it to build up and reinforce teachings and identities shaped by distant theological needs.

8. Both Basil and Theodoret connect this psalm to Jesus's baptism early on, perhaps setting the stage for the liturgical practice Mays notes.

9. Mays 1994b, 138.

PSALM 30

Canonical Context and Themes

Psalm 30 offers a host of familiar themes. An individual supplication, it speaks of a time of trouble and the experience of rescue. Typically, it widens its perspective to encourage the worshiping community not only to join in the rejoicing of the one rescued but also to maintain a confident hope that trouble, when it strikes—even if it signifies God's anger—will soon pass and well-being will return.

The description of an escape from death in 30:4 sparked multiple associations in the minds of commentators, indicating the poem's broad pastoral applicability. Theodore and Theodoret both associate it with Hezekiah's recovery, identifying the trouble behind this psalm as physical illness. *Midrash on Psalms* and Rashi both associate it with the demise of Haman and the reprieve of the destruction of the Jews in the book of Esther. Calvin and Ibn Ezra, however, interpret the near-death experience as a spiritual illness (as does Augustine); they associate it with David's anguish over his sins in the Batsheva affair and interpret the healing as receiving forgiveness. While Theodoret associates it with Hezekiah, he also makes a connection to Christ's escape from death by resurrection, as does Augustine, and both find the hope of resurrection the poem conveys applicable to everyone. Rescue is from illness, sin, the threat of violent death, or death itself, and the various biblical characters associated with one or more of these threats provide models through which readers can reimagine themselves.

Structure and Dynamics

While the distress-rescue dynamic of this poem is standard psalmic fare, its structure is counterintuitive. Psalm 30 opens by exalting God (30:1–3), shifts to addressing the local audience to urge praise for the rescue operation (30:4–5), and then moves into a lament mode (30:6–12). Within that dynamic, it also changes tense and orientation, beginning with how the speaker will extol God when he is rescued and adjuring his hearers to do likewise. It then turns back to the past with a plea for the rescue that has already been reported in 30:1–3 and finally returns to the joy of rescue with which the psalm began (30:11–12). To render the movements of the song more accessible, I will assume poetic license as an interpreter and comment on this poem in a rearranged order that allows the ideas to flow more readily. I retain the Christian verse numbering to reveal the modifications. The translation is my own.

Psalm 30

⁶ When life was easy I said: "Nothing will bother me."
⁷ It pleased you, LORD, to establish me as strong as a mountain.
  [But then] you hid yourself [and] I was overwhelmed.
⁸ I cried to you, LORD, and supplicated my master [saying]:
⁹ "What value is there in my death? If I descend into the grave, will the
  dust praise you? Will it tell your truth?
¹⁰ Hear, LORD! Take pity on me! Be my helper, LORD,
¹² so that my life may sing to you and not be silent. [Then,] LORD my
  God, I will give thanks to you forever.
¹ I will celebrate you, LORD, for you drew me up, and gave my foes no joy
  at my expense.
² I cried to you for help, LORD my God, and you healed me.
³ You brought my life up from the place of the dead, LORD, [and] restored me from being submerged in the pit.
¹¹ You have turned my mourning into dancing, removed my sackcloth, and
  girded me with joy."
⁴ Sing to the LORD, [you] his followers, and give thanks as you recall his
  holiness.
⁵ For his anger is fleeting, while his favor is for a lifetime. Weeping may
  spend the night, but joy comes with the morning.

Using this reordering, I comment on this poem in three segments.[1] Psalm 30:6–7 establishes the life of the speaker before troubles destabilized his life. Psalm 30:8–9, 10, 12, 1–3, and 11 tells the speaker's story, from his troubled time and cry for help to God's response of rescue. Finally, 30:4–5 turns to the local audience in celebration and praise, concluding the psalm on a joyful note.

Both Athanasius and Calvin read the emotional candor of the Psalter as holding up a mirror to the reader, encouraging her to read herself in its light. I follow that

---

1. The reordering in this psalm roughly follows Walter Brueggemann's rendering of the lament psalms, moving from orientation to disorientation to reorientation. My disagreement with Brueggemann's schema in this case is only that I read the experience of reorientation to be more or less a return to the status quo ante rather than a breakthrough to a new orientation along the lines of what Pauline conversion sometimes suggests (Brueggemann 1984, 2007).

suggestion by speaking in the first-person plural. "We," the readers of the song, find ourselves in and through it.

When Life Is Stable (30:6–7)

When life is stable, we think of ourselves as strong. Being untested, we imagine that we can withstand hardship. Even in hindsight, the psalmist's honesty here is admirable as it confesses an unproven strength that crumbled under pressure. It stands as a warning.

When Instability Intrudes (30:8–10, 12, 1–3, and 11)

When trouble comes upon us unawares and we are taken by surprise, as perhaps the psalmist was, we are liable to flounder in shock for a time as we try to get our bearings. Even if one can see the trail of events leading up to the distress, one may become defensive, seeking to offload blame. "This cannot be my life," but indeed "this is my life," says the unwanted voice of difficulty intruding on a hitherto uncomplicated life. Sadly, we often achieve insight about our situation only when pressed. Calvin takes advantage of this teachable moment in what he took to be David's life.

> This served to purge his mind as it were by medicine from the disease of perverse confidence. A marvelous and incredible method surely, that God, by hiding his face, and as it were bringing on darkness, should open the eyes of his servant, who saw nothing in the broad light of prosperity. But thus it is necessary that we be violently shaken, in order to drive away the delusions which both stifle our faith and hinder our prayers, and which absolutely stupefy us with a soothing infatuation.[2]

Calvin believed that by highlighting our wretchedness, suffering subdues the spirit, causing us to throw ourselves on God's mercy and to plead for favor as Ps. 30 does. Yet misfortune may have the opposite effect of hardening us with cynicism so that we focus on seeking personal advantage as we try to exercise any available shred of personal power or material gain. Indeed, believing that divine anger is behind one's difficult plight may turn one against God; by experiencing oneself as an innocent victim, one might blame others for an inclement life. Suffering may as readily drive one away from God.

Although he cries for mercy, the psalmist's behavior does not fit Calvin's characterization of the self-critical attitude he hopes will result from the speaker's troubles. On the contrary, the protagonist tries to argue God into rescuing him (30:9–10). His suffering does not reflect well on God, and it is in God's best interest to remediate the situation quickly. As I indicated earlier, the same argument is made in Ps. 6:5.

2. Calvin 1998, 493.

The suppliant tries to lure God into rescuing him by promising to sing joyously to him forever (30:12). Taking this promise as tantamount to confession, Augustine notes that one confesses two sorts of things: sin and praise. "When things are going badly for us, in the midst of our tribulations let us confess our sins; when things are going well for us, in our joy at his righteousness let us confess praise to God. Only, let us never give up confession."[3] With a comment like this, Augustine moves Christian attention away from the direct engagement with God that the psalmist enjoys and toward the position that Calvin would also take. Self-criticism and praise of God become the two standard forms of piety appropriate for the Christian.

In my reordering, the plea for help is answered. Psalm 30:2–3 and 11 bursts into celebratory song and dance, which is a response to the move from death to life—the fundamental Christian reversal of nature. While the order of nature demands that death follows life, the Christian order of redemption insists that life follows death based on the example of the resurrection of Jesus Christ of Nazareth. This reversal of nature is the order of hope. It challenges the order of nature that provokes despair that death has the final word. Whether the trouble be illness, sin, or death, the Christian message challenges the triumphant reach of them all.

When Joy Returns (30:4–5)

In my reordering, the psalm concludes in much the same way as other laments that draw the community into the experience. It exhorts the local congregation to sing thankfully for the passing of mourning and the dawn of morning. For those who can hold on until divine anger passes and suffering abates, the clothing torn in grief will be exchanged for garments donned in joy (30:11).

If we read the speaker's suffering through the prism of divine wrath suggested by 30:5 (echoing Ps. 6:1), a very high doctrine of divine control over history emerges—one that sees the experience of suffering as the expression of God's anger and the remission of suffering as the restoration of divine favor. Yet, quite unlike Christian theology, God exacts no additional pound of flesh. No further price need be paid to placate or propitiate divine wrath. God is not thirsty for blood to pay the insuperable debt of sin the suppliant owes, as second-millennium Western exegesis of the cross claims. According to Ps. 30, the assumption is that divine anger, fierce as it may be at times, abates of its own accord. As of yet, there is no judgment of an eternal decree regarding each individual that will last forever. Instead, one finds the rather comforting implication that enduring God's displeasure for a moment gives way to the restoration of his good pleasure for a lifetime. Perhaps the theology behind the thought is that suffering and death atone for any past wrongdoing, as in the case of David. In the Psalter, God does

---

3. Augustine 2000a, 313.

not demand death, as Christian theology would later suppose in order to make theological sense of the cross.

However, the message of the story of Hezekiah's recovery from illness has nothing to do with suffering as punishment or the abatement of divine wrath. Hezekiah received a new lease on life because he held fast to his trust in God against great odds. The psalmist conveys that if one can remain strong when pressed—as 30:6–7 implies the speaker could not—one's fortunes will change, for the only constant in life is change. One recalls tragic cases of adolescents mired in the typical despair that can characterize those tender years. Unable to see beyond the acute pain of isolating loneliness and the humiliation of social ostracism, they take their own lives. Perhaps this psalm is for them.

Theological Pedagogy

The theology and the pedagogy of this psalm are different depending on how one fills in the identity and circumstance of the complainant and of those rejoicing. This common observation is one of the great advantages of the Psalter. Its persistent ambiguity invites a wide variety of applications to people in all manner of circumstance, as the various commentators recognize.

The general point of the poem combats the experience of abandonment seen in Pss. 13 and 22 by proposing that God pays attention and is compassionate to those who cry for help and are faithful. The theodicy question is never far from those who suffer. The psalmist celebrates physical and spiritual resurrection in which those whose time of trial has passed look back on their misery to see God's steady hand at work in their lives.

To enjoy God's eventual favor, however, one must be patient—a lesson that pertains not only to individuals but also to whole communities, as the Jewish commentators' association of this psalm with the rescue of the Jewish people in the book of Esther makes clear. A Christian version of corporate rescue appears in Samuel John Stone's hymn, "The Church's One Foundation," which employs Ps. 30:5b in the third stanza:

> Though with a scornful wonder men see her sore oppressed,
> By schisms rent asunder, by heresies distressed;
> Yet saints their watch are keeping, their cry goes up, "How long?"
> And soon the night of weeping shall be the morn of song.

Embedded deep in this poem is a report of the kind of spiritual maturation that Calvin seeks for his readers. In my reordered version of the poem, the speaker starts out as one who thinks he will never stumble, only to uncover his own weakness when he does. Perhaps from the perspective of Christian piety, the turning point is when the speaker realizes that he cannot pull himself out of the pit into which he has fallen and that only divine mercy can pull him out.

PSALM 31

Canonical Context and Themes

"To some, lament psalms may appear as little more than 'lofty language' or shrill rhetoric meant to articulate the suffering of a petitioner."[1] Indeed, by this point in the Psalter, the major themes of the laments have been presented, and one may begin to become numb to their cries, especially without the experience of debilitating circumstances that call forth deep anguish or an inclination toward Stoicism. In the psalms, the idea that whatever comes one's way must be good is absent, as is the belief that one must celebrate one's suffering because God is good and all-powerful. Rather, tragedy is to be mourned, and this psalm both depicts and mourns a tragic circumstance.

Several details in Ps. 31 enable the reader to identify the speaker's situation a bit better than in some of the other psalms. The speaker refers to the offense or the crime (*ba'ăwōnî*) that is causing his suffering, which has been going on for many years (31:10). Furthermore, his affliction is both mental and physical (31:9), but despite his sin, he counts himself among the faithful (31:1, 3, 5, 14). Finally, he has been abandoned and is derided not only by his enemies but also by everyone who knows him (a detail that appears in other complaints); they shun him (31:11), treating him as if he were dead (31:12). Quite simply, he is a sorry mess.

Certainly important parallels can be drawn with Jesus, but not all of the details fit. While Jesus suffered both mentally and physically, his suffering did not last long, and although he was convicted as a criminal, he never admitted to guilt; the tradition staunchly maintains that the Romans executed an innocent man. Indeed, the standard theological argument holds that it is precisely his innocence that enables Jesus to propitiate God on behalf of others. In Ps. 31, the speaker admits his guilt and mourns it. He is aggrieved by his own fault and by the sins of others against him,

1. Tucker 2011, 70.

and he suffers physically as well as emotionally. His sin has damaged him, and the various punishments he suffers, especially the mockery of others, afflict him further.

If this is not a plight that everyone can identify with, perhaps one's understanding can be enhanced by putting more flesh on the wasting bones of the suppliant. Let us envision him as a thirty-nine-year-old African American male serving a life sentence in state prison for aggravated felony murder committed when he was sixteen years old. His stipulated sentence is thirty-five years, so the earliest he could be released is at age fifty-one. He never met his father, and his mother died of hepatitis, which she contracted through drug use. Since his incarceration, his four half sisters have neglected him. For years, he sought to meet with the children of his victim to repent and beg for some sort of reconciliation, but they were not interested. Prisoners receive a state allotment of twenty-eight dollars per month. A number of very low-paying jobs are available for inmates in the prison but not enough for all those who seek them. Prison food is cheap and exceptionally poor, and the prison store is expensive and lacking in variety. The state does not provide toiletries such as toothpaste. Medical and dental treatments are minimal, and inmates must contribute co-pays. All phone calls from inmates must be collect; phone calls to inmates are not permitted, nor are computers. Prison life is harsh, noisy, and ugly, and prison personnel can be lazy, brutal, and callous. Corruption and intimidation among both staff and inmates are rampant, and sometimes inmates are pressured for money or favors to be protected from other inmates as they engage in petty financial dealings to try to get ahead of the curve. Scant vocational or educational opportunities are available, although our inmate managed to earn the general education diploma in juvenile detention while awaiting trial. Desperately lonely, our prisoner contracted HIV-AIDS from another inmate in the twenty-first year of his incarceration. That inmate did not tell our inmate he was sick. Both are receiving medical treatment.

Of course, not every detail of this tragic story fits the psalmist's portrait. The speaker is not literally in prison, although he feels imprisoned by the combination of his sins and the calumny he bears. Still, the analogy is warranted because the psalmist suspends the speaker between the guilt of his sins and his humiliation by others who appear in the psalm as persecutors. Being both a sinner and the one sinned against is no paradox. It is simply an honest report on the circumstance in which most people find themselves.

Among the commentators, Theodoret is the most appropriate interlocutor for this approach to this psalm. He focuses on what he takes to be the historical context—David lamenting his murder of Uriah while being pursued by Absalom. Theodoret "gets inside" the character, and his insights are helpful here.

Structure and Dynamics

Psalm 31 is mostly written as a direct address to God in supplication, although it slips back and forth among supplicating God in prayer, offering gratitude to God for rescue, and speaking to the gathered community about God's goodness to the faithful. Like its immediate predecessor, Ps. 31 breaks sharply in the middle of the speaker's supplication to announce and joyously celebrate gratitude to God for release from affliction (31:5, 7, 8).[2] The plea for deliverance resumes thereafter until the speaker turns toward his local listeners, switching to the third person to speak of God at 31:21. He turns back to God for a minute at 31:22 and finally returns in 31:23–24 to encourage other sufferers to take courage in their own troubles, based on his own experience of being rescued.

To minimize the jarring effect of three verses of exaltation amid an ongoing despairing complaint, I will treat the three celebratory verses in the middle segment with those similarly oriented. I treat this poem in three major segments: the complaint (31:1–4, 6, 9, 10–18), a celebration of God's redemption (31:19–22 and 5, 7–8), and a concluding appeal to the local audience (31:23–24).

I Am Like a Discarded Pot (31:1–4, 6, 9, 10–18)

The bulk of this song pleads for God to deliver the prisoner from his tragic plight.

I PUT MYSELF IN YOUR HANDS (31:1–4, 6, 9)

The first and primary terror for which the speaker asks God's help is the shame he endures. Being faithful because he takes refuge in God's righteousness (31:1), he calls upon God to shame his slanderers by silencing them, even through death (31:17). The phrase 'al-'ēbôšâ appears in both 31:1 and 17. In 31:1 it appears as 'al-'ēbôšâ lĕ'ôlām, "may I not be forever shamed." He is being mocked and scoffed, as the poet makes clear. In both verses, the basis for the plea is his recourse to God. Theodoret captures the thought well: "The sin covered me in deep shame, he is saying, but I pray this may not long remain with me owing to my confidence placed in you."[3]

The implication is that taking refuge in God—in and of itself—should suffice to end the shaming, or at least tamp down feelings of embarrassment at being disgraced. The speaker's reliance on God should supply the strength he needs, which he goes on to explain in detail in 31:2–3. In effect, he is praying for the strength to let his trust be the vehicle of his rescue—not that external circumstances will change but that his ability to handle them will improve.

Wanting to escape humiliation motivates the speaker's cry for the shaming to end. However, feeling his own weakness, the prisoner asks God to attend to him and save him quickly by lending him his fortress-like strength, rescuing him

2. Calvin struggled with the incongruity at this point in the psalm: "I am rather inclined to think that stopping all at once in the middle of his prayer, he promises himself a deliverance, for which he will have abundant matter for giving thanks" (1998, 505–6).

3. Theodoret 2000, 192.

from the invisible net in which he finds himself trapped. The speaker's anxiety at humiliation gives rise to the sense that the coils of the net are the empty lies, the disgrace, and the calumny of those who scheme against him, though he admits to having done wrong.

For our inmate, the denunciations and scoffing may be based on fact, but the murmurings and shunning that accrue to him as a result, understandable though people's gossiping may be, are deeply painful to bear. As the psalmist tells us, the whispers are especially painful since they come from neighbors and people who know him and are spread through the community by those who no longer have anything to do with him. They dehumanize him, and it takes the strength of God to bear up under such castigation.

Soliloquy (31:10–13)

Within the complaint, Ps. 31:10–13 constitutes a self-reflection that, while still within the segment addressing God, expresses the speaker's conversation with himself as he assesses the state of his life. I commented on some of his thoughts above, but more can be said. As years pass, the prisoner wastes away emotionally and physically, grieving for the life that could have, should have, been. The evil-speakers pierce his self-respect, but that fades compared to the regret and self-recrimination he bears. The "if onlys" and "should haves" pierce him. He experiences himself as a lost or discarded utensil thrown out in the trash; it is as if he were dead.

Theodoret puts the feeling touchingly, commenting on 31:9–10, which recognizes that anguish like this is experienced viscerally in self-righteous anger and anguish deep in the gut to the point that one cannot eat and wastes away from lack of nourishment. "In other words, having provoked you to anger by sin, I must constantly weep, and in fact my soul is filled with distress and alarm. Now, he gave the name *stomach* to the recesses of his thoughts: it was his thoughts that were disturbed, not his stomach. *My life is wasted with pain, and my years with groans* [v. 10]. I have consumed all my life, he is saying, in pains and tears."[4]

In the case of our hypothetical prisoner, being neglected by those who knew and loved his victim may be understandable, but being shunned by those not directly involved, such as neighbors and acquaintances (31:11), expands the circle of adversaries. Theodoret drives the point home: "Everyone has given me up for lost, he is saying, like a vessel mislaid or a corpse occupying a tomb. He brought out the degree of forgetfulness by reference to the worthless vessel: just as when lost it vanishes from the memory of the losers for reason of its worthlessness, he is saying, so too am I in their estimation like someone non-existent and have become deserving of no esteem."[5]

4. Ibid., 194.
5. Ibid.

To make matters worse, even that larger circle expands as those within the prison walls watch him fade away as the fatal illness and hopelessness, its pungent side effect, gain the upper hand. The prison inmates and guards are the immediate community that withdraws from the speaker for their own reasons. The prisoner experiences and perhaps seeks ever more isolation, overcome by listlessness and despondency and perhaps clinical depression with its distractibility, psychosomatic complaints, and exhausting sleeplessness.

Continuing Plea (31:14–18)

In the concluding five verses of the complaint, the speaker manages to rouse himself from his torpor to repair to God. There only does he find acceptance and shelter; indeed, his faith is his strength. The seasons of his life are in God's hands (31:15), hands that he absolutely needs to cradle him, and in which he placed himself all along (31:5). He certainly cannot rescue himself. Everything has conspired to defeat him, but God's loving-kindness and strength may yet shine upon this miserable one (31:16). The supplicant begs God to still the proud and avenging voices that speak contemptuously of him and the rolling eyes that wordlessly dismiss him, be they on the street or within the confines of the now restricted community (31:18).

In addition to his casual and foolish behavior with money, property, and perhaps women, the prisoner now faces the brunt of the thoughtlessly undertaken tragic deeds that have destroyed his life. He has indeed been put to shame, and the only refuge left to him is God's indomitable love, which the prisoner must believe can triumph over the anger, frustration, and disappointment that God must surely feel upon seeing the tragedy of this child's lost life.

Of all the commentators, Theodoret alone recognizes the distinction the psalmist makes between sin and impiety. The speaker, while admitting his sin, still counts himself among the faithful. The belief that sin cannot efface faithfulness is the basis for the speaker's appeal:

> Then he shows the form of the redemption: *Lord, let your face shine upon your servant; save me in your mercy* [31:16]: when you make your appearance, gloom is immediately lifted. *Lord, let me not be confounded, because I called upon you. Let the ungodly be put to shame and cast down to Hades* [31:16–17]. From this we learn that the sin is very different from impiety; hence the mighty David beseeches that he be freed from the shame caused by the sin, but those addicted to impiety be sent in shame to their death.[6]

Although all are sinners, it may be that not all sinners put themselves in God's hands, feeling shame before God. Those who look for relief may seek release not from divine disapproval but from the public shame that accrues from public misbehavior.

6. Ibid., 195.

Celebrating God's Goodness (31:19–22 and 5, 7–8)

The second major segment of this relatively long psalm proclaims that God has rescued the speaker. Whether that means that the calumniating voices have ceased and the invisible net of vituperation has been ripped open is not clear. All that one "sees" is the celebratory mood of the speaker. Perhaps the original speaker's circumstance was not as dire as that of our inmate for whom salvation is harder to envision, so at this point the characterization breaks down. However, the rescue that the speaker experiences at the end of the poem is consistent with the plea for strength issued at the outset. Perhaps rescue is not a radically transformed external reality but the strength to reclaim one's indestructible dignity as one created in the image and likeness of God that not even heinous crimes can besmirch. He remains God's own.

This segment divides into three subsections as the poet changes grammatical voice. Psalm 31:19–20 addresses God as one who rewards the faithful, among whom the speaker counts himself, despite his mistakes. Psalm 31:21 turns to the speaker's immediate hearers, telling them of God's love for him. Psalm 31:22, along with 31:5 and 7–8, turns back to God, forming a unit that proclaims the supplicant has been redeemed; God came to his aid.

You Protect the Righteous (31:19–20)

In 31:19–20, the speaker speaks to God sotto voce so that the local audience is sure to hear, extolling the reward that God stores up for those who revere him and take refuge in him against all odds. Those sheltered in God are safe from the conniving wiles of wagging tongues.

God Rescued Me (31:21)

Continuing the celebration of rescue but changing grammatical voice, 31:21 addresses the local audience directly, telling them that God has rescued him from a "besieged city." The speaker reports how God's love operated on his behalf when he was in dire straits. He is clearly speaking to a later projected audience, not to those who have held him in contempt. Like many psalms, perhaps Ps. 31 began as a personal reflection that was later recast for general use, be that liturgical or personal, although it might also be a purely literary creation.

You Heard Me (31:22, 5, 7–8)

This gerrymandered pericope addresses God directly, celebrating whatever it is that the speaker experienced as salvation—one possibility being that he has developed the psychological strength not to be undone by derisive slander even though caustic voices have not been silenced. He hearkens back to his original cry for help and, behold, is answered.

In his comment on 31:22, Theodoret has a wonderfully realistic and compassionate insight into David as both sinner and sinned against. He precisely captures the situation of the speaker and of our hypothetical inmate who exemplifies him:

> I thought that on falling into sin, he is saying, I was far from your care; but you took account of my humble words and did not despise me in my need. Now, he rightly called his sin *departure* [Septuagint uses *ekstasei*; Masoretic Text uses *běḥopzî*]:[7] after treading the way of righteousness he left it and turned aside; but he stumbled and fell foul of bloodthirsty brigands [in being pursued by Absalom]. This very thing reveals David's virtue: he was not in the habit of sinning, but departing a little from his chosen course he suffered that awful slide.[8]

In the midst of that cry, Ps. 31:5, 7–8 bubbles over with the excitement of the rescue reported in 31:8. Though calm in tone, 31:5 states unequivocally that simply placing himself in God's hands constituted his rescue. In the Gospel according to Luke, Jesus recites the first clause of this verse, "into your hands I commit my spirit," as he dies (Luke 23:46). Quite independently, Ps. 31:5 became enshrined in one of the two major hymns of Jewish liturgy.[9] In addition, it is recited in the daily office of compline[10] and remains associated with the committal of the dead in Christian funerary rites.

While 31:5 is subdued, 31:7–8 (which is also addressed to God) is exuberant. Coming disconcertingly early in this song, 31:7–8 sings buoyantly of the rescue already recognized in 31:5.[11] An atmosphere of elation or surprise is evident here: the speaker has escaped his enemies' grasp. Rather than being constricted in a narrow place, as our inmate is, the speaker's feet are placed in a wide-open space with plenty of room to move. No longer hemmed in, he celebrates his freedom and attributes it completely to God.

Love the Lord and Be Strong (31:23–24)

As in so many of the psalms, the final verses of this poem urge readers to imitate the speaker as faithful adherents of the God who saves. Recapping 31:19–20, they reinforce that what God has done for the protagonist will be done for future suppliants. The psalmist urges classic virtues: strength, courage, and patience.

7. The Hebrew means "to flee hurriedly in fear." It describes the flight of the Israelites from Egypt in Exod. 12:11, which is recalled in Deut. 16:3.

8. Theodoret 2000, 196.

9. Birnbaum 1949, 11, 12.

10. *Book of Common Prayer* 1979, 132.

11. Goldingay deals with the disjointed structure of this poem by offering several suggestions. Either the repeated structure—roughly defined as plea-trust-praise—is a prayer that needs to be prayed twice, or the first declaration of trust and deliverance may refer to an earlier experience of salvation. Furthermore, the two parts might have been composed separately and later joined (2006, 434–37). While these explanations attempt to address the disjointedness historically, my purpose here is not to add to the elucidation of the history behind the text or of the text or of the liturgical use of the text, but to ask how the theology of the text might be helpful to us. It is to this end that I dare to treat the text in a revised order.

Theological Pedagogy

What then is the theological pedagogy of this psalm? What would God have us learn from the artistry of this poet and the heartrending predicament it depicts? Perhaps the most poignant observation is that cavalier divisions of people into saints and sinners should be questioned. In Ps. 31, it is the sinner's faithful clinging to God that catches the reader's attention. One does not either obey or abandon God *tout court*. People fall and recover, dwell in their guilt and cry for forgiveness, pursue and are pursued by turns throughout life. As Jesus said to the leering men crowding around an adulterous woman in John 8:7, "Let he who is without sin cast the first stone." Fuelled by righteous indignation and untempered by compassionate understanding for the weakness of human flesh (tragic though it be), the act of casting stones signals a brittle authoritarianism, the hypocrisy of which Jesus saw through instantly.

Perhaps the poet is inviting us to take our place in several of the roles offered by this psalm, much as Rembrandt invites us to assume the place of the father, the son, and the various onlookers in his painting of the prodigal son. We are David as well as the inmate, both sinner and sinned against. We are the neighbors and acquaintances of 31:11 who ignore the sinner, treating him like an unwanted pot—much like the priest and the Levite who ignored the crushed man because helping him would render them unfit for their sacred duties (Luke 10). But we are also members of the congregation of Israel hearing the story recounted, worrying about whether we will be treated so contemptuously for our misdeeds.

The psalmist hopes to soften us by having us look both inward and outward in order to recognize that the pain and suffering we experience, as well as inflict, leave their mark on us. Quite apart from the speaker's cry for aid is the psalmist's cry to resist dehumanizing sinners by treating them as if they were dead when they cry for mercy. Rather, we must trust that God will draw them to the guilt and repentance that they need to be transformed anew. Only then may we celebrate their true resurrection from the death of sin and failure and welcome them back into new life in Christ, ushering them into the community of light and grace in the company of God and the faithful who share new and unending life in him.

PSALM 32

Canonical Context and Themes

Psalm 32 glosses 31:10b of the previous psalm in which the speaker cries over his sin, having lost years in sorrowful sighing. One of the great penitential psalms of the Psalter, it lends itself particularly to second-millennium western Christian theology, which identifies remission of sin as the soteriological center of Christian interest—perhaps even the core of happiness this side of paradise. Salvation occurs either through sacramental absolution developed in the medieval penitential system, or through belief in a carefully developed interplay of doctrines including grace, faith, justification, and atonement.

Structure and Dynamics

Psalm 31 is bracketed by verses on either end that celebrate the relief experienced by the penitent who has unburdened herself before God and experienced refreshing forgiveness as a result. The middle section speaks of the burden of ruminating on one's sin and narrates the experience of confession and the need for redirection of life that follows it. Psalm 32:1–2 announces the theme to the gathered congregation. The next two verses rehearse the distress of Ps. 31 leading up to confession of sin at the following verse, while 32:6–7 expresses gratitude to God for the forgiveness the suppliant experiences as a result of confessing. The next two verses (32:8–9) are ambiguous. They are either written in the voice of God speaking to the penitent (or possibly over the heads of the congregation), or they are the voice of the one who has been forgiven, who now speaks credibly to his congregation on the experience of his new life. Psalm 32:10–11, like the final verses of Ps. 31, encourages those who trust in the Lord and live righteously. They are a closing parenthesis ensconcing the penitent in joy that radiates outward from him.

Blessed Are the Forgiven (32:1–2)

The repeated opening word of the first two verses of this psalm carries the reader back to the first word of the Psalter and forward to the Matthean Beatitudes. One who believes that one's sins are not held against one is truly blessed by God's grace. This thought is the heart of Luther's doctrine of justification by grace through faith. However, it is also quite close to Luther's doctrine of imputed righteousness, which might be better called a doctrine of imputed sinlessness when one considers the phrase, "blessed is the person whose sin (*'āwōn*) God does not think about."[1] God ignores it. The idea is not that God himself has paid what one owes, as Anselm of Canterbury would formulate atonement soteriology for the West at the end of the eleventh century; Psalm 32:1–2 makes no mention of a price needing to be paid.[2] Still, the opening verses explain forgiveness as having one's sins covered (*kĕsûy*), with the parallel in 32:2 being that sins are ignored by God.

In his core text on justification, Paul quotes Ps. 32:1–2 in Rom. 4:7–8 to advance the position that uncircumcised gentile men may benefit from the forgiveness the psalm promises "apart from works [of the law]," that is, without having to undergo surgery or even symbolic circumcision. The move is to encourage gentiles to become children of Abraham whose righteousness is reckoned to them, just as "David" speaks of having received it and offered it to the whole people of God.

Certainly the point is central to Luther, who wrote on it voluminously. In his 1521 comment on Ps. 32 he writes, "Here David says, in plain words, that all the saints are, and still remain sinners; and that they are justified and sanctified in no other way than this;—God of his free mercy, for Christ's sake, is pleased not to impute their sins unto them, nor to judge them, but, to forget them."[3] Calvin cites 32:1–2 (often together with Paul's use of them in Rom. 4) numerous times in his *Institutes*, in support of the Protestant doctrine of justification.

It may be noteworthy that Theodore of Mopsuestia, a Greek-speaking contemporary of Augustine, presents a rather "Protestant" view of these verses a millennium before the Protestant Reformation. In Ps. 32, David "teaches everyone, even if they are righteous, that they ought not trust in the merit of their actions nor attribute to themselves any good work. Rather, whatever good work they perform they should ascribe to divine grace and confess that God's mercy is necessary for them, and should believe themselves blessed if they deserve to have God well disposed toward them."[4]

To be sure, Jews were also taken with 32:1–2, although they worried less about the uncircumcised than Paul did and were not anguished by the fear of God's

---

1. The word *'āwōn* is the same word for sin used in Ps. 31:10.

2. Anselm 1985.

3. Luther 1837, 91. Luther's first lectures on the Psalms (1513–15) focus on the righteousness of God as punishment for unrighteousness. It was only later (1518–19), after he had been lecturing on Romans in 1515–16, that he worked out the idea "as a righteousness by which a just man lives as by a gift of God, that means by faith." (Oberman 1982, 165). Consequently, Ps. 32:1–2 came alive for him.

4. Theodore of Mopsuestia 2006, 279.

punishing anger as Luther was, as vivid images of hell in art and literature did not exist in rabbinic Judaism. The rabbis of the *Midrash on Psalms* stress the importance of faith, as Luther does, insisting that forgiveness requires people to "look up to heaven" (Dan. 3:31). Yet the rabbis go further. Along the line taken by the medieval church, they follow 32:2's concluding caveat that the forgiven are devoid of deceit or treachery (*rĕmiyyâ*). To them, the phrase "there is no deceit in his spirit" signals heartfelt repentance: "When a man's repentance is so complete that his heart is torn within him, the Holy One, blessed be He, forgives him."[5] Perhaps the most famous citation of this clause is in the Gospel of John. Seeing Nathanael approaching Jesus says, "Here is truly an Israelite in whom there is no deceit" (John 1:47 NRSV).

Jews confess their sins communally in the Yom Kippur liturgy, and Ps. 51:5 admonishes one to keep one's sins in mind. Recognizing how this practice could slide into unseemly virtuosity, R. Eliezer ben Jacob aptly advises that "a man should hold his sins ever before him, but that he need not keep speaking of them."[6]

The Burden of Guilt and Relief (32:3–5)

Psalm 32:3–5 reprises the complaint of the previous psalm and adds detail. While *kî-heḥĕraštî* literally means "when I went dumb" (unable to speak as a result of being deaf), translating it as "when I tried to conceal it" points out the inner stress of trying to hide one's sin—perhaps from God, perhaps from oneself. It will not work, the speaker tells us. Keeping quiet about sin (perhaps to protect himself from the painful gossip or punishment that Ps. 31 relates) only wore him out so that now he is constantly exhausted and wracked with distress. Theodoret, who insightfully understands the mess the speaker is in, reads 32:3 in light of David who concealed his guilt over the Uriah affair until Nathan confronted him. Imagining that the effect of the sin lingered long in David, Theodoret writes: "Since on receipt of the blow he did not at once show the wound to the physician but kept silence in an endeavor to conceal it, he grew old crying aloud and denouncing the sin."[7]

At 32:4, God's hands on the sinner are burdensome, not comforting as they were in Ps. 31:5 and perhaps 31:15. The heavy hand of God on him now dries him out like a hot Middle Eastern summer. When he can deceive himself (or avoid God) no longer, he makes a confession.[8] In some sort of public or at least vocal way, he externalizes the anxiety and, although no transaction or declaration indicating forgiveness occurs, he feels God lift the burden of sin. J. Clinton McCann notes

5. Braude 1959a, 403.
6. Ibid.
7. Theodoret 2000, 199.
8. The cleansing power of auricular confession leads one to wonder whether something was not lost with the Protestant abolition of the practice and its current neglect in the Roman Catholic Church with the liturgical renewal movement of the twentieth century.

that 32:5c is the turning point of this psalm; hereafter things are different. "The psalmist's confession of sin has been a cathartic, healing experience."[9]

Certainly, 32:5 is the psalm's center. The speaker apprises God of his sin; he no longer tries to hide it. The word the psalmist uses to say that he no longer conceals his sin (*lōʾ-kissîtî*) is the same word used at 32:2 to say that God covers his sin (*kĕsûy*). God covering and the sinner uncovering sin, or perhaps first uncovering and then feeling covered by God, is the central dynamic of release from a life organized around deceiving others about one's true identity. Given one's past, perhaps it is release from the self-deception of thinking that trying to conceal the deed does not matter. This trenchant poet shows the harm that comes from the cover-up. At least for people with a healthy superego, it doesn't work.

Joyful Shelter in God (32:6–7)

With the fever broken, so to speak, Ps. 32:6–7 turns from the speaker's personal situation to the joy of all the followers of God who should pray that they not be swept away in a torrent of distress as the speaker was. In retrospect, perhaps if he had confessed sooner he could have alleviated his suffering. After speaking to the faithful, he immediately turns—as is his wont—to address God directly. He who previously laid a heavy hand on the speaker now shelters him. Psalm 32:6–7 is a confession not of sin but of trust, for God now has credibility with the confessant, who feels forgiven even if there is no objective warrant for that feeling. With an alliterative crispness that is impossible to reproduce in English, the speaker exclaims that God now straightens him—he who had been in narrow straits—with the protection that he needs. He is no longer surrounded by threatening foes but by the rejoicing sounds of deliverance.

Instruction for Life (32:8–9)

Psalm 32:7 concludes with *selâ*, perhaps indicating a pause in the performance of the text, and 32:8 is a direct quotation spoken in the first-person singular, although the speaker is not identified. Most commentators read these verses as God speaking either to the one he has forgiven or to the whole community. He offers instruction and counsel for the new turn the speaker's life has taken following his sincere confession. Having been tamed, he must now begin a transparent life.

Since God is not named as the speaker, one can also imagine that the speaker the psalmist intends for these verses is the protagonist. Having been delivered from the shame of sin, he joins the ranks of the righteous (*ḥāsîd*), giving him a measure of credibility. As a teacher in Israel, he is now able to help others avoid the agony his stubborn pride produced. Whether the speaker is God or the jubilant

9. McCann 1993, 109.

penitent, the counselor will keep a careful eye on his charges that they not stray from the way they should go.

The advice he gives warns his auditors not to descend into animal-like stubbornness, like a horse needing to be broken or a mule that kicks. Neither understands what is expected or where it should go, so the trainer must employ the harsh instruments of bit and bridle to rein it in and keep it from coming dangerously close, perhaps to an unmounted trainer or groom. One wonders at the absence of the rider's crop to urge the reluctant animal to advance. The image of a strong and unruly animal that must be broken to serve its owner perhaps seems odd for one who has just picked himself up from grief and celebrated God's forgiveness.

If God is the speaker, the admonishing tone does not bespeak the impression of compassion and mercy that this poem implies at the outset when the speaker proclaims his confidence in forgiveness. Psalm 32:8 sounds angry and a bit resentful that the animal is so willful and independently minded, perhaps to the point of endangering its trainer. If one takes the speaker to be God, the dramatic shift in tone may be theologically instructive. According to the psalmist, forgiveness is not God "going soft" on us but rather God trying to get our attention, holding up a mirror to our most unflattering selves. If God manages to break through our stubbornness—not unlike the obstreperous horse and mule—our resistant behavior might be overcome, giving us a more realistic appraisal and redeeming the long period of languishing. Although the turning point of the song is gratitude at feeling forgiven, the pedagogical point is that those who are broken like rebellious steeds are transformed and made fit for civilized company, ready to contribute to the well-being of the community.

If the speaker is the penitent rather than God, the irritation in 32:9 reflects back on him as one reflecting on himself. Understandably, he tends to view other sinners in light of his own experience of despair and deliverance. A tinge of self-righteousness can be seen in the speaker, as if he is saying that since he overcame his stubbornness, confessed his sin, and is triumphing in God's grace, everyone should do the same; then they could all rejoice together! If others cannot or do not follow suit, he may be less than sympathetic with them.[10]

What then is the lesson here? While the speaker of 32:9 does not countenance violence against the horse or the mule, if the bit and bridle fail to keep the animal at a safe distance and the trainer feels threatened, he may be tempted to strike the animal, perhaps rousing it to kick harder and sparking a downward spiral. If that is what the future holds for the penitent, he did not use his redemption profitably. Consequently, he will lose access to the compassion with which God

---

10. In his dealings with the Jews of his day, Martin Luther is an example of this kind of thinking. When Luther was beaten down by the practices and expectations of the church, he understood why the Jews did not convert to Christianity. However, once the Protestant Reformation was well under way—and to his mind the impediments to conversion removed—he could not fathom how or why Jews withheld their consent to the truth of the gospel, and he turned against them violently (Luther 1971).

rescued him. Being transformed by compassion should move one to become more compassionate, directing the way forward.

Without pursuing these interpretive musings further, it may suffice to suggest that examining the dynamics of the situation—not only at the level of the text but also at the level of the characters portrayed therein—can be a fruitful pursuit. Indeed, the opacity of the text proves valuable for spiritual reflection.

One more question arises when considering these two intriguing verses. This commentary does not offer a definitive interpretation of the text, but invites the reader to consider who the speaker of 32:8–9 is according to the psalmist. That the stubborn animal in his charge could threaten the trainer in 32:9 is theologically noteworthy. If the speaker is God, the possibility that the "bucking bronco" might harm its trainer is jarring to theological sensibilities that hold God to be unharmable by human effort, no matter how violent. If the speaker is the penitent, being hurt by other stubborn mules is perhaps more palatable. Pastors may be insulted by parishioners who do not heed their sermons and admonitions, especially if being ignored makes them feel unequal to their mission. Given that 32:9 betrays the speaker's insecurity vis-à-vis his audience, perhaps it is more likely that the speaker of these two verses is the protagonist of the psalm, struggling to find his way in a new role with public responsibilities.

Let the Upright Rejoice (32:10–11)

Psalm 32:10–11 pulls back to reflect on the insights the speaker has gained from his experience. His ethic of just deserts tells him that good will triumph. Evil people will suffer the pains they deserve, but his readers—those who are righteous—will be secure in happiness by virtue of their trust in God. In short, honest people (*yišrê-lēb*) have no cause to fear and should feel free to sing joyously, secure in their identity.

Theological Pedagogy

Because Ps. 32 is central to western Christian soteriology, it is worth noting how Augustine, western theology's most important voice, interprets it. He wrote two expositions of this text: one a line-by-line commentary, the other a treatise on faith and works in the form of a long sermon probably delivered in the winter of 412–13.[11] The latter includes an extended introduction that articulates Augustine's position on the need for confession of sin that starts one on the path of spiritual growth and transformation. The development of the western doctrine of justification by grace through faith alone is Ps. 32→ Rom. 4→ Augustine→ Luther.[12]

---

11. Augustine 2000a, 362–87.

12. It is perhaps appropriate to note that Thomas Aquinas's doctrine of justification is also by grace through faith, but not necessarily by faith alone.

Augustine begins the sermon by saying that "this is a psalm about God's grace, and about our being justified by no merits whatever on our own part, but only by the mercy of the Lord our God, which forestalls anything we may do."[13] To live rightly one must tread a fine line between presuming that one's moral helplessness frees one from moral accountability and presuming that one does not need divine grace because one is morally adept.

Although the sermon is preached to Christians, it polemicizes against the pagan position that touts moral strength. Perhaps pagan psychology remains in the hearts of Augustine's auditors. He argues against this view using Rom. 4, where Paul teaches that Abraham pleased God only by his faith, proved by his willingness to slay his son at God's behest. If Abraham was justified by faith and not by any other aspect of his life or character, how can anyone claim moral virtue before God?

At the same time, faith as simply believing that God exists is not sufficient. It is not even relevant in a presecular age. Augustine takes up the ostensible disagreement on this point between the apostles James and Paul. James, who seems to support pious behavior as important, is actually correcting a common misunderstanding of Paul. "Good works" are the fruit of faith and cannot be achieved apart from it.

Turning back to pagans, Augustine argues that before coming to faith moral actions may seem praiseworthy, but they are sterile. An action is deemed praiseworthy by its intent, and that depends on whether it is informed by pure love, that is, love of God and neighbor. Deeds motivated by love are hopeful because they promote a good conscience. By contrast, those who suffer guilt regarding the motivations of their actions are without hope and can expect damnation.

Augustine braids the teaching on forgiveness in Ps. 32 with the three Pauline virtues—faith, hope, and care (*caritas*): "So it is through being forgiven that you begin to live in faith; that faith gathers to itself hope and the decision to love and begins to express itself in good actions."[14]

The sermon proper offers pastoral guidance to enhance Augustine's hearers' understanding of these matters. The first step is admitting that one is a sinner. The second is receiving the gift of faith, and the third is choosing to love following the humble example of Nathanael whose opposite number is the Pharisee of Luke 18:9–14 who is self-possessed. Reminiscent of R. Eliezer ben Jacob's comment on modesty, Augustine notes that the Pharisee failed to show the physician his wounds, and thus he commits the self-destructive error of concealment by talking about the wrong thing: "He should have kept quiet about his merits and shouted his sins; but he got it all wrong: he was silent about his sins and shouted his merits."[15] Augustine continues, "Yet, after all, he does come to recognize himself.

13. Augustine 2000a, 362.
14. Ibid., 370.
15. Ibid., 375.

In a minute he will gain understanding, for he will turn his gaze on nothing else but himself; and in knowing himself he will find himself unlovely. You are going to hear about this, for your own healing."[16]

This is the moment God waits for. Immediately after the Pharisee declares against himself, God forgives him: "My words were not yet in my mouth, but already God's ear was in my heart."[17] Augustine is at pains to explain that declaring against himself is a personal decision, not an act of fate controlled by his horoscope.[18]

The next step in spiritual growth is baptism (properly understood), which is the opposite of the "flood waters" of 32:6—that is, heretical doctrines that keep people from drawing near to God rightly: "This is the water that urges us to confess our sins, the water that humbles our hearts, the water of a way of life that leads to salvation, of those who abase themselves, do not presume on themselves at all and refuse any proud attribution of their achievements to their own strength."[19]

Augustine's immediate audience are baptized members of the body of Christ who should be dancing with happiness (as 32:7 puts it), even as they patiently endure the groans of misfortune awaiting the redemption of their bodies (Rom. 8:23). The faithful now have a special responsibility—to lift their eyes to God all the time (as *Midrash on Psalms* also admonishes) so that they are not like obstinate loose-tongued people who need to be reined in with bit and bridle. Taking God as the speaker of 32:8–9, Augustine understandably adds the whip to God's arsenal for subduing sinners "so that later, when they have been broken in, they may walk without the whip, and hold to their course without the need for bit and bridle. If you refuse your rider, it is you who will fall, not he."[20]

Yet again Augustine preaches against the crooked-hearted who resist God by raising the theodicy issue in opposition to a proper understanding of divine sovereignty. Right-hearted people (32:11) align themselves with the divine God. "Do likewise yourself," Augustine urges in conclusion, "and rejoice in the troubles that befall you; and if your last day is upon you, rejoice. If any of the frailty of your human will tries to take over, surrender it swiftly to God."[21]

Grace, then, is a strong tonic in the bishop's pharmacy. The psalmist's final verse that encourages trust in the Lord's kindness so that people might celebrate forgiveness and shout joyfully becomes a stern admonition against enjoying one's righteousness, even when it is not self-righteousness but properly God-given righteousness through confession, forgiveness, and subsequent good works. Augustine's pastoral pedagogy means to intimidate his hearers into deciding to join the straight-hearted and distance themselves from the crooked-hearted by following the steps he lays out.

16. Ibid., 375–76.
17. Ibid., 377.
18. Augustine constantly warred against astrology, which held powerful sway in his time.
19. Augustine 2000a, 380.
20. Ibid., 384.
21. Ibid., 387.

This, however, is not the theological pedagogy of the psalmist. By ensconcing the speaker's story in two sets of two verses each celebrating being freed and surrounded by divine loving-kindness, the message of grace triumphs over the penitent's anguish. The psalmist is able to encourage the enjoyment of faithful living in a way that Augustine apparently could not, the latter being ever vigilant against the daunting specter of vanity in his auditors. This fear fuelled his war against Pelagianism, which he waged until the very end of his life, and it has haunted the western theological tradition ever after. Thus, while Ps. 32 articulates theology that would become essential in western Christianity, the psalmist offers it in a far less anxious "tone of voice."

PSALM 33

Canonical Context and Themes

The absence of a superscription for Ps. 33 suggests that at one time it may have been a continuation of its immediate predecessor. Even if that is not the case, the mention of straight ones (*layšārîm*) in the first verse, which follows the straight-hearted (*yišrê-lēb*) who celebrate confidence in the Lord in the closing verse of Ps. 32 (32:11), links the two linguistically and offers a clue to the canonical ordering.

In either case, Ps. 33 elaborates 32:11 on the rejoicing of the righteous. The righteous celebrate the forgiveness they have received and proclaim it both within and far beyond Israel. Psalm 33 steps beyond Ps. 32 to establish God's authority unto the ends of the earth so that not only Israel but also all of humanity is responsible for revering God. The psalmist puts Israel's celebration of the righteousness that follows forgiveness in a universal setting, classifying it as another psalm that teaches Israel its global responsibilities beginning with the personal experience of one Israelite. Recognition of God then proceeds to the Israelite community at large and outward to embrace everyone. The psalmist teaches that the God of Israel is the maker of heaven and earth. Many centuries later, the structure of the Jewish liturgical blessing enshrined this bifocal theology as the core of all Jewish prayer with, "Blessed are you Lord, our God, king of the universe." God is God of Israel and the entire world. Psalm 33 is about the vocation of ancient Israel and of the Jewish people following it.

Poetically speaking, this psalm is exquisite—studded with alliteration, rhyme, creative diction, and beautifully balanced clauses that heighten its literary beauty. I will note some of these poetic features along the way.

Structure and Dynamics

Not being a supplication, Ps. 33 lacks the typical changes of audience; it addresses God directly only at the very end. Most of the poem addresses the psalmist's immediate audience, urging them to sing to God (33:1–3) the creator (33:4–9). The main section of the poem is 33:10–17. Within that, 33:10–11 teaches Israel that God's scope is global while 33:12–15 encapsulates the identity and mission of Israel and the Jewish people. Psalm 33:12 reinforces the standard biblical assumption that Israel constitutes the elect of God, but that identity sets the stage for appreciating the global theater within which God actually operates. Psalm 33:13–15 establishes God's worldwide authority; both Israel and its surrounding neighbors must properly understand God's international authority and power (33:16–17). The next two verses (33:18–19) announce God's providential care for those who revere him, while 33:20–22 speaks in the first-person plural of hope, joy, and trust in the Lord. Psalm 33:22 invokes God's love for those who hope in him, hearkening back to 33:18.

Sing, Praise, Rejoice (33:1–3)

The poem opens with the psalmist urging the righteous to sing triumphantly, lifting both their voices and their musical instruments in a "new song" that shouts joy. Just as Ps. 32 is bracketed by two celebratory verses, Ps. 33 is bracketed by three verses on either end, giving a clear introduction and conclusion that sing of trust, hope, and joy. This is the first of six canonical psalms that sing a "new song" to the Lord.[1]

Walter Brueggemann classifies Ps. 33 as a creation psalm, a song of "orientation" in his tripartite scheme of orientation, disorientation, and reorientation. However, if it is a gloss on Ps. 32, it is more nearly a psalm of reorientation that reestablishes the penitent's jubilation for having been restored among the righteous in Israel. The reorientation warranting a new song involves a turn or return to a life of "straight-heartedness" by one who erred and strayed from the right way like a lost sheep. Perhaps the celebration of one who was lost and now is found is even greater than that of one who never strayed.

God Speaks the World into Existence (33:4–9)

This subsection acclaims God as creator and governor of the world and all its inhabitants, as Pss. 2, 9, 18, and 22 have already attested. Divine sovereignty is not limited to Israel, for God exerts control over nature and history. The earth itself exudes the love of the Lord, and the straight-heartedness of those who revere God corresponds to the straight-heartedness of the works of the Lord that are all honorable since he loves righteousness and justice. Thus creation itself expresses

1. The others include Pss. 40, 96, 98, 144, and 149.

God's love of everything that is well-ordered, seen in the celestial bodies as well as the way oceans and seas function within proper limits. God's effortless capacity to create through speech should arouse everyone to awe and wonder.

Israel and the Gentiles (33:10–17)

DIVINE AND HUMAN PLANS (33:10–11)

The nations in particular are supposed to sit up and take notice of the one who speaks and breathes things into existence, for Israel's God created the world that sustains them. Perhaps echoing Ps. 2, the nations must attend to God's power that will frustrate their plans unless they comply with God's own design that will never be undermined. While the uprightness of the faithful (33:1) matches the uprightness of God's word (33:4), conversely the counsel ('*ăṣat-*) and plans (*maḥšĕbôt*) of the nations (*gôyim*, 33:10) are no match for the counsel and plans of God that will stand forever (33:11). The Israelite psalmist clearly views the plans of the nations as nefarious, perhaps directed against Israel. Theodore and Theodoret both read this psalm as David's prophecy of the miraculous fall of the Assyrians in 2 Kgs. 18–19, especially in light of 33:16–17. This puts Israel on notice concerning God's designs on the nations and restructures Israel's relationship with them. The poet uses three different phrases to identify non-Jews as central to God's plans: "all who inhabit the universe" (*kol-yōšĕbê tēbēl*, 33:8), "all human beings" (*kol-bĕnê hā'ādām*, 33:13), and "all who dwell on earth" (*kol-yōšĕbê hā'āreṣ*, 33:14).

THE BLESSED CHOSEN (33:12–15)

These four verses constitute the core of this poem. The opening half-verse of this subsection (33:12a) reappears verbatim in Ps. 144:15b with the substitution of one word. Psalm 33 reads, "Blessed is the nation (*haggôy*) whose God is the LORD," while Ps. 144 reads, "Blessed is the people (*hā'ām*) whose God is the LORD." The two words are often translated as if they were synonyms, but in this case they may not be. While 33:12 might well refer to Israel, as the second clause of the verse strongly suggests with the mention of God's chosen heritage, 33:13–14 is about gentiles, and 33:15 concludes the segment by adding that God has made all people and watches over all they do. The phrase "people of Israel" ('*am yiśrā'ēl*) appears in 2 Sam. 18:7 and 19:41 as well as Ezra 2:2 and Neh. 7:7, but the phrase *gôy yiśrā'ēl* (nation of Israel) never appears in scripture; however, the phrase *gôy qādôš* (a holy nation) does appear in Exod. 19:6 in reference to Israel. One further clue to the intention of Ps. 33:12a is that the word *gôy* appears in the plural (*gôyim*) just two verses earlier where it clearly means gentile nations. Given these several linguistic considerations, it is possible that the two clauses of this verse refer to the gentiles as belonging to God along with Israel, the people (*hā'ām*) God has chosen as his heritage. While standard Hebrew parallelism usually repeats the same idea using different words in each clause of the verse, it may also amplify the basic idea. That this poet uses words so carefully is reason to think that the latter is the case.

If 33:12 does group the gentiles with Israel as having the Lord as their God, both Israel and the gentiles must change their self-understanding as well as their understanding of each other; a strictly adversarial relationship between them would be obsolete (which is hinted at in Ps. 2), albeit in a circuitous way. According to Ps. 33, Israel is chosen as God's means of "choosing" all humanity. This theology does not match up with Deut. 7, for example, in which God sets Israel apart from and over against gentiles:

> For you are a people holy to the LORD your God; the LORD your God has chosen you out of all the peoples on earth to be his people, his treasured possession. It was not because you were more numerous than any other people that the LORD set his heart on you and chose you—for you were the fewest of all peoples. It was because the LORD loved you and kept the oath that he swore to your ancestors, that the LORD has brought you out with a mighty hand, and redeemed you from the house of slavery, from the hand of Pharaoh king of Egypt. (Deut. 7:6–8 NRSV)

Psalm 33 does not set this theology aside, but it does carry it in a dramatically different direction. Here, God sets Israel apart from gentiles for the sake of gentiles, to show the way to God. In Deuteronomic theology the military and political struggles between Israel and gentiles—as well as the Deuteronomic injunctions to Israel not only to avoid gentiles, lest they pollute Israel with idolatry, but also to destroy their religions and their military power, even to the point of annihilation—sanction deep and lasting hostility between Israel and its neighbors. This attitude is reinforced by passages like the encounter between Hezekiah and Sennacherib that treat Judah and Assyria as deadly enemies. Against this strong biblical precedent, the psalmist teaches both Israel and its neighbors a radically different theology, one in which Christians would later be inscribed.

In Ps. 33, God is more than Israel's protector, and Israel is called to more than simple faithfulness to covenantal precepts. God is using Israel to be the Lord of the universe, and Israel is to be obedient in service to that end. The point of there being but one God is that other ways must be abandoned; all must revere and worship the one who sees everyone. This belief in universal divine authority and power may be the product of the exile, during which Israel discovered that God could be worshiped in Babylonia without the temple and perhaps could even be brought back upon their return. No indication is given here concerning what the conversion of the gentiles might look like or how it might happen, but 33:16–17 does make clear how it should not happen.

NOT BY MIGHT (33:16–17)

Again, the story of Hezekiah and Sennacherib lingers in the background. These antimilitaristic verses strike against Deuteronomic injunctions to conquer territory militarily. Instead, the counsel of Ps. 44 and Zechariah ring in one's ears: "Not by their own sword did they win the land, nor did their own arm give them victory; but your right hand, and your arm, and the light of your countenance, for you delighted in them" (Ps. 44:3 NRSV); "He said to me, 'This is the word of the LORD to Zerubbabel: Not by might, nor by power, but by my spirit, says the LORD of hosts'" (Zech. 4:6 NRSV).

But by Love (33:18–19)

Psalm 33:18–19 draws the reader away from the politics of the triangle of God, Israel, and the gentiles to shape the expectation of those who hope for God's loving-kindness. If my read of 33:12 is warranted—for this is, indeed, a postexilic theology that focuses on the universality of God—those who revere the Lord and to whose needs God tends include both Jews and pagans, even though they remain two distinct communities. The psalmist holds out the promise that God will have such love for those who revere him and that he will save their lives, be it from famine or some other threat.[2]

We Hope in You (33:20–22)

The final segment of Ps. 33 speaks in the first-person plural. Again, the poet connects the verses linguistically, although the poetic flair is difficult to capture in English. In 33:19, the hope that God will save people from death immediately shifts to "our lives" in 33:20 as all wait hopefully for the Lord. The poet joins his voice to those of whom he has been speaking in the third person. He and they are willing to wait for the Lord, who protects them because they joyously trust. At the last, the poet invokes the Lord's loving-kindness on those who hope expectantly.

Theological Pedagogy

From Israel's perspective, this poem is about Israel's vocation in the world—its ministry to gentiles as the people chosen by God to acknowledge and revere him in covenant faithfulness, proclaiming him to all the nations. Therefore, when Israel is opposed by the nations, Israel must be against the nations for the sake of the nations rather than against them for its own advantage.

From the perspective of the gentiles, this theology is humbling, even a bit humiliating. For those who are confident in their national, religious, moral, and political identity, the idea that Israel (who is deemed their enemy and is perhaps the power that has taken their land) possesses knowledge of and access to the one

---

2. English translations that render 33:19a as "deliver their soul from death" may misleadingly suggest immortality of the soul. That idea did not exist in ancient Israel.

true God (whom they must come to acknowledge and revere) is destabilizing. Ironically, these "sworn enemies" turn out to be the source of each other's life and hope. For Israel, the gentiles enable them to fulfill their divinely ordained mission. For the gentiles, Israel provides the way to God, the way to life, and deliverance from death.

PSALM 34

Canonical Context and Themes

Psalm 34 is a sermon in the form of an acrostic poem and is often considered a wisdom psalm because of its central section. Its influence is confirmed by its citation in both John's Gospel and 1 Peter as well as at various points in Jewish liturgy.[1]

From a canonical perspective, Ps. 34 follows its predecessor by inviting its hearers to join the ranks of both the righteous who revere and celebrate being God's own and the speaker who has experienced rescue and redemption. It is a motivational speech, being perhaps the ancient analog of an altar call that invites people to commit themselves to the Lord in what may well be a setting of public worship.

This psalm's superscription is a bit odd in that its assignation is neither patent nor accurate. It reads, "For David, when he feigned madness before Avimelech who drove him away, and he departed." The allusion is to 1 Sam. 21:14 where David saves himself from Achish of Gath by acting deranged. The psalmist's mistaking Avimelech for Achish may perhaps be accounted for by the fact that 1 Sam. 21:8 mentions Avimelech, but that too would be an error.[2] Perhaps the editor was working from memory.

Apart from this, the connection to this event in David's life is still not clear. Robert Alter suggests the following: "In all likelihood, the connection [the editor] saw was the psalm's emphasis on God's rescuing power, even when the just man is threatened with imminent death by his enemies. Particularly pertinent are these lines near the end of the poem:

1. This chapter is based on Charry 2010, 208–12.
2. Commentators have attempted to account for this error. Rashi suggests that Avimelech is not a personal name but a title for all Philistine kings. Ibn Ezra suggests that Achish and Avimelech are two names for the same person.

Many the evils of the righteous man,
>   yet from all of them the LORD will save him.
He guards all his bones,
>   not a single one is broken.[3]

Whatever the rationale for the superscription and its assignation to Ps. 34 may be, this poetic thanksgiving for rescue (with the usual moral exhortation to righteous living on the part of the afflicted) is connected to a story of subterfuge, itself worthy of comment. This poem's energy impresses the poet's hearers with the speaker's reliance on God. And yet its example is a king who successfully used deception to save himself from danger. Does that encourage reliance on God? Obviously, the editor was not cowed by the mixed message. In contrast to a piety that would counsel passivity when under duress, waiting patiently for God to *do something*, the editor is quite comfortable having David act on his own behalf without drawing the conclusion that self-help in any way detracts from the power of God to rescue. Indeed, the poet is determined to instill reverence for God into his hearers precisely because he trusts that God surely hears and rescues them. No tension can be discerned here between acting on one's own behalf—even employing trickery—and relying on God. Perhaps the point exemplifies the old adage, "God helps those who help themselves." The message of the superscription seems to be that God wants his people to act on their own behalf; God acts in and through acts of self-preservation.

This attitude contrasts with passivity on the part of the pious that Augustine seems to promote with his comment on the opening verses of this psalm, especially "let the humble hear and be glad" (Ps. 34:2). "The Lord wants gentle, compliant animals for his use; so you be the Lord's beast; be gentle, I mean. He sits on you, he himself controls you. Do not fear that you may stumble or fall headlong. Weakness is characteristic of you, certainly, but think who your rider is. Donkey's colt you may be, but you are carrying Christ."[4]

Structure and Dynamics

This entire poem addresses the local audience. I consider it in three parts. Psalm 34:1–10 alternates between the poet lavishing praise on God that explains how God works on behalf of those who revere him and urging his hearers to seek the Lord based on the speaker's positive experience with God. Psalm 34:11–14 gives concrete advice for a morally good life in the form of proverbial wisdom. The next segment, Ps. 34:15–22, further elaborates God's way, both with the righteous who take refuge in him and with the wicked who will be condemned. Following the advice of the psalmist, taking refuge in God is living wisely.

3. Alter 2007, 117.
4. Augustine 2000b, 26.

"Taste and See" (34:1–10)

The first ten verses of this poem alternate personal testimony, in which the speaker tells the story of his rescue and of God's protection of those who revere him (34:1, 2, 4, 6–7, 10), with a staccato series of doxological exhortations to join the speaker in a holy life free from shame and want (34:3, 5, 8–9). Psalm 34:2, 3, 5, and 7 all have six words in two clauses each, giving a clipped dynamic rhythm to the recitation that conveys the speaker's excitement. His joy overflows, and he eagerly shares both his experience and his elation as he moves rapidly from praising God to telling his story and then exhorting his hearers. In telling them why he blesses and praises God continuously, the speaker means to comfort and encourage the humble who, upon learning of his experience, will be happy (*wĕyiśmāḥû*).

The opening salvo (34:1–2) is two clipped declarations of what the speaker is doing now: blessing and praising the Lord continually, with words and in silence. He immediately turns to invite his audience to join his doxology and share his joy by magnifying and praising God together (34:3).[5] Psalm 34:4 explains this praise and adoration of God in terms of the speaker's own experience and uses it as an offering of encouragement. He sought the Lord, and the Lord relieved his terror (*hiṣṣîlānî*).

Again, the speaker stares intently at his hearers. If they will also look to God (by living a wholesome life), their faces will not flush with shame. Perhaps he is implying that they will not be ashamed when trouble strikes because no one will say that their trouble is justly deserved. While it is clear that the speaker's enemy is terror, he does not explain what causes it. However, he turns to his auditors and assures them that their confidence in God (literally "radiant faces") will protect them from the comparable emotional distress of shame. A face radiant with confidence in God will not flush, for the person has nothing to hide and so nothing to fear, shame being the object of fear. Another interpretation might be that no manner of humiliation can touch the radiance of those whose moral strength comes from their confidence in God. The speaker is building up his hearers' confidence in their ability to withstand trouble by assuring them that they already have the strength they need, for they share the humble, reverent life that God favors.

Psalm 34:7–9 offers protection for these pious ones. The scene changes, or rather emerges. Until now there has been no scenery, no images to locate the narrative spatially. With 34:7 the reader finds herself encamped. It might be in a military theater, or, as 34:10 suggests, the jungle; it does not matter. The place is danger-filled. The pious who have heeded the singer's advice are protected by an angel (their humility?) and saved, whereupon a peal of rejoicing goes up in one of the most famous lines in the Psalter. The poet applauds his audience: "O taste and see that the LORD is good; happy (*'aśrê*) is the one who takes refuge in him"

---

5. Psalm 34:3 is canonized in Jewish liturgy and generally sung aloud by the congregation after reading from the Torah scrolls.

(*yeḥĕseh-bô*, 34:8). He continues building his hearers' confidence, reassuring them that they are God's holy ones; they revere him, and so they lack nothing. Living wisely is all that they need; it is their protection. To reassure them once more, the speaker employs a dramatic and unexpected image. He contrasts his attentive listeners with young, hungry lions prowling for food; it is meant to comfort them. They need not worry that they might become prowling lions.[6] The high ground on which they stand is firm, and they are prepared for what may come.

Living Wisely (34:11–14)

In this strophe, the psalmist speaks as a moralist striking the classic didactic pose of Proverbs.[7] While he cultivates his hearers' interest through empathy and encouragement in the first part of Ps. 34, here he carries the holy ones (*qĕdōšāyw*) deeper into their reverence for God and gives their piety concrete form and content. Though taking refuge in God to avoid terror is necessary, it is not sufficient. Perhaps a connection, albeit an oblique one, can be made here to the idea posed by the superscription: trust in God must be complemented by acting in one's best interest.

The opening verse of this segment (34:11) invites the reverent to gather around the teacher as he delves into the nature of their reverence. A strong theme in this poem, reverence, appears in 34:7, where the reverent are protected by God's angel, and twice in 34:9. Reverence is holiness, and those who practice it lack nothing. As in the first half of this psalm, the students are avid learners. The teacher's work will not be difficult; the students want his teaching.

The lesson begins when all are gathered, and it takes the form of direct address in the style of 34:3, 5, 8–9. The core of the lesson consists of two straightforward rules (which remain unsurpassed) for a happy life. First, one must guard the most unstable organ of the body: the tongue. Second, one should avoid evil and do good by pursuing peace. Herein is "reverence for the LORD" (34:11).

God's Attentiveness (34:15–22)

Most of Ps. 34 presses the point that a morally good life is the best protection against the fear of shame. In the third part, the focus turns to God, lest one think he has dropped out of the equation. The preacher and the moralist combine to encourage the audience to stay the course because God is watching and listening and will take action (33:15–17). The poet explains God's attitude and behavior toward the upright and the wicked, emphasizing the former. Once again the territory of Ps. 1 comes into view with its classic just deserts morality and an *ex cathedra* mode of operation. The righteous flourish, the wicked perish, not only by virtue of their way of life but because God intervenes either to rescue or to

---

6. Psalm 34 is quoted by 1 Peter: Ps. 34:8 at 1 Pet. 2:3; Ps. 34:12–16 at 1 Pet. 3:10–12.

7. Psalm 34:12–16a is quoted verbatim in 1 Pet. 3:10–12.

punish. He attends to both the upright and the wicked—to save the former and sternly erase the memory of the latter from the face of the earth.

The final six verses (Ps. 34:17–22) reveal that God has a soft spot in his heart for the brokenhearted and for his afflicted loyalists. Although troubles will assail the righteous, God will protect their bodies by fighting for them so that not one of their bones will be broken; furthermore, the poet assures them that their enemies will die condemned. In a reprise of 34:8, the poet assures the pious that God redeems those who cover themselves with him (*kol-haḥōsîm bô*, 34:22).

Theological Pedagogy

John 19:36 reads Ps. 34:20 as prophesying a detail of Jesus's crucifixion, since he died without needing to have his legs broken to speed up his death. Augustine, who often seeks to spiritualize material references in scripture, warns not to take this promise in a material sense: "The 'bones' are the firm supports of the faithful. In our bodies the bones provide strong support, and in the same way faith provides firm support in the heart of a Christian; and endurance born of faith is like a spiritual skeleton. These are the bones which cannot be broken."[8]

Theodore of Mopsuestia has a telling insight into the apparent tension between the suffering of the righteous and the statement that none of their bones will be broken. He writes:

> Far from simply allowing even those in tribulations to suffer under those distressing them, he rescues them after allowing the tribulations for a while to their advantage, keeps those in the midst of tribulations free from harm, and preserves their strength completely. This is the meaning of *all their bones*—that is, so that they incur no severe risk. Hence, *will not be broken* was well put, meaning "they will incur no risk," since what is broken naturally meets with complete destruction.[9]

By distinguishing suffering from harm, he may have in mind physical suffering, from which one may recover, as opposed to the possibility of destruction, from which there is no recovery. But the distinction also may be between physical suffering and moral and psychological suffering—a distinction made briefly in my comments on Pss. 3 and 23.

While Jesus suffered physically from being whipped, carrying the tree, and being pierced with the nails, the experience of being abandoned by those he loved, who neither lifted a finger to object to his being seized nor sought to rescue him, is another kind of suffering entirely. He experienced the indignity of being abandoned by God and by those who loved him and whom he loved. However, Jesus did not experience degradation; he experienced physical pain in the one case and

---

8. Augustine 2000b, 41.
9. Theodore of Mopsuestia 2006, 335.

the spiritual anguish of betrayal in the other. What may look like degradation is not. It was his executioners and those who abandoned him from timidity who degraded themselves; they could not rise to the occasion even to protest. It is the shame of having one's moral weakness disclosed that is humiliating. Psalm 34 has a Stoic ring to it, though that philosophical school did not exist at that time.

One might consider the horrible beatings and torture experienced by slaves during the American slavocracy, which are detailed in a narrative such as the *Life and Times of Frederick Douglass*.[10] In such cases, the one enduring pain is the slave, but the one being morally harmed is the master who administers the beating. By doing so, the master denies his own dignity, not that of the slave. With the perpetrator's sinfulness in plain view—even if only to the victim and God—the victim may be physically injured but not morally harmed.

Looking at this from a theological perspective, human dignity is a gift of God through which one understands oneself to be made in the divine image; according to the Christian perspective, it means becoming a child of God through baptism. Although the cases of Jesus and Frederick Douglass are far from identical, in both cases shame accrues to the perpetrators of violence, not its victims. Jesus and Douglass were anguished at their treatment, but they were not degraded. They were insulted; they suffered, but they were not vanquished. They retained their integrity, standing for their principles. Indeed, their moral stature was enhanced by the treatment they endured. Moral dignity is something over which one has control, and Ps. 34 calls us to guard it well. No one can take it away or damage it; only we can do that.[11]

To put a more doctrinal edge on the point, sin degrades—not political, economic, or social oppression, not accident or illness. Such stressors are damaging and can lead to self-degrading behavior. Certainly they can become harmful if they press one into untoward patterns of behavior and action. Yet in and of themselves they do not harm however much they hurt. Redemption from sin is the restoration of moral integrity after having degraded oneself by harming others.

10. Douglass 1962.
11. See also Chrysostom 1889.

PSALM 35

Canonical Context and Themes

Psalm 35 presents another personal complaint with a strong imprecatory element. It implores God for vindication, asking him to punish the speaker's tormentors and repeating the cry for justice that is heard in Pss. 7, 12, and 28. Psalmic poetry in Jer. 18:18–23 and 20:10–13 that contains the same themes and tone as this psalm prompted Theodore to attribute Ps. 35 to Jeremiah, albeit as David's prophetic utterance about what Jeremiah would later write.

Commentators often contrast the psalmist's emphasis on God's justice with Christianity's interest in the attribute of mercy, in which case this psalm seems to be discomfiting. Theodore and Theodoret both struggle with the problem. The latter cautions readers not to be misled:

> I beseech those reading it not to incur even the slightest harm from the prayer of the righteous man nor make it the occasion for curses against one's enemies, but realize that the inspired author was adopting the way of life sanctioned by the Law, not by the Gospels.... Looking at this difference, therefore, realize what is in keeping with the Law, and what with grace. In particular, it was not to deliver a curse that David said this; rather, in inspired fashion he foretold what would clearly come to be.... even he did not take vengeance on those who wronged him.[1]

Theodoret points out that David is leaving the administration of justice to God and not taking matters into his own hands. This is an especially important point for societies without effective judicial systems where tribal loyalties tempt people

---

1. Theodoret 2000, 216–17.

to do just that, inciting round after round of tribal vendettas. God will act as and when God will, and it is appropriate for people to urge God to act in accord with the justice proper to his character.

It would be shortsighted, however, to contrast a biblical focus on justice with a later Christian focus on mercy. While Christians are wont to stress divine mercy and forgiveness as chief traits for human emulation, justice is never far from Christian concern and is often articulated in terms of God's hatred of sin in order to stimulate humility and repentance. The centrality of the themes of atonement and justification in second-millennium western theology attest to the importance of satisfying the demands of justice in a Europe struggling its way through the lawlessness that followed the collapse of Mediterranean civilization. Although like Jeremiah the psalmist seeks harsh punishment for his persecutors, the sting of this imprecation abates at least somewhat when one considers that the psalmist is not taking revenge on his enemies but asking God to repay injustice sternly, perhaps as a deterrent. Yet there is more.

Structure and Dynamics

Following the customary segmentation, I treat this poem as three laments run together: 35:1–10, 11–18, and 19–28. Each concludes with a promise to celebrate God, following the pattern observed numerous times in these poems. Of these, only the first and third laments seek the downfall of enemies. The second testifies to the speaker's own exemplary way of life, which has netted him only derision.

Fight My Fight, O Lord! (35:1–10)

The first mini-lament is the harshest of the three. It asks God to take up instruments of war against the opponents, shaming and dishonoring them (35:2–3). As noted earlier, the shame-honor dynamic is at work in Pss. 4, 6, 22, 25, and 34, where shame is the great calamity that terrifies the speaker. Like Ps. 6:10, Ps. 35:4 asks for shame to beset his antagonists, even as the protagonists in the earlier poems beg to have shame lifted from them. Turnabout is fair play in the service of justice; the wicked, not the righteous, should rightly be dishonored. Similarly, the speaker asks God to trap his pursuers in the very snare they have set for him, treating him like an animal (a theme seen in Ps. 9:15). The psalmist appeals to God's sense of justice. The wicked should experience the evils they have devised for others.

Psalm 35:8 sustains the intense anger of this call for revenge, and the speaker asks that unanticipated disaster strike his foes. Twice repeated, the word "disaster" (šô'â) is particularly chilling to today's readers because it is the word used of the Nazi genocide.

Previous psalms also reverberate in this mini-lament's concluding promise to celebrate the power of God if indeed his enemies are thwarted. Sustaining the theme of reversal in which his enemies are shamed in his stead and fall into the trap they have set, 35:10 reverses the terror of quaking, melting, and disjointed bones reported by the psalmist in Pss. 6, 22, and 31. In the event of vindication, both his spirit and his bones will praise God, who is the incomparable deliverer of the poor and needy.[2]

But as for Me . . . (35:11–18)

The second mini-lament takes this poem in a quite different direction, escaping the notice of some commentators. Along with condemning the adversaries, it touts the virtue of the speaker. For later Christians (for whom humility is the chief virtue), seeing the speaker point to his righteous deeds may be off-putting, but the scene calls for a thicker hearing. The psalmist is almost defiantly identifying admirable behavior that would be most seemly if pointed out by someone else. His social ineptitude may damage his admirableness, but at least he leaves his reader with behavior to emulate. Still, there is more to be said.

Lest one conclude that these are three unrelated laments, it is noteworthy that the poetic use of reversal to press a point connects this mini-lament with its predecessor. While 35:8 asks God to bring destruction on the enemies caught off guard (*lō'-yēdā'*), 35:11 finds the protagonist caught off guard (*lō'-yāda'tî*). The phrase *lō'yāda'tî* recurs at 35:15, where unknown strangers assail the speaker. Being taken by trouble unawares is a central feature of the terror that besets the righteous when assailed by enemies. Indeed, those who abjure Ps. 35 as morally inferior to the Christian preference for mercy and forgiveness may yet be taken aback.

The poet makes the strategy of reversal explicit in 35:12 as he begins his defense by identifying the egregious behavior of his adversaries against which he measures himself virtuous. He acted justly; they repaid him with injustice. As the central motif of the psalm, he enumerates his pious deeds, saying that he donned the accoutrements and postures of mourning and fell to prayer, perhaps beating his breast, ostensibly for the sin he admits to committing. Although he mourned as if for a close relative, his penitential sincerity was met with scorn in the faces of unknown ruffians.

As in the case of Ps. 32, the speaker admits to falling; his penitential demeanor is not only warranted but also praiseworthy. What is not warranted is the glee of strangers in the face of one who is humbled by his sin, for it packs humiliation upon humility. It feels like teeth sunk into raw flesh. In light of his mortification, the penitent pleads again for rescue, and this mini-lament concludes with a promise of public thanks and praise.

---

2. The phrase depicting God's incomparability, "who is like you" (*mî kāmôkā*), is from Exod. 15:11 in the Song of Moses, which is sung at the deliverance of Israel at the defeat of the Egyptians at the Red Sea. The quotation would certainly not be lost on the psalmist's hearers.

Do Not Let Them Win! (35:19–28)

The final mini-lament of Ps. 35 returns to the anguish of experiencing baseless hatred (35:19).[3] It is one thing to jeer at an unrepentant sinner in order to get him to repent but quite another to revile the sincere penitent the speaker has shown himself to be; he has admitted his fault, on account of which he limps (35:15).

Feeling justified in pleading with God to defend him against his mockers, the protagonist calls on God for vindication (35:19–25) and offers one last cry that God would shame and dishonor those who persist in sneering (35:26). God must awake and restore moral propriety in Israel; penitents should be respected, not jeered. This is not just a matter of one maligned individual specially pleading on his own behalf. Rather, it involves the broader problem of disrespect for decency and moral order.

The issue is not that the righteous do not sin but that the community should honor those who repent, lest there be no hope for the moral integrity of the whole. The poet points this out by turning to his supporters who magnify the Lord and desire peace for the protagonist (35:27). Like the other two mini-laments, 35:19–28 concludes with the speaker's vow to tell of God's justice continually (35:28).

Ultimately, this poem is not an affront to Christian values of humility and self-deprecation but a spur to the more central concern of respect for the integrity of those who live into the honor of repentance and the healing of the community's integrity. Those who sneer at sincerity dishonor Israel; indeed, they are ensnared in the very trap they set for others, for they look foolish in their mockery.

Theological Pedagogy

Pedagogically this poem invites the reader to probe beneath the surface of words that may seem angry or vengeful. Deeper down is a dynamic not disclosed by the seesawing rhetoric of snare and ensnare, shame and be shamed. The Psalter's opening rebuke of cynicism (Ps. 1:2) reverberates here with an admonition to those who would dismiss sincere regret and guilt appropriately expressed. The psalmist's message is that God prefers sincere penitents to those who stand on the high horse of unblemished piety.

At the same time, this poem is sometimes read through the lens of revenge. While that may be difficult for forgiveness-oriented Christians to comprehend, Dominick D. Hankle suggests that the imprecatory psalms may be therapeutic in Christian counseling when handled well.[4] If used to cling to anger and hurt, they may support unhealthy states, but employed judiciously they may provide for catharsis and a way beyond pathological grief and anger, leaving God to resolve complicated situations.

---

3. The anguish of experiencing baseless hatred is quoted in Jesus's farewell speech in John's Gospel (15:25) in which Jesus prepares his followers for the persecution that will follow his death.

4. Hankle 2010.

PSALM 36

Canonical Context and Themes

Just as "straightness" connects Ps. 32 to Ps. 33, the word "smooth" connects Ps. 35:6 to Ps. 36:2. While having a "straight-arrow" character identifies the righteous in Pss. 32 and 33 (as well as Ps. 36), smoothness or slipperiness captures what one might call the "greasy" character of the wicked. Though Ps. 36 is another elaboration of Ps. 1's juxtaposition of the wicked against the straight-hearted, its distinctiveness consists of its penetrating psychological insight into sociopathy.

The absence of historical markers to identify a context for this poem stimulated the imagination of various commentators. The superscription, *lamnaṣṣēaḥ*, usually translated as "to the director," can also mean victory in a controversy.[1] For the rabbis, it brings to mind various biblical incidents, including David slaying Goliath. Theodore and Theodoret both associate it with Saul's state of mind when he tried to murder David; Theodore notes, however, that disclosing the inner life of the characters is more important than identifying them.

Structure and Dynamics

Psalm 36 easily falls into three quite distinct segments: 36:1–4, 5–9, and 10–12. It begins by penetrating the perverse mind, then shifts suddenly to praise God,

---

1. In translating *Midrash on Psalms*, Braude translates this superscription as "To the Lord of victories" and adds the following note: "Generally interpreted *For the leader*. But since the stem *nṣḥ* can mean either 'lead' or 'conquer,' the phrase is interpreted here *To the Lord of victories*, as determined by the context that follows" (Braude 1959b, 469).

and concludes with a plea to God to protect the straight-hearted from the wicked, extending the straightness theme of Pss. 32 and 33.[2]

Self-Deceiving Audacity (36:1–4)

The grammar of the opening segment of Ps. 36 is odd. The poet starts out with a personification of sin. Sin speaks lies to the wicked heart, deceptively telling it that mischief will not be discovered. The fear of God does not deter his impious plans.[3] After one clause of a self-reflective soliloquy by the evil-hearted, the poet slips into the third-person singular, advising the reader about the character of evil ruminations.

Sociopathy here is characterized as a rejection of a proper fear of God; modern-day readers might recognize it as a defective superego, which results in a cunning embrace of evil.[4] In their own eyes, such people seem sleek, spurring themselves on in evil by persuading themselves that they will not be discovered and reviled because of their sins. At least two sins are operating here—the nefarious behavior being planned and the self-deception that powerfully protects the perpetrator from anxiety that would both deter his evil deeds and indicate moral health. Calvin captures the thought well: "When a man becomes hardened in committing sin, ungodliness at length reduces him to such a state of insensibility that, despising the judgment of God, he indulges without fear in the practice of every sin to which his depraved appetite impels him."[5] Augustine presses the issue further:

> *In pretending to find his own iniquity and hate it*: this suggests that he acted in such a way as to make sure he would not find it. Some people make a show of trying to find their iniquity, but they are afraid of finding it, because if they do find it, they

2. "Straight" as a synonym for righteousness also appears in Pss. 7, 11, 64, 94, and 97. Augustine's teaching on original sin makes him uneasy with this thought, as is evident in his sermon on Ps. 36, which presses humility. On the occurrence of "straight" in Ps. 36:10, he explains, "This deals with a subject on which I have often talked to you: those people are right of heart who in this life obey the will of God. . . . His will is straight, yours crooked. Your will must be straightened by alignment with his, not his bent to correspond with yours, and then you will have an upright heart. If things in this world are going well, bless God who gives you consolation; if things are going badly, bless God who corrects and tests you. Then you will be right of heart, and you will be able to say, *I will bless the Lord at all times; his praise shall be in my mouth always* [Ps. 34:1]" (Augustine 2000b, 86–87).

3. Paul cites the crucial phrase of Ps. 36:1, "there is no [dread] of God before their eyes," to conclude a long catena of scripture citations arguing that Jews have no advantage over pagans, for all are under the power of sin (Rom. 3:18 NRSV).

4. The phrase "dread of God" (*paḥad ʾĕlōhîm*) in Ps. 36:1 is its only biblical occurrence. The phrase "dread of the LORD" (*paḥad yhwh*) appears a few times, but this is to be distinguished from the far more common phrases *yirʾat ʾĕlōhîm* and *yirʾat yhwh* (the most common), which denote reverence and combine fear with love rather than terror. Here, the selection of *paḥad* suggests that those without this fear lack a healthy sense of danger in the face of God's power to punish them, which should deter their nefarious plots and deeds. The phrase points to a character defect or perhaps a lack of knowledge of God.

5. Calvin 1996, 3.

will be challenged: "Give it up. . . . [The sinner][6] pretends to seek it here, seek it there, but always he is afraid of finding it. His search is a sham."

One wonders if Augustine is not reflecting on his own struggle to give up sex prior to his baptism.[7]

Countered by Divine Love and Judgment (36:5–9)

The opening dark reflections end abruptly with a seemingly unconnected outburst of effusive praise for God's loving-kindness (*ḥasdekā*), faithfulness (*'ĕmûnātĕkā*), and righteousness (*ṣidqātĕkā*). Calvin explains it this way: "After having spoken of the very great depravity of men, the prophet [David], afraid lest he should become infected by it, or be carried away by the example of the wicked, as by a flood, quits the subject, and recovers himself by reflecting on a different theme."[8]

According to Calvin, pressing divine goodness encourages those who take refuge in God to avoid potentially bad influences by reassuring them that both God's love and God's justice operate throughout the natural world, even among animals. Yet for the rabbis, attributing divine love to heaven raised the important question of mercy on earth, since Ps. 33:5 says that the earth is full of the loving-kindness of God. An answer the *Midrash* offers is that "the deeds of the wicked . . . force the loving-kindness of the Lord back to the heavens."[9]

Psalm 36:5–9 also prompts reflection on the unfathomability of divine providence and raises the question of theodicy, where moral intuition expects mercy for the righteous but harsh judgment seems to prevail as they suffer. Commenting on 36:6, which says that divine judgment is like great mountains and deep oceans, Ibn Ezra sounds a note of pious agnosticism: "People cannot bear Your righteousness, for [it] is like the mighty mountains. However, in reality its meaning is that God's righteousness is beyond comprehension. It is like the mighty and powerful mountains that no man can reach. The knowledge of God's judgments is similarly like the great obscure deep, which man cannot see."[10]

However, the poet assures the righteous that they will feast delightedly at God's table, "for the core of life is with you and in your light we see light" (36:8–9). That last (famous) phrase is tantalizingly ambiguous and invites speculation. Theodore interprets the light literally, insisting against other commentators that the light is not Christ but rather the physical gift of light, which is, indeed, the fountain of life. "[David's] meaning was to present the utter generosity and abundance of God's gift—hence his mention of these two things in particular: the light . . .

6. Augustine 2000b, 73–74.
7. Clerical celibacy was well established in the Latin tradition before Augustine was born. Perhaps anticipating clerical leadership, he equated baptism with becoming chaste.
8. Calvin 1996, 8.
9. Braude 1959a, 417.
10. Ibn Ezra 2006, 413.

and enjoyment of the light."[11] God is therefore shown to be both "creator" and "provider"; he gives "some [of those things] for our continuance and sustenance, some for us to have a pleasurable and beneficial enjoyment of life."[12]

Feasting in God's house (36:8), which refers to salvation for those who take refuge in God, speaks to Christians of heavenly reward after this life although that idea is not in the text. While Theodore denies that these verses allude to Christ, Augustine is sure that they do. Eschatologically, Christ is the fountain of life.

> The reality is that a fountain is light also; you may call it what you will, because it is not what you call it. You cannot find a suitable name, because it is not captured by any one name. If you were to say that it is light, and only light, someone might object, "What then was the point of telling me that I am to hunger and thirst? Can anyone eat light? That other hint that was given me was obviously more apt: *Blessed are the pure of heart, for they shall see God* (Matt. 5:8). I had better prepare my eyes, then." Yes, but prepare your throat too, because the reality that is light is also a fountain: a fountain because it drenches the thirsty, light because it illumines the blind. . . . Here below the two may be separated; but there you will never flag, because there will be the fountain for you, and you will never walk in darkness, for there is light.[13]

That the Arrogant May Fall (36:10–12)

The last three verses are a prayer that the loving-kindness of God will prevail with justice for the straight-hearted so that they will not be stepped on by the arrogant or the wicked and be made to wander from the straight way that they have mastered. Looking back to the beginning of Ps. 36, the fear is apparently not of the righteous being directly oppressed by the wicked but the more harmful danger of being seduced into evil thinking and acting, in which case the wicked win. As the speaker strives to hold to the straight way, his final plea is that the workers of iniquity will fall, unable to rise, so that the righteous can prevail in their way.

Theological Pedagogy

In Ps. 36, the struggle is not between the righteous and the wicked but rather the struggle of righteousness and wickedness in the heart of each of us. The fear is that wickedness, rather than the wicked, will vanquish those who know that they ought to hold to the straight way. As every parent whose children keep bad company knows, the struggle is psychological. The temptation to give in to wickedness can be strong, especially based on the fact that in rooting for the good guys against the bad guys, one's sense of fairness is often frustrated. Wrongdoing can be more fun than rightdoing, and the poet is eager to dissuade us from the wrong path.

11. Theodore of Mopsuestia 2006, 407.
12. Ibid.
13. Augustine 2000b, 86.

PSALM 37

Canonical Context and Themes

This acrostic psalm is a mini-guide for the theologically and psychologically perplexed. Like the book of Proverbs and Pss. 1, 25, 32, and 34, it is a moral exhortation that urges wise living. It goes beyond general moral encouragement, focusing on the negative effects of angry jealousy and replacing it with patient piety. Psalm 36 raises the issue of theodicy, and Ps. 37 remains focused on this universally troubling concern of classical theism. In theological perspective, if God prefers wholesome living to disgraceful living and is able to reward and punish, why do evildoers flourish and harass the pious? The psalmist has no distinctive answer to this ageless problem, but knowing that civility, indeed civilization, depends on believing in a just moral order, the question must be addressed. Behind it lurks the possibility of atheism, which amounts to moral despair in the eyes of the psalmist (as I noted at Pss. 10 and 13); without the theistic sanction, moral living is jeopardized.

In psychological perspective, the psalm addresses jealousy. The poet counsels patient waiting and begs his listeners to persevere in a morally lofty life, trusting that a just moral order will prevail and vicious people will eventually be foiled. Following the path set forth in Ps. 1, Ps. 37 details and urges wise living while shaming wickedness. It speaks to the perplexed in an encouraging rather than a threatening tone, trusting that living wisely will be materially rewarding and psychologically strengthening.

The material promise concerns land possession. The pious are not promised a postmortem life in a heavenly hereafter but secure and prosperous living on earth. This should not be read literally as life without death, postmortem bodiless immortality, or postresurrection life but rather living in peace and abundance and being able to bequeath that security and prosperity to subsequent generations. Possessing land offers the promise of stability, especially for those who have known exile.

Voluntary geographic mobility, built into the fabric of modern societies, is unknown to scripture. This land-based eschatology influenced the Matthean Beatitudes that promise land and prosperity along with, or better put, *as* the reign of heaven. With the exception of Augustine, most classic commentators I consider here respected the worldly eschatology of the text.

Structure and Dynamics

The opening two verses announce the message of the poem, and the remainder of the opening segment offers advice on how to avoid falling into an untoward life (37:1–8). The long main body of the poem (37:9–33) articulates the Psalter's basic doctrine of providence. Good will triumph; evil will fail. The final segment (37:34–40) offers further advice on the theme.

Do Not Fret (37:1–8)

The opening segment speaks in the second-person singular imperative. It begins and ends with an injunction not to become angry that the wicked flourish, for they are as evanescent as summer's grass. The phrase "do not be incensed" appears three times in this segment (37:1, 7, 8), and the parallel phrase in the opening verse is "do not become jealous." Angry jealousy is a dangerously unstable emotion with its combination of aversion to the wrong being done with a desire to imitate the wrong in order to get ahead. It sinks the self into its own underside—a peril the poet is eager to guard his listeners from. Theodore opines,

> The general run of people, you see, especially when observing the wicked prospering, grind their teeth and claim that there is no benefit in being righteous: most righteous people are under pressure from disaster, even suffering this at the hands of villains. This it is that particularly renders the experience of calamity more depressing, whereas vice brings no harm to those guilty of crimes from which many villains are found to be living a life of wealth and prosperity without succumbing to any disaster. To dispel this ailment, he devotes most of this psalm to treating of it at length.[1]

Ibn Ezra, appreciating the aggravation of one who feels sidelined by vicious characters, who "get ahead" unscrupulously writes: "Do not join with him and show him love and goodwill when your intention is to harm him."[2]

Not fretting, however, does not simply mean trying to ignore bad behavior. Much more is required. The psalmist wants his listeners to enlist in a strenuous commitment to the opposite way of life. Psalm 37:1–8 is full of imperatives;

1. Theodore of Mopsuestia 2006, 413.
2. Ibn Ezra 2006, 425.

Ps. 37:3–5 repeats the same advice—trust in the Lord, do good, and all shall be well. Ibn Ezra understands how trying this can be. Against other interpretations of these verses, he writes, "In my opinion people are envious of those who work unrighteousness because of the wealth in which they put their trust. Hence the psalmist now says, trust in the Lord and do not refrain from doing good."[3]

The psalmist admonishes his listeners again in 37:7, knowing that anger threatens to destabilize the complainant. The poet counsels patience, trusting that the godly way will win the day. However, not being jealous of the wicked is easier said than done. If sustained, angry jealousy can embitter and devour the soul and infect other relationships. Perhaps some personalities are able to withstand such stress better than others. Commenting on 37:7–11, Calvin's pastoral psychology is insightful:

> The accumulation of terms which occurs in the next verse [37:8], in which he lays a restraint as with a bridle upon anger, allays wrath and assuages passion, is not superfluous; but, as is necessary, he rather prescribes numerous remedies for a disease which it is difficult to cure. By this means, he reminds us how easily we are provoked, and how ready we are to take offence, unless we lay a powerful restraint upon our tumultuous passions, and keep them under control. And although the faithful are not able to subdue the lusts of the flesh without much trouble and labour, whilst the prosperity of the wicked excites their impatience, yet this repetition teaches us that we ought unceasingly to wrestle against them; for if we steadily persevere, we know that our endeavors shall not be in vain in the end.[4]

The Righteous Will Inherit the Earth (37:9–33)

While the opening segment of this poem urges controlling unstable emotions, the long middle section offers comforting encouragement in the form of a discourse on divine justice in eschatological perspective. It is noteworthy that the poet does not appeal to God's punishing anger either to convert the wicked or to keep the pious in line. Rather, the vicious will simply meet a deserved end, and the godly will prosper long after their adversaries self-destruct, as 37:15 puts it.

To stabilize the jealous, the psalmist anticipates the impending fall of the wicked and promises that those who hope in God and do good "will inherit the land" and thrive abundantly long after the short-lived success of the wicked ends. The promissory phrase picked up in Matt. 5:5 appears in Ps. 37 five times (37:9, 11, 22, 29, 34) and is stated using different words in 37:18. This and other promised rewards for living blamelessly, being generous, and speaking wisely and justly interlace with repeated promises that the wicked will lose what they have. They will wither like grass. They will be cut off; they will vanish. God will laugh at them; they will fall on the swords they prepare for others. Their arms will be

3. Ibn Ezra 2006, 421.
4. Calvin 1996, 24–25.

broken; they will disappear like smoke. That is, the vicious self-destruct in a blaze of infamy. Like public figures suddenly caught in compromising circumstances, they disappear from the scene almost overnight.

The just deserts framework for encouraging moral endurance contrasts with Augustine's doctrine of providence that elaborates Rom. 9's use of the birth of Rebecca's twins in Gen. 25. Augustine develops Paul's depiction of the birth of Jacob and Esau into a theological determinism, suggesting that God's wrath and favor toward people has nothing to do with their moral life. In an apparently arbitrary way, "he has mercy on whomever he chooses, and he hardens the heart of whomever he chooses" (Rom. 9:18 NRSV). The Psalter does not entertain the philosophical question of free will versus determinism; it never doubts that people are responsible not only for the moral caliber of their own lives but also for the moral cohesion of society. Psalm 37 typifies the Psalter's conviction that moral living, grounded in allegiance to God, strives for communal well-being rather than the eternal salvation of individuals. God sustains those who cling to him emotionally; he supports their self-respect and laughs at those whom he sees will damage themselves through unsavory lives, presumably when their bad behavior is publically exposed.

Augustine spiritualizes the promise of prosperity through his schema of two cities: the future heavenly Jerusalem that the saints will eventually enjoy after this life and the earthly city for everyone else.[5] He comforts the saints for whom the promises are made by diverting attention from the promise of material prosperity and urging saintly people to be satisfied with God alone:

> Your God will be your peace. Peace will be for you whatever you long for. In this world gold cannot also be silver for you, wine cannot be bread for you, what gives you light cannot provide you with drink [cf. Ps. 36]; but your God will be everything to you. . . . He will possess you whole and undivided, as he, your possessor, is whole and undivided himself. You will lack nothing with him, for with him you possess all that is; you will have it all, and he will have all there is of you, because you and he will be one, and he who possesses you will have this one thing, and have it wholly.[6]

Designed to protect God from human disaffection and promote patient endurance of life's inevitable hardships, Augustine's spiritualized eschatology came to dominate western theology. As a result, concern for health, safety, economic security, and respect for personal achievement ceased to have much purchase on the Christian imagination. Indeed, poverty and self-denial were valorized, and prosperity distrusted; humility—often in extreme forms—became the chief Christian virtue. Not so the psalmists; lacking a heavenly afterlife that would compensate the righteous for ills suffered during life, they promoted godly living as the way to achieve material well-being, respectability, and self-respect.

5. The two-cities schema comes from Rev. 21:1–2.
6. Augustine 2000b, 101.

The poet is at pains not only to differentiate the fates of the wicked and the righteous but also to identify behavior and attitudes that separate them. In the sphere of finance, their paths differ greatly. Before banking, financial transactions were personal agreements between individuals rather than between an individual and an impersonal financial institution with rules and policies to be followed as a matter of course. The poet points out that the wicked borrow but fail to repay their debts, while generosity in both giving and lending characterizes the righteous (37:21, 26). The personal nature of financial transactions in the ancient world guaranteed that untoward financial behavior would seriously damage the community as well as the individual and his family.

Another distinction between the wicked and the righteous can be discerned in the way each uses that most vulnerable organ of the body, the tongue. "The mouth of the righteous speaks wisdom and his tongue utters justice" (37:30), while the wicked stalk the righteous, seeking their destruction (37:32). The divide between the two is cavernous. Divine teaching suffuses the heart of the righteous, sustaining them in time of need, while the wicked are denied divine aid because they have not internalized the right way to live. As a result, the contrast can be expected to permeate every aspect of life.

Amid this discourse, the poet pauses to offer a personal aside to assure the righteous that they need not worry about their children's well-being. Throughout his life, he has never seen the children of the righteous go hungry. Their parents' reputation for generosity and justice seems to assure that their children will be taken care of should the need arise.

Patient Waiting Pays Off (37:34–40)

The last segment of this psalm returns to the imperative of the opening segment (37:1–8) and is interrupted by a first-person recollection of personal experience in which the speaker assures his listeners of the promises spelled out in the preceding theological discourse. To reinforce the promise that the wicked will soon be gone, he adds that he has seen the wicked operating at full strength and watched them disappear. He adjures his listeners to "hope in the LORD," "keep his way," "remain innocent," and "look at the upright," for peaceable people are blessed with a future—unlike the wicked who are soon gone.

Theological Pedagogy

Psalm 37 concludes with the resounding theological conviction of the Psalter: God rescues the upright who take refuge in him (37:39–40). Salvation is rescue from "the enemy's" clutches; in concrete terms, what does that mean? Given the opening reflection on angry jealousy and frustration at seeing the wicked flourish, the damage the wicked inflict is psychological. They stir up these dangerous emotions in the heart (or perhaps better, the belly) of those longing to abide in God—those who are able to resist being pulled down by such raw negativity but struggle nonetheless. In this context, rescue is protection from becoming lost while walking the Lord's way; even if one stumbles—perhaps by making cunning plans and strategies to take matters into one's own hands—rescue is still possible (37:24). I suggest that the psalmist engages here in a high-stakes struggle for the hearts and minds of those who seek to cling to God yet are understandably torn between keeping faith with God's way and becoming what they hate. The psalmist proffers a realistic and helpful scenario.

PSALM 38

Canonical Context and Themes

This gripping poem is the third of the seven penitential psalms so designated by Cassiodorus. More precisely, however, Ps. 38 is a penitential lament. Combining penitence with lament is odd, almost oxymoronic from a Christian perspective, because penitence implies confession of wrongdoing while lament complains about being unjustly afflicted. The logic of Ps. 38 implies that the speaker's critics abjure him because of his sin. Christian piety might expect the truly penitent to bow humbly before their critics rather than complain at being persecuted without cause (38:19).

One reason for the perplexity is the different understandings of sin that operate in scripture and later theological tradition. For the psalmist, sin refers to a discrete event or incident. One commits sins that are to be dealt with in one way or another. For the later western Christian tradition, commencing with Augustine, religious thinking about sin migrated from focusing on the incident to focusing on its perpetrator. The sinner became "sin-ful." Concern was not only with individual incidents but also with the sinfulness of the sinner. Though sinfulness was once a reparable state, it became an inherent identity, an ontological condition of human existence that defines each person quite irrespective of actions, attitudes, and virtues. According to this view, God is warranted to perceive human beings in terms of their failure to live rightly; therefore, divine condemnation is the appropriate response. Sinfulness so infests everyone's personality that it is referred to as "the human condition" or "the human predicament." Augustine's notion of original sin, extended by Calvin with the phrase "total depravity," means that moral weakness—often construed as self-absorption, vanity, or arrogance—permeates all that humans are and all that they do. This is not the case for the psalmists or for Judaism, which never thematized the fall of Gen. 3 as Paul led later Christians to elaborate.

According to the Augustinian view, a sinner complaining of being sinned against is somewhat of an affront, as if one were trying to sidestep one's basic identity—that calls for sorrowful remorse rather than complaint. From the psalmist's perspective, a person's identity is fluid. One may be a sinner in one setting yet sinned against in another. In this view, tension does not exist, for each moment of life is judged on its own terms.

By braiding the pain of regret together with the pain of oppression, this brilliant poet paints a picture of a person squeezed with pain from within and without to the extent that he is scarcely able to breathe. It is so pungently real that it is difficult for one even to look upon the afflicted, whose torments are at once physical, psychological, and spiritual. One beholds a person at his nadir; God is the only possible source of help, but that help is not assured.

Through the prism of the poet's searing candor, the commentators have dwelt richly in this poem, offering a wealth of insights into the somatic and psychological dynamics of sin, suffering, and comfort. In what follows, I can offer only a sample of their wisdom.

Structure and Dynamics

The poem could be variously segmented, although as a whole it is a great soliloquy that lets us in on several forms of the excruciating pain the speaker endures. In the psalms, one cannot assume that the poet is speaking in personal terms, but the depth of insight into the texture of pain suggests that the writer knows whereof he speaks. The soliloquy includes a piecemeal plea to God in the second-person point of view (38:1–2, 9, 15, 21–22). It constitutes a seamless part of the deep soul-searching that is the psalm's backbone. Segmenting Ps. 38 by point of view would interrupt the flow of the thoughts. The first and last two verses are easily marked off as pleas to God. Within the body, 38:3–10 explains why God need not punish the penitent further; he is already experiencing the psychological and somatic effects of deep self-confrontation. In addition to his physical affliction, Ps. 38:11–12 details his social suffering, while 38:13–14 tells how he handles himself in such straits. The last segment turns back to God in self-reflective meditation and a plea for help (38:21–22).

Before proceeding to the body of the psalm, the much-commented-upon superscription deserves a word. "A song to David, for remembrance" stimulated varied comments from writers who understood the pedagogical importance of remembering. Rashi infers that "remembrance" is meant to bring Israel's troubles at the hands of gentiles to God's attention.[7] Although the poem is written in the first-person singular, Rashi reads it as a communal lament by Israel that intended to fend off insults directed at the community by gentiles, primarily Christians. Before him, Augustine takes the remembering to be remembrance of the Sabbath rest from which humanity

7. Rashi 2004, 319.

has been torn by Adam's fall. He interprets Sabbath as eschatological rest in God in the hereafter—when we possess God and God fully possesses us.[8]

I Am Already Punished (38:1–2)

The opening two verses introduce the speaker as he pleads with God for lenient discipline because he has already been pierced for his sins by the arrows of remorse. Although he is depleted, one sees maturity in his deeply penitent rather than defensive posture. The poem goes on to demonstrate the depth of his repentance; additional punishment on God's part would be vindictive rather than medicinal and, hence, counterproductive. Theodoret artfully depicts God as physician rather than judge, and he sides with the penitent's plea for mild, not harsh, remedies for his transgressions; punishment is meant to cure sin rather than mete out retribution that might harden the offender whose guilt, shame, and regret are adequate. Any further punishment would portray God as malicious. *Midrash on Psalms* takes this opportunity to teach measured discipline:

> Chastisement is good—as Scripture says, *Blessed is the man, whom Thou chastenest, O Lord* (Ps. 94:12)—but we cannot long suffer it. . . . He who is not skilled in giving lashes, after binding a man, strikes him upon the head or between the eyes with a stick; but he who is skilled in giving lashes, after binding a man, strikes him upon the back, not upon the head or between the eyes; in order not to blind the man's eyes, he strikes him upon a part of the body where there is no danger.[9]

Perhaps the psalmist is discouraging the use of discipline when one is angry because the discipline might prove counterproductive, causing the wayward one to hate the administrator of appropriate discipline but also protecting him from discipline administered in anger, which is an exercise in personal power rather than medicinal treatment.

My Body Is Punished (38:3–10)

The next segment of the poem expands on 38:2 to depict the various somatic expressions of genuine contrition, perhaps mixed with the dread of further punishment implied by the opening plea. The speaker writhes with the somatic effects of extreme emotional distress, identifying unsound (perhaps aching) bones, festering sores, pain that leaves him stooped, abdominal distress, groaning, sighing, and heart palpitations. Body and spirit are of a piece.

Not only are physical symptoms caused by emotional distress, but such states also have physical expressions. Stress can somatize as rashes, knots in the stomach, palpitations, headaches, and high blood pressure, among other features. Depression

8. Augustine 2000b, 146–47.
9. Braude 1959a, 425–26.

can somatize as sleep and eating disorders, difficulty concentrating, and so on. The poet is gloomy all the time, retains no sparkle in his eyes, and feels no health in his body (*'ên-mĕtōm bibśārî* expresses the deadening feeling, which appears in 38:4, 8). His symptoms express spiritual death.

Johann Sebastian Bach set Ps. 38:3 to music in the opening movement of Cantata BWV 25 (*Es ist nichts Gesundes an meinem Leibe*): "There is no soundness in my body because of your anger; there is no wholeness in my bones because of my sin." The cantata was written for the fourteenth Sunday after Trinity Sunday (the first Sunday after Pentecost) and first performed in Leipzig in August 1723. The opening movement uses Luther's translation of the text: "*Es ist nichts Gesundes an meinem Leibe vor deinem Dräuen, und ist kein Friede in meinen Gebeinen vor meiner Sünde.*" It is set in E minor, the traditional key for penitential texts, and the layered music is hauntingly sorrowful and filled with grief and long deliberate sighs. It is a double fugue for SATB (soprano, alto, tenor, bass) voices set over an instrumental chorale for strings and oboes that alternates with trombones and recorders. Many people are familiar with the chorale of "*Herzlich tut mich verlangen nach einem selgen End*" of this cantata in the hymn "O, Sacred Head Sore Wounded." Thus the death of Christ hovers in the instrumental parts, tying the penitential agony of the sung text to the cross.

Like Bach, Augustine also counterpoints the sinner's sins (which he portrays as malodorous) with the fragrant offering of Christ. Augustine was very attentive to the role of the five senses in spiritual matters and so hones in on the psalmist's graphic portrayal of his sins as wounds filled with pus: "You only need a healthy sense of smell in spiritual matters to be aware how sins fester. The opposite of this reek of sin is the [good odor of Christians] of which the apostle says: We are the fragrance of Christ. . . (2 Cor. 2:15)."[10]

My Relationships Are Decimated (38:11–12)

To explore the full range of suffering, the psalmist now turns to its social aspects. The sinner is alienated not only from his own body but also from the body politic. As he experiences it, his support system—even his family—seems to be harming him. Psalm 38:12 pounds home the experience of abandonment with alliterative force that escapes translation: *waynaqšû mĕbaqšê napšî.* The opening phrase of the verse pounds out four feet, three feet, two feet': ′ ′ ′ , ′ ′ ′ , ′ ′. Each word stresses its final syllable, giving the phrase a staccato ring. He broods on those who seek to strike him down and go around slandering him.

At this point, the pious Christian might raise her eyebrows. What? The one agonizing over his sins suddenly takes umbrage that he is shunned for his misdeeds? Should he not be begging for forgiveness and heaping penitential coal and ashes on his head? Further, is it not meet and right that the community sides

---

10. Augustine 2000b, 153.

with righteousness against the sinner? By bringing the question to the reader's attention, the psalmist seems to have something else in mind.

The speaker's intimates should encourage and comfort him; they should be helping to rehabilitate the fallen member of the community, especially since Israel does not practice shunning as a formal expression of corporate discipline. The sinner's dismay at being abandoned by those who love him moves the poem from the consideration of what constitutes adequate punishment by God (with which it begins) to what constitutes adequate punishment on the human level. When unsavory financial, sexual, or physical behavior that is not punishable by law becomes known, people are likely to draw back from the perpetrator, perhaps unsure of how to respond or surprised to see another side of the person. The same is true in cases of physical illness.

The speaker craves to be helped, not ignored. Perhaps he can be helped to confess and work through the events and emotions that led up to the ill-fated incident. Perhaps he can be helped to anticipate circumstances that could precipitate similar temptations and be given techniques to avoid them. Today people seek professionals for therapeutic aid, but that does not justify the abandonment of companions who need well-tempered love, uncomfortable as the demand may be. A ministry of silent presence is preferable to self-serving gossip, the goal of which is to separate oneself from the sinner as a means to boast of one's piety.

I Fall Silent (38:13–14)

The speaker's response to his troubles is telling. He falls silent before criticism, goading, and disapproval, able to ignore the taunts, questions, and insults. He takes the higher road rather than engaging in vituperative debate—an argument he will surely lose. Throwing back countertaunts to opponents is a sure path to self-destruction. Given how often the Younger Testament portrays Jesus quoting psalms, one wonders whether his silence before the high priest and Pilate recorded in the Synoptic Gospels was not inspired by this psalm and perhaps verses 1 and 2 of the next. Rashi counsels the same to Jews being taunted by Christians: "We are silent, for we think to ourselves, 'If we answer them with harsh words, perhaps they will see our defeat and *rejoice* over us *when* our *foot gives way*, and they will *vaunt themselves against* us.'"[11] As the Miranda law kindly advises, it is preferable to remain silent when one is certain the argument will be lost.

I Confess, Pray, and Wait (38:15–20)

Since human agents are liable to be as fickle as the speaker's friends and family, the speaker strategically turns from human assailants to eschatological hope in God's power to answer in the long term. Augustine aptly sums up the situation:

11. Rashi 2004, 320.

In saying this he has advised you what to do, if you find yourself in trouble. You seek to defend yourself, and perhaps no one undertakes your defense. You are extremely worried, and think you have lost your case because you have no counsel for defense and no evidence on your side. Guard your innocence within yourself, where no one seeks to undermine your case. Perhaps false evidence has swayed the verdict against you, but this is so only in the human court; will it have any weight with God, before whom your case is to be heard? When God is judge, there will be no other witness than your own conscience.... Simply arm yourself with a good conscience, so that you may say, *You will hear me, O Lord my God, because in you, Lord, I have trusted.*[12]

Heavenly vindication proved to be the answer for Christians finding themselves unable to win in frequently corrupt courts.

However, the situation is not cut and dried. The speaker is remorseful for his dreadful sin, whatever it was, yet claims that the opposition he experiences is unwarranted because his opponents are unprovoked. Perhaps his sin did not involve or affect them. At the very least he believes that he has relationships with these people that should be able to absorb his wrongdoing in a wider context of care and concern, especially since he is penitent. Those who vaunt themselves at the penitent's expense fail him by magnifying his pain rather than helping him to regain moral and social equilibrium. They have betrayed their love for him.

Come, Lord; Save Me (38:21–22)

In conclusion, the protagonist begs God not to stand apart from him as his companions have but to show himself to be bigger-spirited than they are by rescuing him. Needless to say, salvation for the psalmist has nothing in common with Christian salvation—neither its eternal bliss nor its eternal punishment. Rather, salvation involves the situation at hand. God's abandonment (about which Jesus cried out from the cross) or worse, the thought that God is the true enemy, is perhaps the most frightening possibility of all.

No resolution can be found here, no indication that God has or will rescue the penitent. While the psalmist leaves his readers hanging, the final ambiguity is realistic and honest. Patrick Henry Reardon articulates the crisis well: "Whether physical, emotional, mental, or spiritual—or all of them together—what we suffer in this life are incursions of death, and death is simply sin becoming incarnate and dwelling among us."[13] The protagonist in Ps. 38 portrays himself as a dead man walking who wants to live. Christian theology that puts most of its energy into the dynamic of shame and release will read the speaker's plight as a craving for the atoning work that the cross of Christ provides; it enables the penitent to rest in the forgiveness wrought for the unjust by the unjust death endured by

12. Augustine 2000b, 162.
13. Reardon 1975, 73.

God himself. The belief that God accepts the death of Christ to pay for one's sin would release the penitent from the humiliating shame that plagues him. Not only that, but it would also confront his companions and family members who estrange themselves from him with the fact that judgment and forgiveness are God's, not theirs, to give.

Theological Pedagogy

In Ps. 38, the psalmist teaches compassion for those who join their voices with the vengeful self-righteous who unreflectively take the high moral ground and distance themselves from compassion when the occasion arises. The psalm is for the "kith and kin" who turn against one of their own as much as it is for all of us who may one day find ourselves walking in the death of remorse, without hope apart from God.

God is strangely quiet in this poem. While the suppliant appeals to God in the opening and closing couplets, the bulk of the poem is about the suppliant himself. He is ambivalent about God, who is both the source of his suffering—the hand behind his alienated friends—and the source of his healing. The speaker pleads for God to change his attitude and strategy toward him. The "arrows" that God has sunk into him have succeeded in arousing remorse and regret. Now that the suffering of shame has achieved a therapeutic effect, it is time for the punishment to complete its medicinal course so that healing can begin.

Although repentant, the speaker still thinks that his companions hate him wrongfully; at the very least, in light of his remorse their contempt is unwarranted. Perhaps they have overreacted, which is how the protagonist experiences their shunning of him. Because the situation in Ps. 38 is not simply between God and the speaker but among God, the speaker, and the community, healing constitutes the mending of damaged horizontal relationships as well. The stilling of divine anger, resulting in a changed attitude toward the sinner, would need to express itself through the changed attitude of the foes that are the visible instruments of divine anger.

Psalm 38 ultimately looks toward the rehabilitation of the penitent. The lingering question is how to discern when sanctions for bad behavior have effectively brought about change, or at least a resolve to behave differently, so that they are no longer needed. Indeed, if they persist beyond effectiveness they may take on a life of their own, inflicting further social and psychological damage. The individual who is prevented from resuming constructive personal relationships dwells in bitterness, and the community that denies healing may become self-righteous and callous. Many inmates who languish in prison under mandatory sentences exemplify this difficult case.

PSALM 39

Canonical Context and Themes

The canonical link between Ps. 39 and Ps. 38 is the way in which the speaker takes refuge in silence (a central theme here) even though he admits that it does not help him (39:2). As with Ps. 38, the public audience is gone; it is just God and the speaker, who offers another soliloquy and a rather desperate plea to avoid humiliation as a result of his sins. This anguished poem has often been compared with Kohelet (Ecclesiastes), not only in its use of the phrase *kol-hebel* (all is in vain) but in its despondency at life's evanescence as cause for depression and despair, exacerbated perhaps by the crushing blow of seemingly unremitting divine chastisement. Walter Brueggemann notes that this poem, like Ps. 88, is one of the very few psalms that offers no resolution of the pain, no light at the end of the proverbial tunnel.[1]

Structure and Dynamics

This poem begins with a soliloquy and changes orientation at 39:4 to address God directly throughout the rest of the poem. The soliloquy permits the reader to overhear the speaker's self-conversation, in which he prudently calls himself to refrain from harmful speech amid inner turmoil, while the main body of the poem turns to God in a philosophically recumbent position. Psalm 39 asks a perennial question: How long will I have to endure this pain and humiliation (39:4–6)? The speaker pleads to be spared public exposure and to have his punishment mitigated by death, hinting that the thought of suicide might be lurking in the background (39:4–5). The morose reflection on the hopelessness of his situation (39:4–11)

1. Brueggemann 2001, 25.

gives way to a last despairing gasp for air, in which the despondent speaker begs God not to rescue him, as so many psalms do, but to *leave* him so that he may smile again before he dies (39:12–13). God is deliberately identified as the enemy, and the speaker wants to be rid of him.

Stuff It Down (39:1–3)

The opening verses of this poem find the speaker struggling to maintain his composure and act prudently under pressure. Being too distraught to respond to those who torment him in a way that might improve matters, the speaker struggles to remain silent, knowing that they watch and wait for him to feed them ammunition should he attempt to defend himself against their punishing judgment. Perhaps his propensity for speaking rashly is part of the problem for which he is remorseful yet in which he feels trapped. Sensitive souls often brood on untoward comments that slip out unwisely and then cannot be taken back. Frustratingly, the reader has no idea what circumstances have precipitated this chagrin. Perhaps the poet omits background information so that readers may identify with the speaker through their own contexts.

To protect his dignity and exercise some control over his situation, the speaker vows nonresponse to his tormentors, much as Jesus remained silent before his accusers. His dignity hangs on his silence—on his refusal to give in to his emotions and speak back (39:1). He determines not to engage on that level, knowing that he would lose. Muzzling himself is the best way to protect whatever shred of poise he has left, and yet, as Brueggemann points out, he craves giving voice to a claim for himself against "ruthless and indifferent" power.[2] To speak or not to speak? Which is the more eloquent act? While silence is preferable to protect himself, the speaker's dignity cries out to address the unfairness of the situation and to summon his persecutors to reflect on their behavior toward him in shame for treating him this way. When to keep silent and when to speak is one of life's weightiest challenges.

By beginning with a meditative soliloquy in an unspecified setting, the poet inducts his readers into a space that they can easily make their own; drawing from personal experiences, they can approximate the speaker's situation. How is one's personal authority best used in debilitating circumstances? On the one hand, to speak will release anger and hurt and perhaps engender self-reflection on the part of the perpetrator. Yet catharsis in the presence of those who inflicted the pain only weakens one's stature in their eyes because it acknowledges their success in causing injury. On the other hand, the refusal to speak sustains one's dignity in public and disinvites further abuse, though perhaps it allows the oppressor to walk away from the situation feeling victorious, even if from the outside he looks vicious. Either option might satisfy those inflicting harm, thereby denying

2. Ibid., 24.

the victim even the chance to stem their smugness. Opening the poem with a soliloquy is stunningly effective.

The speaker's emotional candor is compelling. While retreating into silence may serve his dignity and poise, stuffing down hurt and anger only increases his distress, for it renders him unable to call his oppressor to account. That is, silence inhibits doing anything to restore the righteousness that he craves from his opponent. He roils, and his resolve to remain silent finally fails him. He is overcome with the need to externalize his pain and speak on behalf of righteousness by articulating the insult he has received. Fortunately, he has the presence of mind to pour his heart out to God rather than to his tormentors. That his words now resound in our ears strengthens their impact beyond anything the original poet could have imagined.

Depression, Despair, Death (39:4–13)

The remainder of this poem is sometimes referred to as a melancholic reflection on the transience and futility of the human condition rather than an expression of personal suffering.[3] However, separating the two genres denies the causal link between them. The poet begins analyzing his immediate situation in terms of how he should respond to it, but as he does so he is able to look beyond his immediate tormentors and see God standing behind them. The point of the turn to God is to hold *him* responsible for this paralyzing suffering in which death begins to be inviting.

WHEN WILL I DIE? (39:4–6)

Life has become pointless and the sufferer looks to death for escape. He may well be experiencing what modern-day readers know as clinical depression; this may include suicidal thoughts, or at least the hope that natural death will come soon to release him from his humiliation. He experiences life as vapid yet fleeting, not in the philosophical sense that Kohelet bemoans but in terms of his depression, which empties his life and makes even simple tasks overwhelming. The speaker turns to face God and admits to himself and to God that his life means nothing to God: "My lifetime is as nothing in your sight" (39:5). In the face of life's fragility, self-despair casts a pall over others' busyness, revealing it also to be vanity. Life is a bleak shadow-play, or as Shakespeare would put it in *Macbeth*, "a tale told by an idiot, full of sound and fury, signifying nothing" (5.5.26–28).

GOD, YOU ARE THE TORMENTOR! (39:7–11)

In one of the most searing statements in scripture, the poet's anger at God explodes through his high doctrine of divine sovereignty as it dawns on him that God, in whom he has placed his trust, has not only not answered him but has

3. Mays 1994b, 165.

also betrayed him. The complaint is not so much against his human tormentors as against God: "I am worn down by the blows of your hand" (39:10). The human agents in the drama fall away and God is confronted in a confused profusion of thoughts and emotions that assail the speaker, who is seeking someone against whom to vent his anguish. While Ps. 39 opens with the speaker seeking to hold his tongue, this shocking realization about God leaves him in stunned silence. God is exposed as both powerful and harsh, and the psalmist offers no evidence that the speaker believes God's punishment has pedagogical value. If it did, the speaker would praise God for it, as some might argue, to protect divine benevolence. But this is not the case. The one who might prevent him from the sins that make him the object of ridicule—presumably the sins of the tongue he tries to stifle at the beginning of this poem—has turned against him; he is exhausted.

He begs for a reprieve and turns back to a general reflection on the frailty of human life. Perhaps he comforts himself by locating his suffering in the emptiness of facing divine punishment, which destroys him as a moth eats his clothes. Life is empty when God acts like a devouring moth! This segment reveals deep ambivalence in the speaker, perhaps even the poet himself. On one hand, he believes that his situation will not improve, and he looks forward to death; on the other hand, he bemoans the fleeting character of life. Such confusion gives the poem a realistic tone as the reader watches this tortured soul thrash around in his pit of despair.

Please Leave Me! (39:12–13)

In a final summoning of strength drawn from his fleeting life before God, the speaker implores God to leave him. God's presence in his life is so destructive at this point that the most he can manage is to ask God to let him go peacefully into death. "Look away from me," he begs poignantly (39:13). One is left with the sense that God has strangled this person with punishment and humiliation and that death is his final hope.

Theological Pedagogy

By unapologetically admitting that he experiences God as cruel—that is, without trying to make the suspicion of God go away—this reflective poet, like Qohelet, encourages candor among those who suffer remorselessly. It may be, as James L. Mays puts it, that "the Lord reigns in the Psalter," but that is not to suggest that we can always appreciate that reign.[4] In life, one is sometimes haunted not only by the fear of the absence of God but also by the fear of the presence of God. This is a permission-giving poem that allows us to be repelled by God's actions. It is not a definitive statement on the divine character, but it does respect human

4. Mays 1994a.

experience by not repressing negative feelings or subordinating them in a desire to protect the perfect goodness of God. In the poet's theology, room is made for genuine theological doubt, and no experiences or emotions are ruled out because they do not fit a preexisting set of theological assumptions.

Of course, theological assumptions are also made, the most salient being belief in the power of God and in his awareness of and involvement with human life. What is not assumed is that God is reliably beneficent. The admission that God can permit or actively facilitate personal harm is painful to behold in print but consonant with the God construed in both the Older and Younger Testaments—a God who nearly wiped out creation in the great flood, threatened to destroy Israel for worshiping its golden calf, and required the death of Jesus to enable forgiveness.

Marcion of Sinope, a second-century Christian bishop, rejected Hebrew scripture because it contained theology such as that of this psalm and he in turn was rejected by the church. By formally embracing the whole of Hebrew scripture, the church endorsed these texts that, though jarring to later Christian sensibilities, countenance a full range of human emotion, even hostility toward God.

At the same time, blaming God is an emotionally healthy response to suffering because it protects other people. Venting at God allows anger to be deflected into a safe space. If God truly is beneficent, he surely prefers to receive the blame rather than watch violence erupt from the one in anguish, which could potentially mar civil society. In this sense, God serves as a pressure valve, releasing destructive emotions that simply will not be suppressed.

PSALM 40

Canonical Context and Themes

The first ten verses of Ps. 40 function as an antidote to or, perhaps better, a resolution of the psychological and pastoral calamity undergone in Ps. 39. A song of joyful praise written in the third person redeems the despair that drove the speaker to beg God to leave him alone, replacing it with jubilant celebration at having waited (and waited) for God to send relief. Yet the poet soon backtracks in confusion, and the second half of the poem devolves into another pained plea for deliverance and a call for the divine punishment of adversaries, leaving the impression that the relief was short-lived and that the speaker is trapped in a vicious cycle. Like Sisyphus, he pushes his heavy burden up a hill and finally reaches the summit, only to watch it roll back down again. However, the poem concludes on a hopeful note of trust that rescue will be forthcoming.

Structure and Dynamics

As in numerous other psalms, the poet addresses both his immediate hearers and God in direct address. It segments into three parts. Psalm 40:1–4 is directed to the community and speaks about God, beginning this poem on a contented note of confidence that recalls the blessedness of those who follow God (as proposed by Ps. 1). The following six verses (40:5–10) shift into the second person to address God directly. The last segment, 40:11–17, remains in the second person and continues to address God but reverts to a complaint.

A Report and Editorial Comment (40:1–4)

This poem begins with a happy report from the speaker about God rescuing him. It is written in the first-person singular and addressed to his local audience. He tells them that after a long period of anxiety and despair he regained his footing and has emotionally stabilized. The Hebrew duplication of the opening verb *qawwōh qiwwîtî* ("hoping I hoped" or "waiting I waited") indicates the intense stress during this period and ties these verses to the preceding poem. The report goes on to witness to a new song of praise that comes from his mouth, perhaps contrasted with the agonizing attempt to remain silent in Ps. 39. As with previous psalms in the canon, the public report intends to broadcast knowledge of God's graciousness so that others may benefit from his redemptive experience and "put their trust in the LORD" (40:4). Again one can see the evangelistic interest of the poet. He appends an editorial comment to his report of good news about how fortunate people are who remain faithful to God and do not turn away. As an aside, perhaps it recalls the contrast between the righteous and the wicked of Ps. 1, here pointedly placed in the context of a long wait for relief that may tempt many to give up on God (as in Ps. 39).

An Insight (40:5–10)

At this point the poem moves into a second-person direct address to God in effusive praise of the incomparable rescue operation that has enabled the speaker to resume his place as a faithful leader in Israel. The praise is as effusive as the distressed despair over God's silence in the previous poem. But it is not unreflective praise. Psalm 40:6–8 offers an insight apparently gained from having waited so long for God and having finally received an answer.

Perhaps the psalmist is trying to educate Israel on the nature of proper worship of God. God does not need or want the temple sacrifices that can be offered relatively easily at scant personal cost.[1] Rather, God wants what the speaker himself has done. He has internalized God's teaching (torah) and delights in following it; he sees himself described in the scroll as the model Israelite who endures adversity in hope and trust. The theme of faithfulness to torah carries the reader back again to Ps. 1, which divides the righteous from the wicked according to their faithfulness to God's teaching.

Reflecting on the inscrutability of God, especially when one experiences suffering, Calvin reaps as much pastoral guidance as possible from his high doctrine of divine sovereignty with these words:

1. Correcting an understanding of sacrifices is a prominent theme in Ps. 50. See also Jer. 6:20 and 7:21–23. The author of the Letter to the Hebrews zooms in on Ps. 40:6–8 to highlight the futility in thinking that cultic sacrifices could possibly be effective for cleansing sin; he puts the verses in Christ's mouth. While the poet may be leading Israel's understanding of proper worship in a fresh and interiorized direction, this psalm does not inaugurate a clear break with the sacrificial system that Hebrews claims happens only with Christ.

From this we learn how foolish and vain a thing it is to say, by way of caution, that none should speak of the counsels or purposes of God, because they are high and incomprehensible. David, on the contrary, though he was ready to sink under the weight, ceased not to contemplate them, and abstained not from speaking of them, because he felt unequal to the task of rehearsing them, but was content, after having declared his faith on this subject, to finish his discourse in admiration.[2]

Further, the speaker continues the now familiar response of publicizing his positive experience with God, assuming his rightful place as a public proclaimer of God's saving faithfulness. No one has grounds to scoff at him now. He is completely vindicated and no longer embarrassed by his proclamatory vocation; his tongue is loosened. Rather than restraining his lips from speaking, he gives public testimony in praise of God. This fired up Augustine to pen the following:

> The lips must proclaim what is in the heart: this is an injunction against fear. But the heart must have in it what the lips say: this is an injunction against insincerity. Sometimes you are afraid, and dare not say what you know to be true, what you believe; but at other times you are tempted to be insincere, and say something that is not in your heart. Your lips and your heart must be in agreement. If you seek peace from God, be reconciled with yourself; let there be no harmful conflict between your mouth and your heart.[3]

But Yet . . . (40:11–17)

Lament resumes with a second-person plea to God as the poet's human audience listens. The second-person address to God continues for most of the rest of the poem, but the topic changes dramatically. From rejoicing the reader is plunged back into the speaker's suffering for his sins depicted as blinding pain and a sinking heart. A spiritualized reading of the text by later Christian commentators suggests that the poet is not necessarily lashing out at other people but has so internalized the ubiquity of his sins (as many as the hairs of his head) that he personifies them as his enemies. He is angry at them, for his sins dishonor and torment him; he seeks God's revenge upon his sins. The effect of such a reading dramatically reshapes the text's dynamic. Drenched in self-recrimination, he desperately tries to alienate himself from his sins, begging God to crush them. His sins shame him, robbing him of his dignity in a different way than if the enemies were external. If he is his own enemy, his position of leadership in Israel is undone, for how could he uphold the message of Ps. 1 if he is mired in sin?

Whether one understand the enemies as external or internal, the bottom line is the same; clinging to God's ultimate faithfulness through cycles of elation and dejection has never been easy. This poem, like many others, turns away from

2. Calvin 1998, 97–98.
3. Augustine 2000b, 211.

the complainant's personal circumstance to remind his local audience that they should praise God's divine greatness, come what may. In this way, it typifies later Calvinist piety. The poem ends with a quietly humble plea for speedy deliverance.

Theological Pedagogy

The canonized form of Ps. 40—on one hand, separated from its predecessor whose tension it resolves and, on the other hand, receding back into angry frustration at God, who is apparently not hastening to help—seems confusing. If it is a contiguous piece, it seems that the two parts should be reversed, as I suggested with Ps. 30. Yet realistically speaking, life buffets us with anxiety, embarrassment, and shame in one season of life and then offers a firm foundation through the certainty of God's supportive presence and care for us in another. One need not interpret this poem (perhaps along with its predecessor) as a portrait of manic-depressive illness to appreciate the poet's insight into the vicissitudes of human life. Perhaps, over the long haul, these psalms can enable us to prize equanimity when we can manage it. If this is the case, Ps. 40 calls us to be gentle with ourselves, knowing that we will have seasons of strength and seasons of weakness.

PSALM 41

Canonical Context and Themes

Canonically speaking, Ps. 41 completes the first of the five books of the Psalter with a concluding doxology and the formulaic "amen and amen" (41:13). This phrase also appears at the conclusion of Books 2 and 3 of the Psalter, in Num. 5:22 and Neh. 8:6, and on Jesus's lips in the Gospel of John (often translated as "very truly").[1] Psalm 41 embraces two topics, tied together by the theme of illness, that pervade the whole. The first topic is that God safeguards those who care for the poor, even when they are ill. The second is the familiar prayer for deliverance from enemies, in this case, when the complainant is ill.

Structure and Dynamics

I treat this psalm in three segments. The first, 41:1–3, reassures those who care for the poor that God will take care of them when troubles befall them. The second segment, 41:4–12, the bulk of the poem, assumes the posture of a typical lament psalm but uncharacteristically we do know the situation causing the distress: illness through which God upholds him. The final verse seals this first book of the Psalter with a common doxological formula.

God Protects the Compassionate (41:1–3)

The poet begins not with a direct cry to God, as is common with complaints, but with a motivational speech to his hearers advising them that it is in their best

---

1. The canonical division of the Psalter into five books, which imitates the five books of the Torah, appears in the Septuagint, suggesting its ancient Jewish origin.

interest to care for the poor, for God will richly reward that care in four ways. God will keep them alive, bless them in the land, refrain from giving them over to their enemies, and heal them if they become ill—all strong incentives to tend to the common good.

Although the poet talks about visiting the sick only at 41:6, the rabbis of *Midrash on Psalms* comment on the importance of visiting the sick at 41:2, in which they interpret "the poor" as the sick.[2] "R. Johanan said: He who visits a man in poor health removes one-sixtieth of his illness; and he who does not visit adds one-sixtieth to his illness. R. Abin observed: If what R. Johanan says is true, let sixty persons come to visit a man who is in very poor health and so rid him of his illness!"[3]

Confiding in God (41:4–12)

The bulk of this poem now becomes a rather standard lament, with the additional note of the illness of the speaker beset by enemies, former intimates who have betrayed him. It presents as a report to the audience of the speaker's confidential first-person address to God in which he pours out his heart unstintingly. The speaker is suffering multiple types of pain and humiliation simultaneously: shame and regret if the illness is punishment for sin, which he considers as a possibility; the pain of the illness itself, which apparently could be fatal; and betrayal by those closest to him who pretend to be concerned for his well-being when visiting him but who gossip about him as soon as they leave his sickroom, expecting or hoping that he will die.

This quintessential Hebrew image for betrayal—"Even my bosom friend in whom I trusted, who ate of my bread, has lifted [his] heel against me" (41:9 NRSV)—flows heartrendingly from Jesus's lips at John 13:18, foreshadowing his being handed over to the police by Judas. Jesus tells his stunned friends that this future act will be to fulfill the psalm, but the reader knows that such betrayals are not as rare as one might wish, even if they do not carry the high stakes that Judas's betrayal did. To experience such disloyalty from within a community of like-minded comrades who have banded together as a tiny minority in the presence of harsh opponents is a deeply sobering awakening. Not only are these Jews disaffected from the majority by virtue of following Jesus, but even their little band

2. Judaism highly values visiting the sick, adhering to the talmudic instruction (*Shabbat* 127a), which elaborates the mishnaic text (*Pe'ah* 1:1) that there are activities for which no proper limit can be ascribed. One such activity is visiting the sick. Although one cannot know for certain that the rabbis of *Midrash on Psalms* had that text at their disposal, it is noteworthy that it was inserted into the morning service so that worshipers would daily be reminded of the importance of this and other acts of kindness.

3. Braude 1959a, 436. Sixty may be a standard number that is understood to dissolve the illness into small enough increments that it dissipates. For example, in determining whether meat into which milk has accidentally spilled can be eaten (Jewish dietary laws prohibit them to be mixed), the rule is that if the ratio of milk to meat is 1/60, the milk is considered an insignificant enough amount that the meat (or broth) does not have to be discarded as polluted.

is suspect. The psalmist identifies a situation in which anyone might find herself both physically and emotionally threatened and suddenly alone, abandoned by those she trusted, perhaps for many years.

It is utterly embarrassing to misjudge people, trusting those who end up turning their back when one is unaware and undeserving of such treatment. A thousand thoughts must be rushing through the suppliant's mind. Despite his sins, he has lived with integrity, he tells God. He searches his memory, asking himself what he might have done to warrant such treatment from people he loves. Is he such a bad judge of character that he could not have seen this coming? Reverting to the first person, he muses that his closest associates seem to want him dead and that they might get what they seek! He is hurt and angry; for the sake of his honor, he wants to repay them for this treachery.

All these questions and doubts swirl through the sufferer as he turns to God, who is his only lasting means of support now that human companions have proved fickle. Psalm 41:10–12 admits that, while people are unreliable God, is his last reliable hope, and the speaker throws himself on God's grace. This poet does not hold God accountable, as others do, for the abandonment he is experiencing. On the contrary, he consoles himself with the thought that God is pleased with him—despite the sins he mentions in 41:4—because his enemies have not yet fully triumphed over him. He is still alive and fighting with all he has. Whatever deadly disease has entered his system, it hasn't won the day. The speaker turns warrior on his own behalf. He will not live by his enemies' perception of him but by the perception that he believes God has of him, which may be the most difficult struggle of all. The complainant strives to hold on to the self that he is in God's eyes—the self that cannot be obliterated by the vision of himself that his enemies project onto him. Ultimately, his dignity depends upon the image he has of God's vision of him. At the end of the poem he finally breaks free of the power that his taunters hope to exercise over him, even if they cannot recognize the psychological power that they actually exert.

Concluding Praise (41:13)

As suggested at the outset of this chapter, the final verse of Ps. 41—"Blessed be the Lord, the God of Israel"—is a formulaic doxology indicating the ancient designation of the end of this book of the Psalter. It also appears toward the conclusion of Book 2 (Ps. 72:18), Book 3 in a variant form (Ps. 89:52), Book 4 (Ps. 106:48), and in other biblical texts in shortened form unrelated to psalms.[4] The ambiguity of this verse in this particular location is tantalizing. While it clearly functions as a placeholder separating books of the Psalter, it also praises God for the strength he has given the suppliant, who now knows not to rely on flesh-and-blood companions but on God alone.

4. 1 Sam. 25:32; 1 Kgs. 1:48; 8:15; 1 Chr. 16:36; 2 Chr. 6:4.

Theological Pedagogy

What is the psalmist teaching about God's ways with us? Perhaps the most painful lesson is that God is more faithful than people. While other psalms suggest that even God is not to be trusted (particularly when he lies behind cruel treatment suffered at the hands of flesh-and-blood companions), Ps. 41 teaches that even if our dearest companions forsake us, God knows the truth of our innermost self and forever holds us fast.

In the context of other laments whose speakers alternate between hoping for relief from human foes by God's gracious intervention and resigning themselves to being abandoned by God (at least temporarily), Ps. 41 takes the unexpected turn of urging us to care for the poor, even amid our own inexplicable suffering. Perhaps this is the most profound exhortation of the poet. Amid confused humiliation, the way forward is not to dwell on the degradation experienced at the hands of our loved ones but to care for the poor; God rewards such care. Being a faithful Israelite is a demanding undertaking. No sweet comfort here. Only by striving beyond our hurt and affliction can we attain to that realm of light wherein God sustains us happily in the land.

PSALM 42–43

Canonical Context and Themes

Psalms 42 and 43 seemingly constitute a single powerful poem based upon various literary features, the most salient of which is the thrice-repeated refrain in nearly the same words at 42:5, 42:11, and 43:5. Together they frame a three-stanza poem of sixteen verses (according to the Christian numeration) that is punctuated by this repeated searching self-reflection summoning the reader to hope in God to calm a perturbed spirit. Treating these two psalms as one is also warranted because Ps. 43 lacks a superscription, which is common in other psalms of this second section of the Psalter (Pss. 42–72). Further, the distressed cry of 42:9 is repeated almost verbatim at 43:2—"Why must I walk about mournfully because the enemy oppresses me?" Here, in keeping with the consensus of modern scholarship, I treat Pss. 42 and 43 as one poem that opens Book 2 of the Psalter, which generally, though not exclusively, identifies God as *ʾĕlōhîm* (or a variant of this word) rather than as the Tetragrammaton, as is the case in Book 1.[1]

Following the superscription, this poem opens with a soliloquy addressed to God; the suppliant longs to be with the living God who waters him. The power of fresh-flowing or living water, essential for life, connects the water imagery with the repeated identification of the living God (42:2 and 8), for whom the speaker sheds tears (42:3). The remaining verses soliloquize memories of better days and carry the reader deep into the emotions of the conflicted suppliant, who is confused and constantly questioning both himself and God. From the opening verse, water images dominate the first half of this psalm (42:1–7).[2] In the second half (42:8–43:5), the suppliant despairs, feeling cast off by God. He remembers better days when all was well and he processed in festival worship; perhaps he

---

1. This word or a variant of it appears eighteen times in these sixteen verses.
2. Brown 2002, 132–34.

held a leadership role in the temple[3]—a fond memory that only increases his despondency. For now he is unnerved by the taunting of those who ridicule his faithful past as naïve, sparking a raw spiritual emptiness that leaves him wishing that his past memories were powerful enough to keep him strong now. He pleads with God to vindicate his faithfulness and enable him to regain his previous stature in the community so that he can worship joyfully among the throng of those observing the festival.

The thrice-offered tortured refrain expresses the speaker's consternation that he cannot control his feelings. He is embarrassed not only in front of those who taunt him but also in front of himself and perhaps in front of God. As I noted earlier, being mocked seeps into the soul and breeds self-doubt. Was his trusting and worshipful self hoodwinked into believing that God is truly there? Psalm 42–43 pulls the reader tautly between the speaker's exaltation in celebratory worship and the desperate fear that God has truly abandoned him or perhaps was never "there" at all. It probes the tormented heart. Perhaps the celebratory moment is more about enjoying one's own leadership (or at least public-spirited energy) than about one's faith in God!

Structure and Dynamics

As noted, the three segments of the unified poem are Pss. 42:1–5, 6–11, and 43:1–5, each punctuated by the refrain, "How depressed I am and growling. Yet I wait for God and still expect his rescue" (42:5, 11; 43:5).[4] The refrain indicates the conflicted disposition of the speaker mired in self-doubt, seemingly forgotten by God, and taunted by scoffers who mock, "Where is your God?" (42:3). He yearns to remain faithfully hopeful, but the mocking question hits its mark.

Thirsting for God (42:1–5)

The opening stanza of the poem likens longing for the living God to the thirst and hunger of an animal. Though the speaker seeks water from God, he languishes with only his tears to drink; God is absent. While *be'ĕmōr* in 42:3 is customarily translated as "they say to me," suggesting that the speaker is being taunted by "the wicked" hinted at in Ps. 1 (a theme redolent throughout the poems), the form of the verb is ambiguous because it is an infinitive construct. It could also suggest

3. The word *'eddaddēm* (Ps. 42:4) can mean either "process," "walking deliberately," or "to lead," which would catapult this poem into an entirely different framework of a leader torn from honor and thrown into disgrace.

4. Several translations translate *mah* in 42:5, 11, and 43:5 as an interrogative "why," yet Alter is more to the point by translating it as a declarative "how," which expresses the stress under which the suppliant labors. This translation is my own. The Hebrew, terse as ever, uses but twelve words in the refrain, whereas the NRSV uses twenty-nine. My sixteen-word translation captures the tautness of the poet and the distress of the speaker.

that the speaker is constantly plagued by asking himself where God is, for self-doubt is more unnerving than the sneer of adversaries, although being sneered at will surely affect tender souls adversely.

To counter nagging self-doubt, the poet has the tormented speaker admit his former confidence among the throng of Israelite worshipers in the temple. It is a picture of stark contrasts—humbling and perhaps even embarrassing. The speaker is not defensive but genuinely tortured, and the poet lets the reader in on the pain of this ingenuous soul. Can his former exaltation in worship speak now to his disquiet about trusting God? He admonishes himself with the thrice-repeated refrain, trying to reassure himself to get back on the track he wants to follow: "How depressed I am and growling. Yet I wait for God and still expect his rescue" (42:5).

Hoping for Hope (42:6–11)

The poem's second stanza expands the water imagery from the personal experience of tears to the geography of Israel. God is remembered in the lands surrounding the Jordan River and the nearby mountains of Hermon and Mitsar, in addition to the great waterfalls whose gushing streams playfully call to one another, overwhelming the speaker.[5] Even if God is not evident through personal rescue, his hand in nature stills fear, at least temporarily. Nature itself seems to reassure him so that at night song and prayer to God are again possible, perhaps reminiscent of the public worship he once led.[6]

Yet the speaker and the reader with him are tossed from hand to hand, from trust to despair by turns. In hopeful moments, the speaker castigates his own despair: "By day the LORD commands his steadfast love, and at night his song is with me" (Ps. 42:8), but when his taunters' voices rise in a crescendo of gloom, he mourns again for his life: "I say to God, my rock, 'Why have you forgotten me?'" (Ps. 42:9), for they strike what feels like a mortal blow to the speaker's body. As other psalms indicate, stress vitiates the body. The speaker repairs to his mournful refrain: "How depressed I am and growling. Yet I wait for God and still expect his rescue" (42:11). The poet presses for hope.

Confronting God (43:1–5)

Moving from the self-scrutiny of Ps. 42, a more familiar plea to God appears in Ps. 43. The speaker turns from self-doubt and the tussle between hope and despair to entreat God for vindication against the ungodly, a refrain in its own right. Here, the speaker finds his footing as one who has overcome his fear that

5. *Midrash on Psalms* personifies the upper and lower falls as male and female united in fertile sexual embrace (Braude 1959a, 443–44).

6. For a fuller treatment of this theme see Brown 2002, 132–34.

either God has abandoned him or that he (the speaker) is not confidently able to ask God to deliver him from his mournful trembling (Ps. 43:2).

Theological Pedagogy

Psalm 42–43 is one of many that endear the Psalter to Jews and Christians for personal devotion. Who manages to get through life without faltering when an important foundation gives way? The speaker undergoes this crisis in public no less! Christians have hesitated to voice doubts about God's benevolence and power as this psalm so candidly does. Reformed "federal theology" of the seventeenth century, later elaborated by Karl Barth, assumes that the covenant between God and the people of God (the church) is an act of unilateral grace on God's part and that God sets its terms. On these terms, the pious assume that whatever happens is within God's covenantal commitment and so is for the best. This justifies events, even suffering, as the sovereign will of God.

The psalmists have a different understanding of covenant as a bilateral arrangement. According to that view, they do not hesitate to call God to account, so convinced are they of God's responsibilities to Israel. The poet does not fear brutal honesty in that relationship because God and Israel are both responsible for protecting it. The mutuality of that understanding may serve as a salutary model for tutoring people in sustaining healthy human relationships in which both parties must attend to the needs of the other.

Furthermore, the response of the speaker is a model for later readers who resonate with his experience. He does not become defensive. He is more hurt than angry and does not go after his enemies, even though they have touched him to the quick. Instead, he engages in deep self-examination, taking seriously the taunts aimed at him as painful as that process surely is. To be able to say to himself "they may be right" is a humbling admission for a public leader, but he is strong and mature, clinging to hope for stability.

That he simply cannot let go of God, whatever the empirical evidence may warrant, is also a model for the poet's readers. Faith is not a calculated commitment but is organic to a person's emotions and attachments. Even coherent arguments cannot unseat God from the speaker's body. God is embedded there; as such, the afflicted can seek "the peace of God, which passes all understanding."[7] Perhaps withdrawing from the position of leadership is warranted and a period of retreat and repair needed. The speaker's life may need to take a fresh direction. If it does, it will be a tested way forward, lived with integrity.

---

7. *Book of Common Prayer* 1979, 339, quoting Phil. 4:7.

PSALM 44

Canonical Context and Themes

As we have seen, the laments continue into Book 2 of the Psalter. Psalm 44 is, however, the first communal lament. The voicing shifts back and forth between first-person plural, speaking for Israel, and first-person singular, an unidentified individual,[1] but it is predominantly written in the first-person plural, with the nation directly addressing God. In addition, the poet also puts words in the mouth of the people to remind desolate Israel of the true source of its safety and well-being. The poem cries out to God to rescue the nation from whatever military or political humiliation it has suffered on the world stage. A text like 1 Sam. 31, in which King Saul and his three sons die in battle and Israel is routed and humiliated by the Philistines, might have been in the psalmist's mind, although the psalm does not suggest that. The kingdom was taken from Saul and Israel punished because Saul refused to destroy the finest possessions of the Amalekites, giving these spoils of war to Israelites who wanted them, apparently unaware that God would consider this a grave sin (1 Sam. 15).

This poem radiates bewilderment and confusion as both community and individual voices fumble to express consternation at the thought that God would/ could/might abandon them to their enemies. It also urges God to awaken to Israel's extreme need because Israel has been faithful to God in season and out (44:8, 17, 20). While the issue here is theodicy, as it is with many individual laments, Ps. 44 stands apart from individual supplications because the parties to

---

1. Following the assumption of form criticism, Nancy L. deClaissé-Walford assumes that the individual is the liturgical leader for this psalm and that it was written for antiphonal public worship. However, the change of voices need not suggest antiphonal recitation, and the continuous flow of the thought between singular and plural voicing does not suggest public worship as its compositional location (DeClaissé-Walford 2007).

the drama are quite different. Individual laments generally portray the righteous complainant in opposition to wicked Israelites who scoff at the righteous and abjure God's teachings, for which Ps. 1 sets the framework. There and in other laments of individuals, the struggle is between pious and cynical Israelites and serves to spur other Israelites to faithfulness.

In Ps. 44 the struggle is between faithful Israel and the surrounding nations. The nations are not portrayed as wicked as much as in Israel's way, authorizing Joshua's conquest of them for Israel to inherit their land. Israel assumes that if it is faithful, God will protect, defend, and rescue it. Concomitantly, the psalm insists that Israel relies on divine grace rather than its own military strategists and armamentarium—a point that echoes the great model of King Hezekiah who adhered to Isaiah's advice and was vindicated against the Assyrians (2 Kgs. 18–19).

The theodicy question is not resolved, and the poem ends with a fervent plea for rescue. Yet it does point to Israel's deeper strength, which is located in the nation's faithfulness to God, even when humiliated. As in its immediate predecessor, Ps. 42–43, the community cannot give up on God despite empirical evidence that might warrant it. Psalm 44 might have been a rallying cry for victims in the Nazi death camps, and indeed, 44:22 has often been cited in this regard. The theology urges holding fast to God's goodness and power even in dire circumstances. The psalmist's admonition is to resist imploding into a bundle of angry cynicism, that only damages the soul and one's dignity.

Structure and Dynamics

This poem offers an alternative and perhaps controversial construal of Israel's history, contrasting sharply with that of Ps. 78 that portrays Israel as consistently rebellious and perhaps ungrateful and God as regularly forgiving and faithful.[2] Psalm 44 says the exact opposite. Israel is depicted as consistently faithful while God is missing in action. Ps. 44 begins by rehearsing the conquest of the land, presumably under Joshua (44:1–3), that he attributes to divine favor. After this reminder to God of his responsibilities to Israel (44:4a), the poem adverts to a plea to God for a repeat performance to save Israel now from its current enemies on account of Israel's faithfulness (44:4b–8), not simply on account of God's mercy that Ps. 78 stresses. But the third scene of Ps. 44 reveals that God has not yet acted and Israel feels rejected and publically debased despite its loyalty to God (44:9–22). The closing segment of the lament is not a scene because no events are

2. Because Hebrew has a limited vocabulary, many words carry a broader lexical range of meaning than they would in languages with an expansive vocabulary like German and English, which can employ words more specifically. This makes Hebrew difficult to pin down. While it gives freer poetic license to authors, it makes the job of translators and interpreters more difficult. This is especially the case with Ps. 44. Here I try to interpret several words in keeping with the person, number, tense, and voice of nearby words, particularly as these affect the isocolonic verse structure.

portrayed. Rather, it is a concluding plea for rescue, ostensibly grounded in scene two of the rehearsed history where God's preference for Israel emerges. The lament ends with Israel's inability to leave God, even if he acts inscrutably (44:23–26).

In Antiquity You Acted . . . (44:1–3)

The opening strophe of this poem gently chides God by reminding him of his responsibility by calling attention to his past, protecting leadership of Israel in the conquest of the land. Whether the conquest narrative in Joshua is historically accurate is less important for understanding the theology of the poem than is the fact that our poet recalls it to rouse God to action and thereby encourage his hearers to hold on. In prodding God to be his best self the poet is not only reminding God of his track record but also teaching the people of their own proper theological attitude: trust in God rather than their own resources. It recalls the admonition of Zechariah (4:6): "This is the word of the LORD to Zerubbabel: Not by might, nor by power, but by my spirit, says the LORD of hosts."

Statement of Loyalty (44:4a)

The simple proclamation—"God, you are my king"—by an individual (perhaps the worship leader if this psalm was written for public use) is profound, especially following the previous reading of Ps. 44:1–3. It marks a weighty realization that Israel is part of a plan of salvation larger than its own experience and is to be faithful to a history that it neither controls nor can predict.

But Then You Turned to Us (44:4b–7)

After this humbling beginning, the poet carries the reader in an entirely different direction. God now controls Jacob's military might against its enemies. Israel gores[3] its military opponents and desecrates those who challenge it (44:5), yet the poet immediately and cautiously adds that neither Israel's bow nor its sword save it. God is the rescuer; he has defeated those against whom Israel strives. *Midrash on Psalms* strongly highlights the point:

> When the children of Israel went forth from Egypt, they could not offer any works of their hands whereby they might be redeemed. And so, not because of the works of their fathers, and not because of their own works, was the sea rent before them, but only that God might make Himself a name in the world. [Isa. 63:13 is quoted.] . . . When the children of Israel were redeemed from Egypt, Moses said: Not because of your works are you redeemed, but only *That thou mayest tell in the ears of thy son* (Exod. 10:2), that is, only that thou mayest give the Holy One, blessed be He, the glory of having His children declare His praise among the nations.[4]

3. This translation follows Alter (2007, 155).
4. Braude 1959a, 446.

Calvin echoes the point more succinctly: "*For they got not possession of the land by their own sword. . . .* The best means, therefore, of cherishing in us habitually a spirit of gratitude towards God, is to expel from our minds this foolish opinion of our own ability."[5]

Giving Thanks (44:8)

In Ps. 44:8 the community proclaims its constant praise of God, the ground on which it can trust and hope that God will redeem it. It does not prepare us for the next turn of events.

Yet Now You Turned against Us! (44:9–22)

Now the community is shocked at being brought low. It has accepted God's original embrace of the Canaanites—since after all they were the original occupants of the land—God's subsequent rejection of them, and his turn toward Israel. But now the reader (along with Israel) inhabits an utterly new universe. God has apparently betrayed, abandoned, and rejected Israel; formerly he gave the land of the Canaanites to Joshua's forces. Now Israel is vanquished, exiled, taunted, and overcome. The intense communal complaint laments Israel's chagrin at its public disgrace; it is plundered by its enemies, perhaps descendants of those same Canaanites whom God through Joshua previously conquered.

Israel's anger, however, is not directed at the Canaanites but at God. Just as God was the power behind Israel's success, so God is the agent of Israel's humiliation. Israel may be all the worse for having touted God as the source of its strength, in place of its military prowess. Deep ruminations surface again. God, not Israel, is in the hot seat.

Israel is mocked by its neighbors, exiled, slaughtered like helpless sheep, and publically debased. It crawls on its belly like a snake, or perhaps an insect, yet claims never to have forgotten God or embraced a foreign deity. Here the fault lies firmly with God. Israel has never claimed military or political victory for itself but gives all the glory to God, and so now God is responsible for Israel's public shame. Indeed, Israel's shame is God's shame. What foreign nation would take this God seriously? By abandoning Israel God is defeating his own purpose of sovereign rule of the nations, on the assumption that conquest in the name of God is persuasive to the conquered.

Wake Up, God! (44:23–26)

This sad poem offers no resolution of Israel's plight, yet it is not enveloped in hopeless self-pity or (self-)destructive anger. Israel remains as perplexed as ever at God's silence in the face of its suffering, given the intransigent belief that God

5. Calvin 1996, 152–53.

is both faithful to Israel and powerful to save. Psalm 44:23–26 pleads for God to arise, wake up, *do something* to vindicate himself. As the community calls upon God's loving-kindness, the poem ends on this note of tenuous hopefulness.

Theological Pedagogy

On this reading, Ps. 44 is a particularly jarring poem. It presses Israel's self-understanding as the apple of God's eye—an identity on which the nation fundamentally relies—to call God back to his post when Israel is suffering terribly. Moreover, it thrusts into the foreground the possibility that God is unreliable despite Israel's faithfulness. The poem leaves us with the haunting thought that perhaps God has abandoned Israel after all. It is a theme that Christians inherited in the form of Christian supersessionism seeded by Pauline and Johannine ecclesiology that in different ways define the people of God as those who follow Jesus, not Jews who adhere to emerging normative Judaism.

Yet the bottom line of this unsettling poem urges readers to remain faithful no matter how daunting the circumstance. Divine inscrutability ought not affect obedience. Paul is perhaps the first to lift this up as a Christian ideal when he quotes Ps. 44:22 in full to urge persecuted Christians who experience themselves as "being killed all day long; we are accounted as sheep to be slaughtered," to cling to the conviction that no human experience has the power to undermine Christian grounding in the love of Christ. Jews who read this verse would be urged to hold fast to their faith despite their persecution, not infrequently at Christian hands. It is not a stoic "grin and bear it" admonition but what I would call a "cry in order to bear it" mentality. Crying out for rescue acts as somewhat of a pressure valve and enables people to bond together in their suffering.

Another reason that this pedagogy is disturbing is because the poet does not encourage active resistance to oppression in a search for justice, but only apparently to wait for God. While endurance may be relatively easy to urge in the abstract, to those oppressed by horrendous evils like genocide, natural and human disasters, ethnic cleansing, and apartheid, it is certainly a challenging posture to take.

PSALM 45

Canonical Context and Themes

Psalm 45 takes us in a quite different direction than the preceding songs as the first in a series of four psalms that focus on the delicate question of Israelite foreign policy. God's designs on the surrounding nations, especially through the relationship between Israel's king and the nations' kings, bubbles up throughout the Psalter (beginning with Ps. 2) and is focused in this little group of psalms. Israel's problem is how to understand the basic theological conviction that Israel's God is the God of the nations. Like the current State of Israel, ancient Israel struggled to balance this twin challenge. The temptation to tribalism is permanently inscribed in the formula of all Jewish blessings, the liturgical spine of Judaism: "Blessed are you Lord our God, king of the universe." Perhaps the most striking biblical statement of this tension between Israel's calling to be both a people apart and the instrument of God's universal reign is stated inadvertently in Solomon's prayer at the dedication of the temple where he asks God both to protect foreigners in Israel's midst and to give Israel victory in battle against its enemies (2 Chr. 6:32–35).

Psalm 45 offers a strategy for dealing with this tension. It depicts a royal marriage and conceivably may have been composed for or sung at a public celebration. Its heading designates it as a love song to be sung to the tune of *šōšannîm* (lilies). The poem itself, however, is not about just any wedding but about a politically expedient marriage that advances international relations. Its three themes—or better put, three directions—open with the imported bride preparing for her marriage to the king. Next, it instructs the bride in the ways to be a supportive imported wife/concubine. Only toward the poem's end is the bride presented to the bridegroom, who never speaks.

This is the first psalm to focus on women, their place in the royal domicile, and their role in international affairs. It purportedly gives the reader a woman's point of view on these matters; at the very least it gives the author's portrayal of a woman's point of view. Whether the psalm was actually penned by women as 45:1 suggests or whether it presents women's perspectives as construed by a male author, it is still the first time that women's voices appear in the Psalter. Two women are portrayed sympathetically and appear to be speaking candidly.

The bride is from Tyre (45:12), a heavily fortified coastal Phoenician city in southern Lebanon renowned for its maritime prominence and its cedar trees, which were undoubtedly one of its premier exports. The bride may be the daughter of King Hiram of Tyre, a good friend of King David's. Hiram continued that alliance with Solomon when he took office (1 Kgs. 5:1–12), and Solomon purchased cedars from Hiram to build the temple in Jerusalem. Peace reigned under Solomon's wise cultivation of this neighbor.

Alternatively, this psalm could also mark the later marriage of Ahab, king of Israel, to Jezebel, the daughter of King Ethbaal of Sidon, about twenty miles north of Tyre (1 Kgs. 16:31), but that is unlikely since the psalmist mentions Tyre. Marriage has been a standard foreign policy strategy to secure peace throughout history.

Because it seems to make better historical sense of the story told here, I will assume that the psalm is about Solomon and his household. Solomon was renowned for his imported wives, who led him and then Israel into paganism (1 Kgs. 11:1–8). This psalm not only marks but celebrates Solomon's admittance of one of Hiram's daughters to his harem, perhaps gifted to him to sustain the alliance. Scripture does not mention an acquisition of Hiram's daughter specifically, but it does say that as a result of Solomon's importation of these women he worshiped Astarte, the chief Sidonian goddess (1 Kgs. 11:5, 33). This historical context enables one to better assess how politics and religion interact in real life, offering insight into the theology embedded in the text and the theological reading given to it by later readers. In this way, present-day readers can appreciate its subtlety in their own context.

Structure and Dynamics

Psalm 45 reads like a short play in two acts (45:1–9 and 10–17). The first act has two scenes, and the second has three. The speaker in the first act is the bride preparing for union with the king, while the speaker in the second act is the chief consort or queen mentioned in the last verse of act 1 who prepares for her entrance as the speaker in act 2.

Act 1 opens with the bride preparing for her new status in life, while act 2 has the king's chief consort first instructing the bride in proper courtly behavior (45:10–13), then acting as the mistress of ceremonies for the presentation of the new acquisition to the king, then speaking to those waiting outside the palace or the general public (45:14–15), and concluding with a celebratory salute to the longevity and success of the dynasty (45:16–17). Psalm 45 presents not only women's voices (purportedly) but also the demonstration of their responsibilities and authority as members of the governing household.

Act 1 (45:1–9)

The bride primarily addresses the king, but her speech begins with a brief soliloquy as she steadies her for that meeting.

Act 1, Scene 1: Soliloquy (45:1)

The bride is excited and not fearful about what is about to happen when she is formally presented to the king. In what may be an interview examining her fitness to join the royal household, her words to him will trip off her tongue with confident calm. The reader is fortunate to be privy to her emotions, for they set the tone not only for what follows in the poem but for the import of this marriage for the monarchy and for peace between Israel and its northwest neighbor. The bride is happy to be where she is because her role in Israel enables her to forward peace for her own people.

Act 1, Scene 2: The Bride Speaks! (45:2–9)

The next scene shows the bride addressing her new lord in what is probably their first meeting to prepare for the liaison. It is noteworthy that the king is silent; only the bride speaks, and she is not interrogated. She flatters him, hoping to impress him as a loyal and trustworthy new member of his household. Bringing outsiders into an imperial house is always a delicate affair. She flatters him appropriately. He is morally beautiful and a grand and successful military commander respected both militarily and because his integrity makes him both beloved and prosperous as God's anointed.

Her recognition of the king's religious authority makes clear to the overhearing public that the king is God's obedient servant and that the new female acquisition will not bring her national gods with her but will embrace his God. Pleased to review the various forms of the king's wealth, the bride mentions his wealth of foreign daughters, who manifest the king's peace-seeking foreign policy. He may demand tribute in the form of building materials, precious metals, and women from those he has vanquished. Alternatively, the marital alliances may pave the way for trade agreements. But aside from simply amassing wealth, marital alliances are designed to establish international peace. The take-away message is that military and moral power in obedience to God bring God's blessings in the form of wealth and peace. The bride speaks as one confident in her ability to enhance international peace.[1]

1. A Christian spiritual reading not surprisingly depicts the throne as occupied not by Solomon or Ahab but by Christ—who loves righteousness, hates wickedness, and is anointed, not with spices (which would portend death) but with oil of gladness (Heb. 1:8–9).

Act 2 (45:10–17)

Now that the bride has had her say, the king's chief consort and director of women's services in the household (introduced in the last verse of the bride's speech) takes center stage. In scene 1, she instructs the newcomer in her duties. Scene 2 narrates the proceedings of the wedding to the waiting public. Finally, in scene 3 she leads the people in tribute to the dynasty. While scene 1 and scenes 2 and 3 could be spoken by two characters, since scene 1 (45:10–12) is direct address while scenes 2 and 3 refer to the principle characters in the third person (45:13–17), the ready flow of the speech suggests a single voice turning to different audiences.

ACT 2, SCENE 1: THE QUEEN INSTRUCTS THE NEOPHYTE (45:10–12)

Act 2, scene 1 is between the bride and her mentor. The queen or novice mistress enters the play to further the newcomer's ability to meet her responsibilities as the newest addition to the harem. The novice mistress impresses upon the neophyte the requirements of her new status in the house of the king. She must relinquish attachment to her community of origin, including its religion, which the bride has already done by acknowledging her obedience to the God of Israel. If she pleases the king, it will bode well for her people in their alliance with Israel. While on one level she must abandon her heritage, on another she is not abandoning it at all but using her new position to protect her own people. This scene is the inverse of the story of Esther, here told from the perspective of a Canaanite bride brought to an Israelite king. In contrast to God's order to commit genocide in order to maintain the purity of Israel's worship and God's punishment of Solomon for his foreign policies of alliances with and religious tolerance of non-Israelites (1 Kgs. 11), Ps. 45's policy of toleration appears humane. And while this psalm sympathizes with the situation of imported women, which may offend current sensibilities regarding women and international relations, in its context it appears benevolent. The moral questions that face Israel in response to God's call for strict devotion to him surface starkly in Ps. 45, as they do in the following three psalms of this group (Pss. 46–48) that focus on Israel's foreign policy.

ACT 2, SCENE 2: THE AUDIENCE WATCHES (45:13–15)

Now the speaker addresses the psalm's wider audience by narrating the pageant taking place, as the bride, bedecked with pomp and imported finery and accompanied by a retinue of virgins, proceeds to the palace where the king awaits her to consummate the union and the political alliance with double pleasure. Assuming that the king is a gentle and skilled lover worthy of the praise his new bride has showered on him, pleasure serves the cause of peace. It is an unusual note for scripture to sound and is reminiscent of the Song of Songs, for which no dating is clear.

Act 2, Scene 3: Dynastic Tribute (45:16–17)

In conclusion, the mistress of ceremonies then addresses either the king or perhaps the bride—the grammar is a bit confusing here—anticipating the children to be born of this union. They are expected to further dynastic reach and power.

Theological Pedagogy

As one might expect of a text that oozes with the importance of sex—not raw sex but sex in the context of loyalty, public responsibility, and personal stamina as vehicles of empire—neither Jews nor Christians have been particularly comfortable with this psalm. Time and again pious commentators sanitize away its plain meaning with ingenious interpretations, beginning with Hebrews itself (as previously noted).

On quite another front, considering that both Israel and the nations are God's own, although in different ways, one need not repair to allegory or other strategies to symbolically obviate the text in order to universalize its import. The potential for this psalm to speak its own voice theologically as part of the ebb and flow of the conversation to understand God and obedience to him calls for exploration.

Jonah, Ruth, 1 Kgs. 17:8–24, 2 Kgs. 5, and Ps. 45 all protest a narrow construal of Israelite ecclesiology, objecting to the belief that God is bent on establishing the extent of his global reach through violent conquest rather than persuasion, as other parts of the Tanakh assert. Indeed, this soft view of inviting non-Israelites into the people of God boldly opposes Deuteronomic and Deuteronomistic theology (e.g., Joshua) that drives home a militaristic understanding of God's determination to establish global authority by intimidation and force. In contrast to Deuteronomic theology, the approach here is grandly conciliatory. Perhaps it was written in an optimistic time before, or at least apart from, the events that gave rise to the somber conclusions of Deut. 17 and 1 Kgs. 11 that the only way for God's authority in the world to triumph is by intimidation (Exod. 12:32 and Ps. 2:10–11) or brute force.

On the one hand, this prompts a discussion about what to do when foreign policy, carried out in the name of God, yields unanticipated negative consequences. A policy of toleration and relatively gentle incorporation of foreigners into Israel advocated by the abovementioned texts designed to integrate foreigners into worship of Israel's God, proved ill-advised according to those who sought absolute purity of worship as the highest priority. These more strident voices may have won the day in Judaism by maintaining the Jewish people as a people set apart from the nations. On the other hand, other voices—notably the authors of Ruth and Jonah, along with many other incidental comments throughout the Tanakh, welcome non-Israelites. Paul and the authors of other Younger Testament texts take the side of these minority voices and invite foreigners into the household of God. The bride of Ps. 45 was welcomed into the king's household as a faithful and loyal princess, following the more open tradition.

While the novice mistress advises the young wife to abandon her family of origin and assimilate into a new one, the reader knows that in doing so the imported bride serves her people by protecting them from harm, as does Esther (although Esther must operate in a hostile setting). In analogous Christian terms, those Jews and pagans who join together under the ensign of the cross of Christ further the worship of God in fresh ways. These may look like treachery to some but are redemptive for those willing to venture beyond the comfort zones of family and friends on both sides of the Jewish–pagan divide. Thankfully, scripture preserves both perspectives for our edification.

The theological pedagogy of this psalm pushes in two quite different directions, both of which are instructive. Like the book of Ruth, Ps. 45 espouses an inclusive ecclesiology that invites foreign wives into Israel, but it is a minority voice in the Older Testament. The majority voice holds to an exclusive ecclesiology in which Israel is set apart by God and required to sustain ethnographic purity that requires harsh measures. In Ezra 10, families are broken up on a grand scale; Israelite men are forced to divorce their non-Israelite wives, and children are sent away with their mothers (Ezra 10:44). Ethnic purity reigns here. It may undergird current Israeli-Jewish sentiments.

The inclusive ecclesiology exemplified by Ps. 45, by contrast, urges Israel to risk diluting, even polluting, the ethnic purity of the community for the sake of domestic and international peace. Perhaps the most salient Christian text here is 1 Cor. 7:12–16. It directly counters Ezra's nationalistic demand to send away all foreign wives to protect the purity of Jewish worship. Paul flagrantly violates that policy on the grounds of his radical view that purity purifies impurity. His optimistic policy is that in the intimacy of marriage partners sanctify each other. On the view that both Esther and the bride of Ps. 45 are secretly working on behalf of their own people, the larger point here is that marriage, in both its sexual and political dimensions, can be a sanctifying instrument that God uses for good.

The intrigue of sex and politics is sure to get readers' attention. Having set the stage with this little drama, we proceed to the stronger stuff of facing Israel's responsibility for its mission to the pagans once the wedding meats are consumed.

PSALM 46

Canonical Context and Themes

While Ps. 45 uses intermarriage to bring the nations into God's household, Ps. 46 resumes a nationalistic outlook on Israel's foreign policy and ecclesiology.

Structure and Dynamics

Strophing Ps. 46 is not easy for two reasons. First, it offers two inherent sets of strophic markers—the ambiguous *selâ*, which appears after 46:3, 7, and 11, and a twice-repeated refrain (46:7 and 11) that also naturally distinguishes stanzas. Two of these markers appear together, which is helpful, but the *selâ* after 46:3 muddies that clarity. Additionally, the refrain of 46:7 does not mark a thematic shift in the poem, for a new theme has been introduced at 46:6, suggesting that if the refrain followed by *selâ* is meant to separate segments of the poem, it should come before the new theme is introduced. Given this lack of clarity, I will strophe the poem according to the use of *selâ* but treat 46:7 with the preceding verses and 46:6 with the following verses to yield three stanzas: 46:1–3; 46:4–5, 7, and 46:6, 8–11.

We Take Strength from Your Strength (46:1–3)

These verses, spoken in the first-person plural by the gathered company, presumably at prayer, depict God as willing and able to protect Israel from natural catastrophes—primarily earthquakes and other geological eruptions that can topple mountains or that occur under the sea. Earthquakes are not common in Palestine but were not unknown in ancient Israel.[1] Many commentators regard

1. Earthquakes are mentioned at 1 Kgs. 19:11–12; Isa. 29:6; Amos 1:1; and Zech. 14:5.

this language as either mythological or metaphorical, but it may simply be poetic description by people who lacked precise meteorological terminology. The poet's point is that natural disasters are fearsome, and God is expected to protect people from their destructive power. While Ps. 45 is a drama about sex and politics, Ps. 46 is a drama about the use of natural disaster for political ends. Israel expects to be shielded from the destructive power of natural disasters like earthquakes. Indeed, God *is* the only hope in the face of earth-shattering events that could not have been predicted. Contrary to militaristic psalms that depict God backing Israel's king against other competing monarchs, this one portrays God defeating dangers that affect everyone. It is more like the battle between Elijah and the priests of Baal than a military encounter that Israel might wage in God's name.

God in the City (46:4–5, 7)

These verses switch to the third-person singular as if addressed to the gathered community, perhaps by a preacher. They identify an unnamed city of God, not Augustine's celestial city but a very tangible one located in Israel's territory.[2] While in 46:2–3 water terrorizes people, in 46:4–5 water is an essential friend. And so it is; water is both the fount and the destroyer of life. An underground spring and water shaft, today a national park in Jerusalem, enable the earthly city of God to survive, for Jerusalem is landlocked. Flowing, life-giving water shows that God favors the city and helps it when needed.

Since these are the only two verses in the psalm that speak of the city of God, perhaps the refrain with its concluding *selâ* (46:7) belongs here, for it speaks in the first-person plural like the opening three verses and states the basic message of the poem (identified in 46:1): "The LORD who commands armies is with us; Jacob's God is our citadel."

The Nations Are Involved (46:6, 8–11)

While Ps. 46:1–5 seeks to calm Israel in the face of impending "acts of God," the poet uses the threat of natural disaster at 46:6 to show the nations what is happening between God's power and Israel's well-being. The poet or narrator speaks in the third-person plural, probably addressing Israel about the nations who customarily threaten it. The poem informs Israel that the forces from which God protects it shake the nations to their foundations. God's power will not protect them! The nations roar (using the same verb as for the roaring sea in 46:3) not from natural causes but at the commanding voice of God that "melts the earth" (46:6). The nations are warned that they will melt down before the power of God. Here God arrays natural forces to protect Israel while other nations are made desolate.

2. It may well be Jerusalem, but it may also be the town of Dan, the center of the tribe of Dan in the far north of Israel near Aram, whence Israel traces its geographical descent into Egypt (Deut. 26:5), located on a tributary that flows into the Sea of Galilee.

Psalm 46:8 instructs all hearers and addressees of the poem to attend to the destructive power of God as much as to the protective power of God, highlighted in 46:1–3. One effect of natural disaster is to put an end to war. In effect, nature fights Israel's battles for it; military activity cannot be sustained in light of domestic crisis.

The final two verses of this poem (46:10–11) bring the message home. Psalm 46:10, spoken in the plural imperative used by 46:8, implores Israel to desist from aggression and attend to God's sovereignty looming over Israel, nature, and the nations. The song reaches its climax in perhaps the most famous and wise words of the Psalter: "Be still, and know that I am God" (46:10). Its conclusion repeats the refrain of 46:7 that summarizes the song's message: "The LORD who commands his forces is with us; Jacob's God is our citadel."

Theological Pedagogy

In accord with the nationalist construal of Israel's mission resulting from its election by God, this antiwar poem counsels Israel to desist from military action and to wait for God to deal with its foreign enemies. Trust in God is more important and perhaps more powerful than trust in military might. While the scene of the nations tottering into desolation is not pretty (and seems to invite *Schadenfreude*[3] from Israel), God's might is bigger than Israel's; it is not a bad lesson to learn. The message recalls Israel's exodus from Egypt, accomplished not by Israel's might but by God's use of natural forces to advance his aims.

3. Pleasure in another's downfall.

PSALM 47

Canonical Context and Themes

This psalm brings to a head the issue of the two preceding poems: the triangulated relationship of Israel caught between God and the nations. Is God the God of Israel only or also the God of all the nations? If the latter, Israel must be able to steer past the nationalism of empire as suggested by an inclusive ecclesiology. The question that bubbles up here is how Israel is to construct and conduct its foreign policy knowing that its goal is not to enhance its imperial power for its own sake but to enhance the recognition of God's universal rule far and wide.

Holding religion and empire apart (like holding ideology and empire apart) is not easy for those in power. Psalm 2 suggests that Israel's king is a mighty warrior selected as God's own to subdue the nations and intimidate them into acknowledging God and Israel's power. Psalm 46 portrays nature as intimidating the nations. However, other characters and stories mentioned previously read the situation differently. God's deeds persuade non-Israelites of God's power. In some cases (the widow of Zarephath, Naaman, Ruth), persuasion comes from having God's merciful deeds extended to them. Other times, Pharaoh approaches God after seeing God's actions on Israel's behalf, and the Ninevites are spared because they heed Jonah's preaching of impending destruction should they fail to repent. In all of these situations, God uses Israel to reach beyond Israel.

Psalm 45 employs a new strategy to the same end. By marrying the house of Tyre to Israel, Tyre begins to acknowledge Israel's God. Yet the wealth and power of Israel's royal house betray the difficulty of being clear-eyed about Israel's theological mission and not confusing it with Israel's imperial designs on its neighbors for its own enrichment. Psalm 46 makes the separation clear by eschewing violent conquest and all wars of domination so that Israel's God can become the God of all nations, perhaps fulfilling the universal promises of Gen. 12:3; 17:4–6; and 35:11. To press the point one step further, perhaps in spite of itself Ps. 47 raises the perennial question of how enmity might be put away, as Ps. 46 hopes it will, despite its unsavory circumstance.

Structure and Dynamics

This poem divides into two segments (47:1–5 and 6–9), each beginning with an imperative call to vocally celebrate God's awesomeness followed by an encomium.[1] Psalm 47 fairly shouts that God reigns over all the earth. On one level, that message is directed at the nations Israel has previously conquered, but on another it reminds Israel that God's purpose for its military success is to extend the knowledge of God across the earth, not to spread Israel's empire for its own sake.

Shout: For God Shouts (47:1–5)

These five verses tersely focus the tension between mission and empire. This segment starts boldly, urging the nations to celebrate God's greatness with noisy joy. They are to shout (*hārî'û*), loudly extolling God because his awesome reign is over the whole earth. The section concludes with a parallel response from God's side. Trumpets triumphantly shout out God's "going up" (47:5), using the same root 47:2 uses for God's exaltedness (*'ālâ*). This strophe is bracketed by the image of the nations and God shouting joyfully to one another, clapping and singing, mirthful in their embrace of one another.

The two verses (47:2–3) sandwiched in between the celebration identify the deep tension underneath the celebrating. The nations now bidden to celebrate God were taken for God by military conquest and their land given to the people of Jacob as an inheritance. They may be looking back to the conquest described in Joshua. Although Ps. 46 does not say so explicitly, it may be that the poet expects the nations shattered by natural disasters to claw their way to God on their knees. Calamity is a blunt instrument, but Israel may rely upon it. On the face of it, the nations are expected to celebrate and enjoy celebrating their own dispossession, worshiping the God behind the catastrophe that put them under foreign domination! Psalm 47 adds belated insult to long-suffering injury.

Another narrative might also be possible. Given the spottier picture of the wars of conquest in Judg. 1, it is possible that acquisition of the land was gradual and never complete since half the tribes of Israel (Manasseh, Ephraim, Zebulon, Asher, Naphtali, and Dan) failed to drive out the Canaanites. In those regions, Israelites and Canaanites lived together, not necessarily easily but out of the necessity to get on with life. Sometimes practical necessity forces the past into the past, and

1. Several strophings of this poem have been suggested by various commentators. I agree with Goldingay because the first verse of each segment is a plural imperative adjuring the audience to worship with their bodies and voices, while the following verses that explain why they should speak of God are in the third person (Goldingay 2007, 75).

unless each subsequent generation is carefully socialized into old enmities, the present has needs of its own. Thus, in 2 Sam. 11–12, Uriah the Hittite maintains his ethnic identity while remaining utterly loyal to David unto death. The flip side of Uriah's assimilation is the introduction of pagan cults into Israel through intermarriage. As objectionable as that has been from Judaism's perspective, it is also a way beyond violence, as Ps. 45 suggests. Again, Ezra 10 illustrates the pervasiveness of intermarriage; although it encroached upon the religious purity of Israel, it also advanced international peace.

It could be that Ps. 47 is addressing gentiles who have made their peace with Israel, as seen in Ps. 45, and that the triumphant shout of God in 47:5 no longer has the sting that it once had. Of course, the poet (an Israelite, one presumes) does not let sleeping dogs lie but appears to rub the noses of the nations in their disgrace. Yet 47:1 is the only verse that directly addresses the nations. As a unit, the poem may not be intended for the conquered, or even the assimilated conquered, but as a reminder to Israel of the source of its security in the land and its obligation to be an ensign of God to the nations.

Rejoice: For God Reigns (47:6–9)

Like the first segment, the second begins by calling people to make music celebrating God who reigns, not because Israel has subdued the nations into submission but precisely because God is enthroned above all the nations of the earth. Ephesians 5:19 seems to echo this sentiment, enjoining people to worship in song and music. In Ps. 47 the addressees may be Israelites or postexilic Jews, perhaps with non-Jews listening in. The poet is discreetly admonishing his auditors to tend to their proper theological mission by reminding them that God's reach embraces everyone. Jews may have temporal priority with God (as Paul says in Rom. 1:16, first the Jews and then the Greeks), but that priority translates into responsibility, not privilege. The broader message is that the Jews are not to rule the nations to enhance an empire but to facilitate knowledge of God's sovereignty.

Negotiating between the sovereign on high and the sovereign on earth haunts Ps. 47 (as it does most of the Psalter), although the issue is not directly addressed. The tension between religion and empire fades behind the joyous celebration of God. Of course, subsequent history has battled through this question time and again as church and state vie with each other for authority. In the nineteenth century, independent secular democratic states emerged in the West, and in the twenty-first-century Muslim world, they struggle to do so.

The last verse (47:9) of the poem has the last word. The leaders of the nations gather along with or assimilate into the people of the God of Abraham, fulfilling the Genesis promises to Abraham. The phrase "the people of the God of Abraham" denotes a rather different reality today. Jews, Christians, and Muslims all understand themselves to be the people of the God of Abraham, although they may understand this in exclusive rather than inclusive terms. Nevertheless, Ps. 47 beckons its readers and reciters to an inclusive vision of the people of God.

Theological Pedagogy

Psalm 47 sings out hope and joy against a history of fear and violence as theology drives foreign policy, struggling to come to terms with each other in a culture that does not distinguish religion from empire. The West did not make the distinction until the seventeenth century. Given these political realities, the poet is prescient and brave. Now two and a half millennia on, the modern State of Israel still struggles to come to terms with these few verses that call the Jewish people to account before God, who reigns over all the peoples of the earth. While Ps. 47 is jubilant, it is fraught with explosive tension. Israel is chosen to serve the nations whom God claims. When the nations seek Israel's very life, the temptation for Israelites is to consider themselves to be God's beloved in exclusive terms rather than the ones chosen for the sake of God's larger vision.

Psalm 47 is of special interest to Christians, some of whom read it through Paul as being directly about them; they are not brought into the people of God—they *are* the people of God. Christian commentators have struggled to understand the place of the Jewish people in this narrative. While Ps. 47 and the several biblical stories leading up to it portray gentiles being added into or drawn alongside Israel, Augustine of Hippo and many following him, adhering to the assumption of Christian supersessionism, saw the gentiles as replacing the Jews in the divine economy, contrary to the plain meaning of the text.[2]

Calvin, on the contrary, softens Augustine's supersessionism just a tad, suggesting that

> this gathering together will be *to the people of the God of Abraham*, to teach us that it is not here meant to attribute to the Jews any superiority which they naturally possess above others, but that all their excellence depends upon this, that the pure worship of God flourishes among them, and that they hold heavenly doctrine in high estimation. This, therefore, is not spoken of the bastard or cast-off Jews, whom their own unbelief has cut off from the Church. But as, according to the statement of the Apostle Paul, (Rom. xi:16,) the root being holy, the branches are also holy, it follows that the falling away of the greater part does not prevent this honour from continuing to belong to the rest.[3]

Muslims also worship the God of Abraham, but since this poem is not their scripture one can only conjecture what their reading of it might be.

2. Augustine 2000b, 332.
3. Calvin 1996, 215.

As a group, these three psalms try to work out Israel's relationship to God and the nations. It is illuminating and somewhat disconcerting that this question, as pressing as it was in the author's day, is even more urgent today. The prediction that all the nations will gather as the people of the God of Abraham has born amazing fruit. More than half the world is affiliated with either Christianity or Islam, claiming the God of Abraham as its own, while Judaism today claims a scant .23 percent of the world's population.

Where is this "grouplet" of psalms leading its readers? Stepping back from the text, we might gratefully appreciate the hard questions it poses about our own presuppositions of power, authority, and the rightness of our cause. Together they confront us with the delicacy of understanding ourselves in respect to others who are related to us in ways that we may neither desire nor understand. This batch of poems is perhaps a paradigmatic example of negotiating the vast space between self and other. And yet, one more poem must be considered in this grouplet of psalms.

PSALM 48

Canonical Context and Themes

When the author of Ps. 137 piercingly recalls the Babylonians taunting their Jewish captives with "Sing us one of the songs of Zion," he may well have had Ps. 48 in mind. Those mourning their exile not only from familiar surroundings but also from the city of God set on a hill—Jerusalem, Zion, the city of David—could only hang up their harps and still their voices. Humiliation feeds grief.

Against this chastening event in Israel's history, Ps. 48 (and its immediate predecessor) becomes a flashback to a far better time when Mount Zion was beautiful because God's presence triumphed there, not because its landscape was particularly attractive. That Zion's beauty may be theological rather than aesthetic enhances the ironic cadences of Ps. 48 that praise God's dwelling in David's capital amid Israel. Whether referred to as Mount Zion, the city of God, God's holy hill (it is scarcely a mountain), or the city of our God, it is fortified with towers, ramparts, and citadels, crowned by Solomon's Temple itself. This stronghold may signal Israel's military strength on the ground, but theologically it irradiates God's authority unto the world's farthest corners (Ps. 48:2, 10). By recalling God's steadfast commitment to Israel, Ps. 48 serves as an inspirational pep talk to harness Israel's energies in its current situation to its high calling.

According to that perspective, Ps. 48 belongs with the previous three psalms, although it is not focused on precisely how to facilitate the universal recognition of God. Like the others, it views God's presence as centered in Jerusalem—that is, in Israel (although Solomon's prayer at the dedication of the temple locates God's authority as emanating from heaven [1 Kgs. 8:23–36])—while God's power and authority encompass the whole world. From this vantage point, Israel's fumbling to understand its role in instrumentalizing universal recognition of God's global empire, so to speak, is understandable as this pack of former nomadic tribes, later slaves, and now imperial power brokers struggles to reckon with having acquired land, wealth, and the authority that accompany them. Those flush with influence need constant reminding that God is the power behind their power—a difficult truth to hold on to.

Structure and Dynamics

In terms of its voicing, Ps. 48 may be segmented into five parts: Psalm 48:1–3 assures the gathered congregation of (probably) worshiping Israelites that God's center of operations is Mount Zion. Psalm 48:4–7 switches topic (but not audience) to explain to or remind the audience of the painful experience of the nations' kings, who tremble at the sight of the power of Israel's God threatening them. Psalm 48:8–9 speaks in the first-person plural reflecting back on God's love for Israel, presumably in contrast to God's intimidation of the nations. Psalm 48:10–11 turns from the immediate audience to God. It extols God's global reach, which is demonstrated by the intimidation of the foreign kings. Psalm 48:12–14 urges locals to familiarize themselves with the streets and strongholds of Zion, that they may instill in their progeny the conviction that God will forever lead them from there.

The Theological Center of the World (48:1–3)

While Christianity localizes God's authority on earth in the life of a single Jew, the psalmist locates that authority in a single city. As God's love and power emanate from Jesus for Christians, they emanate from Zion for this writer and his hearers. Augustine's comment on Ps. 48:1–2 identifies God's holy mountain and Mount Zion in the north as two mountains representing Jews and gentiles respectively who unite in Christ, represented as the stone of the building rejected by the builders to become the cornerstone of the city of the great king. He cites Eph. 2:14 and Ps. 118:22 in support.[1]

The Kings Writhe in Pain (48:4–7)

At this point the subject shifts sharply, contrasting talk of God's universal lordship with a recollection of foreign kings who formed an alliance, ostensibly against Israel, but were confounded and left trembling as if with labor pains or as if shattered by the east wind like a ship at sea. Of course, their conspiring is for naught against God, for David took Jerusalem from the Jebusites (2 Sam. 5) and made it his capital. Use of the *niphal* verb *nôdaʿ* in Ps. 48:3, where God is known as a fortification for Israel, contrasts with the same verb used of the kings, *nôʿădû*, who can in no way defend themselves against God in 48:4. These verses repeat the stance of Ps. 46:5–6 on the relationship of God and the nations, a pose

1. Augustine 2000b, 337–38.

struck by Ps. 2 for the entire Psalter. God is ensconced in his city, from which he intimidates the nations into submission.

While We Enjoy God's Love (48:8–9)

With this, the singer ramps up his hearers' enthusiasm to embrace his message employing the first-person plural. *We* know this story of God's steadfast love for us and *we* rejoice that God's armies, headquartered in this very city (assuming that the song is meant to be sung in Jerusalem), have won for him the victory.

Judah Rejoices in Your Victory (48:10–11)

Still drawing his listeners near, the poet and his listeners now address God together. Given God's history with them (which the poet has summarized) and understanding that they make their own history, they adore God with one voice. This history "telegraphs" God's name across the earth; the daughter villages surrounding Mount Zion will rejoice because of God's works.

Enjoy God's Stronghold and Instruct Your Children (48:12–14)

The psalm concludes with the psalmist bidding his auditors to explore the city and learn its "ins and outs" in order to prepare themselves to instill in their children the confident knowledge that God will guide Israel from Jerusalem's fortifications until the end of time.

Theological Pedagogy

The bricks-and-mortar emphasis of Ps. 48 is striking, perhaps especially to Christians who may expect spiritual rather than physical fortification against life's vicissitudes. Yet the ramparts, citadels, towers, and fortifications that protected Jerusalem in the poet's day, again in Roman times, later in Crusader times, and even into our own, speak of spiritual strength in their own way. Swayed by the powerful pen of Augustine of Hippo, western Christians internalized the enemies that ancient Israel—and the Jews experienced since the legalization of Christianity—and transformed them into sins. Virtually unchallenged until Islam assaulted it militarily and modernity assaulted it intellectually, Christianity has had the luxury of reading enemies as internal enemies (see also Ps. 3)—not as others who would harm them but as those unlovely parts of our selves that would be personified as Satan or the devil.

The bricks-and-mortar staccato of this psalm enables Christians to engage in self-criticism, a luxury permitted by Christian dominance for centuries. Perhaps Ps. 48, in particular, enables Christians to truly thank and praise God for this great fortune, though the political security that makes this gift of space for self-examination possible has been achieved at the expense of others. Freedom accompanies power. Led by Augustine, western Christians have used that space to journey inward to examine the personal sins that absorbed the church fathers' energies.

Now the bricks-and-mortar emphasis of Ps. 48 invites Christians to turn the poem's self-reflective sensibility in a direction that Augustine could not. If the imperial tone of the Psalter is off-putting to Christians given to both spiritual concerns and self-examination, psalms like this one invite them to examine Christian history for the church's sins against humanity: rash condemnations, forced conversions, banishments, executions, wars, and other political and military exploits undertaken from the stronghold of God's holy hill, wherever it be located on earth.

This is to say that Ps. 48 is a tonic of sorts, and it brings us to an assessment of the trajectory of the four psalms that I have identified in this grouplet: Is God the God of Israel only or also the God of the nations? If the latter, how is Israel to manage that delicate interface? This grouplet of psalms struggles with the fundamental issue that confronts Israel and Judaism, as well as Christianity and Islam. How do those who claim to follow God relate to those who make the same claim but for quite different reasons and with different beliefs and practices? Psalm 45 suggests that commerce and intermarriage offer a way of securing peace. The Deuteronomistic history underlying Pss. 46–48 suggests other strategies to overwhelm paganism, perhaps even integrating foreigners into Israel.

For those convinced that God is on their side, the remaining question is how best to persuade others that their best interest lies in aligning themselves with the ones God has chosen. Do they employ disregard, gentle persuasion, miscegenation, military conquest, natural disaster, or political domination? Judaism, Christianity, and Islam have all had to confront this question as they interact with one another. Psalms 45–48 stand as haunting primitive calls to negotiate faithfulness to the call of God while enabling civil society to proceed securely.

PSALM 49

Canonical Context and Themes

Psalm 49 is of a quite different stripe than the preceding four psalms treated here as a group. Here is a wisdom psalm that tempers, perhaps even confronts, the confident just deserts moral exhortation of Ps. 1 (also a wisdom psalm). It urges Israelites to a righteous life on the assumption that the righteous will flourish and the wicked will perish. Psalm 49 protests against this moralizing agenda set for the entire Psalter. Its inclusion in the canon—along with Kohelet whose pessimistic theology it adumbrates—is noteworthy.[1] Together they teach that death, not moral stature, has the last word.[2] In the context of the Psalter, Ps. 49 fits with those poems that do not flinch from facing the theodicy question head-on. Thankfully, the canonizers of the Bible were mature enough to preserve minority voices for the generations to come.

Psalm 49 meditates on the fear of death. Yet its scope is broader, for although the fear of death dominates the poem, the psalm also recognizes anxious anticipation of persecutors, which so many previous psalms ponder. It criticizes—perhaps with a hint of jealousy—the wealthy who seem to hope to forestall the impact of death by financial means. In short, Ps. 49 takes on the psychological burdens of jealousy, anxiety, and worry under the head of fear that transcends culture, religion, and era, yet offers eschatological hope amid trepidation.

Structure and Dynamics

Psalm 49 is often read as chiastic in form after its grand introduction, which proclaims the wisdom of Israel's sage (49:1–4). From a thematic rather than linguistic

---

1. Spangenberg holds Ps. 49 to be earlier than Kohelet (1997).
2. Psalm 49's repeated insistence that death is the great leveler appears at Eccl. 2:16; 3:20; and 9:10.

perspective, if 49:5–20 does exhibit a chiastic structure, the crossing point or climax is 49:15, with 49:5–14 being the inward movement and 49:16–20 perhaps wending out from the climax, although the somber tone never relaxes or resolves. The sobering reality of death is alleviated only at 49:15 and then disappears again, concluding with the mournful refrain first uttered at 49:12. Psalm 49:5–14 disparages ways that people futilely hope to ransom themselves from death, while 49:15 cuts off those hopes and offers another. Psalm 49:16–20 tries to comfort the anxious heart to set aside worry, but finally death reigns triumphant just as it does before the hopeful turning point at 49:15.

Wise Meditation (49:1–4)

This psalm's long introduction boldly addresses the whole world. Israel is transcended as every human being is called to attend to the great mystery of life. Perhaps the preceding psalms, with their interest in the nations, intend to prepare the reader for this global reach in which the tension between Israel and the nations simply disappears behind the apprehension created by ubiquitous fears of death, oppression, and poverty that plague everyone, uniting all people in common unease. The whole world is caught up in these anxieties.

The introduction itself has two parts. It begins with a resounding appeal to the whole world to attend to the words of this sagacious Israelite and continues to assure the would-be audience that his wise words will answer the great conundrum of life. This grand and provocative opening alerts ears and minds to a perspective on matters of life and death that the traditional wisdom of Ps. 1 did not admit.

Wealth Is No Hideout (49:5–14)

This long section explores the attempt to deny death, primarily through wealth and possessions.

No Ransom Can Suffice (49:5–9)

The lament psalms prepare the reader to meet speakers in distress. By contrast, the speaker of Ps. 49 taunts the iniquitous people surrounding him because he can see right through them. Even if caught in a harsh season of life, perhaps in which jealousy of the wealthy threatens to destabilize him spiritually, the speaker steadies himself with the thought that neither bad behavior nor the wealth with which some may try to hide it means anything. Being distressed at seeing the wicked prosper is a waste of energy, he tells the reader. The wicked cannot buy their way beyond death, so why grant them the power to disturb you? Perhaps he is fortifying those tempted by the evils surrounding them or those whose jealousy is aroused by the wealthy who seem to avoid suffering, at least temporarily.

You Can't Take It with You (49:10–14)

Unlike Proverbs and Ps. 1, which urge sagacious living, the message in 49:10–14 is that sagacious living does not pay off, as if it needed a subsequent reward. Wise and foolish alike lose everything; death is the great leveler. The poet is not comforted by the thought that virtue is its own reward or that providing for others—such as one's progeny or the quality of life of others—is a most satisfying and fitting way to conclude one's life and a goal worth striving for. Here is a pessimistic and limited view that concludes with the poem's tart refrain at 49:12 (repeated as the final verse): whatever one's accomplishments or wealth, everyone dies as the brute beasts do. The analogy to animals continues into 49:14, likening humans to sheep shepherded to the grave by death itself. The poet seems to be scoffing at Ps. 23's trust in the good shepherd who leads his sheep through death's fears. This pessimistic poet's tongue forgoes hope and comfort.

But . . . (49:15)

Psalm 49:15 is the only brake on the negative perspective the poet offers on life in the face of death, and it attempts to force the preceding depressing assessment of death's corrosive psychological power back into the basic theological conviction of the Psalter that human safety and well-being are a result of being sheltered in God. Psalm 49:7–8 uses forms of the root *pdh* three times to describe the attempted denial of death by people hoping to ransom or redeem themselves from their fate by means of their wealth. Psalm 49:15 uses this same root to push the Psalter's overwhelming message: only God ransoms the soul from the grip of death.

This single verse places the psalmist's grim outlook in eschatological perspective. God will take me from death's clutches. Of course, the resurrection of Christ that Paul believes is the firstfruit of those who have died (1 Cor. 15:20) is the core Christian hope. After him, Augustine frequently argues that pagans can never be truly happy because they deny immortality.[3] Indeed, Christianity may be the great retort to this poem, and to Kohelet which sings a similar song. Christianity constitutes a monumental denial of death with its hope of either resurrection or immortality, or perhaps resurrection that morphs into immortality.

Be Not Afraid (49:16–20)

One might expect—as in previous psalms that reach a crisis point and then resolve into joyous proclamation of God's redeeming power—the poet to offer the rest of the poem as an antidote to the pessimism in which he steeps his readers. He is not so moved. Instead, he reprises the main message. Psalm 49:16 does begin in a more comforting tone, however. Because God takes one from the grip

3. Christian eschatology rarely attends to the tension between the eschaton as resurrection and the eschaton as immortality.

of death, being fearful or jealous of the wealthy is pointless because they will lose it all. But this attitude is little changed from its prior analog at 49:6—why should one be fearful or jealous, even if surrounded by evil? The tone in both cases is defiant; the poet encourages his readers to defy their own worst emotions in the name of God's redeeming power.

However, the remainder of this section of the poem returns to the more pessimistic, even cynical, tone. Those who live blessed lives and are praised for it are only fooling themselves, for their light will be extinguished before long. Psalm 49:12, slightly rephrased, reappears to close this sober reflection: people may live well, but they will perish like animals.

Theological Pedagogy

Psalm 49 is a renegade in the Psalter. It bucks the overarching moralism of the psalmists, even those steeped in the wisdom traditions who commend obedience to God's commandments, which are not only delightful in themselves but also promote healthy communities and invite surrounding gentile nations to join forces with both Israel and God. With Ps. 49, both wisdom themes and cynicism infiltrate Israel's precincts—a place where trust, even if lacking empirical evidence, is normally expected.

Yet the faith of Israel and Judaism—whether heard in its insistence on the value of life in this world or forced through the sieve of Christ's resurrection, which speaks of life beyond life—will not be stilled by pointing to the ubiquity of death. The poet's pessimism does not succumb to despair. Resilient hope in life and its possibilities must be indefatigable for society to flourish. This titration of hope emerges triumphant, though just barely, from the crucible of death's scourge at the climax of the poem insisting that, contrary to the fact that we die like all other animals, God will take us from cold death. Perhaps Ps. 49 is the Christian psalm par excellence. Perhaps it is the test case for Christianity's final triumph over death.

PSALM 50

Canonical Context and Themes

Concluding the first third of the Psalter, Ps. 50 returns to the basic theology of Ps. 1, although the distinction between the righteous and the wicked is not quite as clear here as it is there. So far, Ps. 50 is the only psalm in which God directly addresses Israel, perhaps helpfully so. It is also the only psalm in which God rebukes the people, perhaps chastising individuals or swaths of individuals whose fealty to the ancestral faith is weak. If they bring gifts to the altar yet do not live out the teaching suggested by the commandments, they are judged inadequate by the poet's standards; they are missing the essential "Sunday to Monday" connection, so to speak. The psalmist does not criticize the sacrificial system as such but knows that it is easily misunderstood, even abused, when people deceive themselves into thinking that they can meet their religious obligations simply by supporting the institution financially. The psalmist is clear that God wants compliance with both the institutional and the spiritual aspects of Israel's religion. In Ps. 50 God takes center stage to press that point home.

God now breaks his silence to confront the people's religious and moral failings. The poem both bespeaks God's patience and answers the lamenters of Book 1 of the Psalter, who bemoan God's silence when they need him. That God does not remain silent but boldly reprimands those who scorn his teachings (50:17) is perhaps the rescue that the complainants have sought all along. God is finally acting as he should. He may be angry with those who do not keep to the path he has set for them, but he does not heed the requests of lamenters who hope for the destruction of their foes. Rather, he seeks to bring them back to his way by shaming them, bluntly laying their bad behavior in front of them, in front of all Israel, in front of the whole world. It is a risky strategy. God shames rather than harms those who go astray in order to embarrass them into reforming their lives.

251

Structure and Dynamics

Psalm 50 has two major parts: a dramatic introduction spoken by a narrator (50:1–6) and God's case against his people (50:7–23). The latter reads like a prophetic reproach, with God heightening the tension by acting as his own prophet. At the same time, God's address simulates a court of law where God is the prosecuting attorney as the world watches with bated breath. There is no defense attorney, and the defendant never speaks. The prosecution reigns in the courtroom.

The case against Israel proceeds in two sections. Each of these sections consists of two parts in turn. The main body of each lays out God's condemnation—first of bad worship and then of bad behavior—followed by a short concluding section in which God offers his listeners a path beyond their failings. Self-deceptive, perfunctory worship in the first instance and moral waywardness in the second are chastised, yet the wicked are not condemned. In both instances, scolding is followed by encouragement. God still threatens punishment (50:22b) but is more interested in rehabilitating his people than in displaying his power over them by punishing them. In the two clauses of the poem's final verse (50:23), the prosecution summerizes its case. Its first recapitulates 50:7–15 to correct improper worship, and its second recapitulates 50:16–22, to reprimand Israel for abusing covenantal responsibility. The structure looks like this:

Introduction: A Public Drama Unfolds (50:1–6)
Prosecution's Case (50:7–23)
    Public Worship (50:7–15)
        Misunderstanding (50:7–13)
        Proper Worship (50:14–15)
    Moral Life (50:16–23)
        Forgetting God (50:16–22)
        Honoring God (50:23)

God's case against his own begins by explaining what public worship is not and what it should be and then digs deeper to attack behavior that violates specific injunctions of the Decalogue. God ends his case on an encouraging note that offers salvation to those who walk aright in both public worship and a morally good life.

A Public Drama Unfolds (50:1–6)

While Pss. 45–49 locate Israel's relationship to God in the context of God's relationship to the surrounding nations, Ps. 50 takes a step back to set this rebuke in a cosmic context. The cosmos, signified by the merism of heaven and earth, is called to witness God's judicial proceedings against his people. The political and psychological import of this setting is striking for Israel's foreign policy. Not only is God rebuking his people, but the rebuke has also been captured in print. The public proceeding is dramatic, and Israel is shamed before the world. Given that Israel is to model faithfulness to God in order to bring the world under God's sway, the public chastisement here is counterintuitive as a means to that end.

Most commentators have paused over the strange trifold naming of God with which this psalm begins;[1] several English translations are suggested. I prefer "God, God the LORD" because it captures the cosmic frame in which this castigation of Israel occurs. The gods of the nations of the world look on from the gallery as Israel's own God prepares to upbraid it publically. The poem portends high drama. Jerusalem/Zion is the earth's beautiful spot that the God of gods has chosen as the center of the world and at which he now appears confrontationally (50:2), following the tone set by Ps. 48. At this moment all posturing and pretense are set aside as the drama unfolds against God's very own (50:4). The decision to speak judgment is accompanied by a display of divine power; fire precedes God; a great tempest accompanies his entrance into the world to make sure that all bystanders appreciate the gravity of the situation (50:3). This is serious, the poet intones.

While the world is invited to watch and testify, God's own, whose ancestors accepted the covenant (Exod. 24) and now offer sacrifices in Jerusalem, assemble in the sight of the attendant invitees (50:5), perhaps innocent of what is about to transpire as God makes final preparations to present his case against his own in order to demonstrate his righteousness before all (50:6). The spectacle is unparalleled. The world assembles in the spectator gallery as God confronts the people he has chosen and who agreed to accept him as their God. The fate of the Sinai covenant hangs in the air. One can almost see the observers smirking in the gallery; the crowded courtroom is eerily quiet.

Prosecution's Case (50:7–23)

The bulk of this poem is God's prosecution of Israel. Psalm 50:7–15 first corrects misunderstanding of the sacrificial system of public worship, and then 50:16–22 moves in on listeners to condemn their unethical behavior in order to encourage proper behavior. The final verse of the poem (50:23) suggests this two-part strophing. The first clause mentions sacrifice as honoring God while the second encourages a moral way of life that promises salvation. Together they indicate two parameters of covenantal faithfulness—ceremonial and moral—which are reflected in the two sections of the divine rebuke.

PUBLIC WORSHIP (50:7–15)

Now publically exposed, Israel stands silent as God instructs it about what not to sacrifice (50:7–13), yet the section concludes with two verses about the proper place of sacrifice in public worship (50:14–15).

---

1. The trifold naming is lost in the NRSV's "The mighty one, God the LORD."

Misunderstanding (50:7–13)

By reminding Israel that the whole created order belongs to God, Ps. 50:7–13 ousts the crude view that God might want or need to drink the blood or eat the flesh of animals.[2] Wild beasts, domesticated cattle, birds, and the mountains and fields that house them all belong to their creator. When measured by these commodities, Israel's wealth is irrelevant. Israel has no claim on these creatures. If God needs food, Israel need not supply it; the human need to eat should not crudely be generalized to God. Psalm 50:7–13 focuses attention on the author of the created order, just as the introduction calls creation itself to attention, rather than specific political entities.

Whatever the dating of this poem, sacrifices were problematic by the time of its composition. God's point in this speech is that sacrifices are redundant; he neither wants nor needs them. Further, given that they are readily misunderstood and misused, what is the reason for retaining them in Jerusalem's public worship? Would that the psalmist had addressed the question directly!

Proper Worship (50:14–15)

As it is, the rhetorical question of the repulsive implication of 50:13—"Would I eat the flesh of bulls or drink the blood of goats?"—is answered by 50:14: "Offer thanksgiving to God and fulfill your vows to the utmost." Whatever may have been the ritual significance of the sacrifice of thanksgiving, the psalmist presses beyond bare compliance with the form to the further goal of promoting genuine gratitude that orients people to the source of their well-being. He is not advocating compliance for its own sake, although insincere compliance, as the object of scorn, is not encouraged either. God's ways must sink deep into one's being; outward compliance is the capstone of sacrifice, not its point.

MORAL LIFE (50:16–23)

Rebuke of insincere worship is just the warm-up to God's more serious reprimand of Israel's moral behavior measured against the standards set by the Decalogue. Those who have defied God's covenant statutes by associating with, or at least not prosecuting, thieves and adulterers and those who slander their kin for personal gain are stung with dishonoring God. Yet even here the psalmist offers hope.

Forgetting God (50:16–22)

In 50:16–22 God speaks directly to those who, even if they voice commandments of the Decalogue, disparage them and despise their guidance by flouting the very commandments they speak. Those who abet thieves, shelter adulterers (50:18), speak evil of others (50:19), and betray family members (50:20) have

---

2. One is reminded of the concern voiced early by pagans against Christians that Eucharistic celebration is cannibalistic, as suggested by texts like John 6.

perhaps aroused God out of silence into condemnatory speech. One has the impression that this has been going on for some time. God does not cherish publically castigating his people but undertakes it in order to arouse the indolent from their moral lethargy. Reform of the wayward, rather than venting the wrath of the powerhouse, is the message here.

Honoring God (50:23)

The final verse of this psalm instructs both the cultically and the morally castigated concerning how to make amends for their previously untoward worship and behavior. As indicated above, Israel's failings can be seen on two fronts: worship and ethics. The former forms people for the latter. Psalm 50:23 tersely compresses the poem's message: the salvation of God requires both honoring God in public worship and following in the way he has laid out for personal life.

Theological Pedagogy

Participation in communal life symbolized by worship and adherence to the teachings that guide personal behavior are of a piece. Both participation in community worship and personal discipline matter; honoring God in public must be accompanied by following his moral precepts. Psalm 50 knows the threat of public display and the hypocrisy it poorly shields. God will see through insincere public shows of faithfulness if individuals privately act as thieves, adulterers, or slanderers of their kin and neighbors.

Those guilty of financial or sexual impropriety or verbal abuse of others cannot hide from God behind shows of public service that claim to serve the common good. It bears repeating that public and private life are of a piece. God's interest in "the right way" penetrates public behavior to the core of the moral life enshrined in the Decalogue. The salvation of God embraces those whose integrity encompasses both public and private spheres.

BIBLIOGRAPHY

Aimilianos of Simonopetra. *Psalms and the Life of Faith*. Athens: Indiktos.

Allen, Leslie C. 1986. "David as Exemplar of Spirituality: The Redactional Function of Psalm 19." *Biblica* 67, no. 4: 544–46.

Alter, Robert. 2007. *The Book of Psalms: A Translation with Commentary*. 1st ed. New York: Norton.

Althaus, Paul. 1966. *The Theology of Martin Luther*. Philadelphia: Fortress.

Anselm. (1098) 1985. *Why God Became Man: Cur Deus Homo*. Translated by Jasper Hopkins and Herbert Richardson. Queenston, ON: E. Mellen Press.

Athanasius. 1954. "On the Incarnation of the Word." In *Christology of the Later Fathers*, edited by Edward R. Hardy, 52–110. Philadelphia: Westminster.

———. 1980. "Letter to Marcellinus." In *Athanasius: The Life of Antony and the Letter to Marcellinus*, edited by Robert C. Gregg, 101–47. Classics of Western Spirituality. New York: Paulist Press.

Augustine. 1991. *Confessions*. Translated by Henry Chadwick. Oxford: Oxford University Press.

———. 2000a. *Expositions of the Psalms: 1–32*. Translated by Maria Boulding. Edited by John E. Rotelle. Works of Saint Augustine: A Translation for the 21st Century. Hyde Park, NY: New City.

———. 2000b. *Expositions of the Psalms: 33–50*. Translated by Maria Boulding. Edited by John E. Rotelle. Works of Saint Augustine: A Translation for the 21st Century. Hyde Park, NY: New City.

———. 2003. "Letter 147: On Seeing God." In *Letters 100–155*, edited by Boniface Ramsey, 317–49. Works of Saint Augustine: A Translation for the 21st Century. Hyde Park, NY: New City.

———. 2004. *Expositions of the Psalms, 121–150*. Translated by Maria Boulding. Edited by Boniface Ramsey. Works of Saint Augustine: A Translation for the 21st Century. Hyde Park, NY: New City.

Basil of Caesarea. 1963. *Exegetic Homilies*. Translated by Agnes Clare Way. Fathers of the Church. Washington, DC: Catholic University of America Press.

Benedict. 1981. *RB 1980: The Rule of St. Benedict in Latin and English with Notes*. Translated by Timothy Fry. Collegeville, MN: Liturgical Press.

Birnbaum, Philip. 1949. *Daily Prayer Book*. New York: Hebrew Publishing.

Boethius. 1999. *Consolation of Philosophy*. Translated by P. G. Walsh. Oxford: Clarendon Press.

Book of Common Prayer. 1979. New York: Seabury Press.

Bosma, Carl J. 2008. "Discerning the Voices in the Psalms: A Discussion of Two Problems in Psalmic Interpretation, Part 1." *Calvin Theological Journal* 43, no. 2: 183–212.

———. 2009. "Discerning the Voices in the Psalms: A Discussion of Two Problems in Psalmic Interpretation, Part 2." *Calvin Theological Journal* 44, no. 1: 127–70.

Braude, William Gordon, trans. 1959a. *Midrash on Psalms*, vol. 1. Yale Judaica Series. New Haven: Yale University Press.

———, trans. 1959b. *The Midrash on Psalms,* vol. 2. Yale Judaica Series. New Haven: Yale University Press.

Brown, William P. 2002. *Seeing the Psalms: A Theology of Metaphor*. Louisville: Westminster John Knox.

———. 2012. "Happiness and Its Discontents in the Psalms." In *The Bible and the Pursuit of Happiness*, edited by Brent Strawn, 95–115. New York: Oxford University Press.

Brueggemann, Walter. 1984. *The Message of the Psalms: A Theological Commentary*. Augsburg Old Testament Studies. Minneapolis: Fortress.

———. 1997. *Theology of the Old Testament: Testimony, Dispute, Advocacy*. Minneapolis: Fortress.

———. 2001. "Voice as Counter to Violence." *Calvin Theological Journal* 36, no. 1: 22–33.

———. 2007. *Praying the Psalms: Engaging Scripture and the Life of the Spirit*. 2nd ed. Eugene, OR: Cascade Books.

Calvin, John. (1854) 1996. *Commentary on the Book of Psalms*, vol. 2, *Psalms 36–66*. Translated by James Anderson. Vol. 5 of *Calvin's Commentaries*. Grand Rapids: Baker Books.

———. (1854) 1998. *Commentary on the Book of Psalms*, vol. 1, *Psalms 1–35*. Translated by James Anderson. Vol. 4 of *Calvin's Commentaries*. Grand Rapids: Baker Books.

Cassiodorus. 1990. *Explanation of the Psalms*. Translated by P. G. Walsh. 3 vols. Ancient Christian Writers. New York: Paulist Press.

Charry, Ellen T. 2010. *God and the Art of Happiness*. Grand Rapids: Eerdmans.

———. 2012. "Rebekah's Twins: Augustine on Election in Genesis." In *Genesis and Christian Theology*, edited by Nathan MacDonald et al., 267–86. Grand Rapids: Eerdmans.

Childs, Brevard Springs. 1971. "Psalm Titles and Midrashic Exegesis." *Journal of Semitic Studies* 16, no. 2: 137–50.

Chouraqui, Andre. 1995. "Introduction to the Psalms." *Liturgy O.C.S.O.* 29, no. 1: 5–31.

Chrysostom, John. 1889. "Treatise to Prove That No One Can Harm the Man Who Does Not Injure Himself." In vol. 9 of *Nicene and Post-Nicene Fathers of the Christian Church*, Series 1, edited by Philip Schaff, 269–84. Edinburgh: T&T Clark.

———. 1998. *Commentary on the Psalms,* vol. 1. Translated by Robert C. Hill. Brookline, MA: Holy Cross Orthodox Press.

Davis, Ellen F. 1992. "Exploding the Limits: Form and Function in Psalm 22." *Journal for the Study of the Old Testament* 53: 93–105.

DeClaissé-Walford, Nancy L. 2007. "Psalm 44: O God, Why Do You Hide Your Face?" *Review & Expositor* 104, no. 4: 745–59.

Dhanaraj, Dharmakkan. 1992. *Theological Significance of the Motif of Enemies in Selected Psalms of Individual Lament*. Orientalia Biblica et Christiana. Glückstadt, Ger.: J. J. Augustin.

Donne, John. 1995. "Fear of the Lord." In *Imagination Shaped: Old Testament Preaching in the Anglican Tradition*, edited by Ellen F. Davis, 96–113. Valley Forge, PA: Trinity Press International.

Douglass, Frederick. 1962. *Life and Times of Frederick Douglass: His Early Life as a Slave, His Escape from Bondage, and His Complete History*. New York: Collier Books.

Fløysvik, Ingvar. 1997. *When God Becomes My Enemy: The Theology of the Complaint Psalms*. St. Louis: Concordia Academic.

Forward Day by Day. The Episcopal Church. Cincinnati: Forward Movement Press.

Goldingay, John. 1993. *Praying the Psalms*. Grove Spirituality Series. Bramcote, UK: Grove Books.

———. 2006. *Psalms, Vol. 1: 1–41*. Baker Commentary on the Old Testament Wisdom and Psalms. Grand Rapids: Baker Academic.

———. 2007. *Psalms, Vol. 2: 42–89*. Baker Commentary on the Old Testament Wisdom and Psalms. Grand Rapids: Baker Academic.

Gunn, George A. 2012. "Psalm 2 and the Reign of the Messiah." *Bibliotheca Sacra* 169, no. 676: 427–42.

Ḥakham, Amos. 2003. *Psalms with the Jerusalem Commentary*. 3 vols. The Bible with the Jerusalem Commentary. Jerusalem: Mosad Harav Kook.

Hankle, Dominick D. 2010. "The Therapeutic Implications of the Imprecatory Psalms in the Christian Counseling Setting." *Journal of Psychology & Theology* 38, no. 4: 275–80.

Harrelson, Walter J. 1999. "Psalm 19: A Meditation on God's Glory in the Heavens and in God's Law." In *Worship and the Hebrew Bible*, edited by M. Patrick Graham et al, 142–47. Sheffield, UK: Sheffield Academic Press.

Høgenhaven, Jesper. 2001. "The Opening of the Psalter: A Study in Jewish Theology." *Scottish Journal of Theology* 15, no. 2: 169–80.

Ibn Ezra, Abraham. 2006. *Rabbi Abraham Ibn Ezra's Commentary on the First Book of Psalms*. Translated by H. Norman Strickman. Brooklyn, NY: Yashar Books.

Jerome. 1964. *The Homilies of Saint Jerome*. Translated by Marie Liguori Ewald. 2 vols. The Fathers of the Church. Washington, DC: Catholic University of America Press.

Knierim, Rolf P. 1991. "On the Theology of Psalm 19." In *Ernten, was man sat*, edited by Dwight R. Daniels et al., 439–58. Neukirchen-Vluyn, Germany: Neukirchener Verlag.

Lampe, G. W. H., ed. 1969. *The Cambridge History of the Bible*, vol. 2. Cambridge: Cambridge University Press.

Luther, Martin. 1837. *A manual of the Book of Psalms, or, the subject-contents of all the Psalms*. Translated by Henry Cole. London: R. B. Seeley & W. Burnside.

———. 1961. "That These Words of Christ, 'This Is My Body,' etc., Still Stand Firm against the Fanatics." In *Word and Sacrament III*, translated and edited by Robert H. Fischer, 3–150. Philadelphia: Fortress.

———. 1971. "On the Jews and Their Lies." In *Christian in Society*, edited by Franklin Sherman, 121–306. Philadelphia: Fortress Press.

———. 1989. "A Meditation on Christ's Passion." In *Martin Luther's Basic Theological Writings*, edited by Timothy Lull, 165–72. Minneapolis: Fortress.

Mays, James Luther. 1994a. *The LORD Reigns: A Theological Handbook to the Psalms*. Louisville: Westminster John Knox.

———. 1994b. *Psalms*. Interpretation: A Bible Commentary for Teaching and Preaching. Louisville: Westminster John Knox.

McCann, J. Clinton. 1993. *A Theological Introduction to the Book of Psalms: The Psalms as Torah*. Nashville: Abingdon.

McCann, J. Clinton, and James C. Howell. 2001. *Preaching the Psalms*. Nashville: Abingdon.

Miller, Patrick D. 1983. "Trouble and Woe: Interpreting the Biblical Laments." *Interpretation* 37, no. 1: 32–45.

———. 1986. *Interpreting the Psalms*. Philadelphia: Fortress.

———. 2000. "The Beginning of the Psalter." In *Israelite Religion and Biblical Theology: Collected Essays*, 269–78. Sheffield, UK: JSOT Press.

Nel, Philip. 2004. "Psalm 19: The Unbearable Lightness of Perfection." *Journal of Northwest Semitic Languages* 30, no. 1: 103–17.

Neusner, Jacob, ed. 1988. *The Mishnah: A New Translation*. New Haven: Yale University Press.

Oberman, Heiko A. 1982. *Luther: Man between God and the Devil*. New Haven: Yale University Press.

Origen. 1957. *The Song of Songs: Commentary and Homilies*. Translated by R. P. Lawson. Ancient Christian Writers. Westminster, MD: Newman Press.

Pardee, Dennis, and Nancy Pardee. 2009. "Gods of Glory Ought to Thunder: The Canaanite Matrix of Psalm 29." In *Psalm 29 through Time and Tradition*, edited by Lowell K. Handy, 115–25. Eugene, OR: Wipf & Stock.

Rashi. 2004. *Rashi's Commentary on Psalms*. Translated by Mayer I. Gruber. Philadelphia: Jewish Publication Society.

Reardon, Patrick Henry. 1975. "Calvin on Providence: The Development of an Insight." *Scottish Journal of Theology* 28, no. 6: 517–33.

Sarna, Nahum M. 1993. *On the Book of Psalms: Exploring the Prayers of Ancient Israel*. New York: Schocken Books.

Selderhuis, H. J. 2007. *Calvin's Theology of the Psalms*. Texts and Studies in Reformation and Post-Reformation Thought. Grand Rapids: Baker Academic.

Spangenberg, I. J. J. 1997. "Psalm 49 and the Book of Qohelet." *Skrif en kerk* 18, no. 2: 328–44.

Steussy, Marti J. 2008. "The Enemy in the Psalms." *Word & World* 28, no. 1: 5–12.

Theodore of Mopsuestia. 2006. *Commentary on Psalms 1–81*. Translated by Robert C. Hill. Atlanta: Society of Biblical Literature.

Theodoret of Cyrus. 2000. *Commentary on the Psalms: 1–72*. Translated by Robert C. Hill. Fathers of the Church. Washington, DC: Catholic University of America Press.

Tucker, W. Dennis. 2011. "Psalm 31:1–5, 15–16." *Interpretation* 65, no. 1: 70–71.

Westermann, Claus. 1989. *The Living Psalms*. Grand Rapids: Eerdmans.

SUBJECT INDEX

SCRIPTURE INDEX